Published in 2022 by Connor Court Publishing Pty Ltd in collaboration with the Centre for Independent Studies

Connor Court Publishing Pty Ltd.
PO Box 7257
Redland Bay QLD 4165
sales@connorcourt.com
www.connorcourt.com

ISBN: 978-1-922815-17-0

Cover image by Ward O'Neill. First published with a profile of Owen Harries by Paul Kelly, "The Man Who Writes Our Foreign Policy", *The National Times*, 23-26 January 1978.

Cover Design by Ian James

Printed in Australia

PRUDENCE
— AND POWER —
THE WRITINGS OF OWEN HARRIES

EDITED BY **TOM SWITZER** & **SUE WINDYBANK**

With an introduction by Dr Michael Easson AM

THE CENTRE FOR
INDEPENDENT
STUDIES

connorcourt
PUBLISHING

CONTENTS

INTRODUCTION

All of us knew Owen Harries, the three instigators of this book: Tom Switzer, Sue Windybank and me. We admired his thinking, his ideas, the craft he applied to wordsmithing, the jesting and jostling in debate, the integrity he displayed respecting others' viewpoints, the originality he brought to important questions.

He was not a "quietly flows the don" intellectual. Owen aimed to pierce armour. He was engaged in making his interlocutors consider, reassess, and calibrate their viewpoints, imagine different conclusions; to evaluate whether their shields were bullet-proof, whether the familiar carapace covering their ideas gave much protection.

Owen, his pipe a distinctive memory, taught me "Australian Foreign Policy" and "International Relations" at the University of New South Wales in 1975. I stayed in touch thereafter. In the early 2000s at Café Sydney, Owen introduced me to Tom Switzer. Before Tom sat at our table, Owen said: "He is an enterprising fellow who has discovered most things I've written including a few best forgotten."

Tom got to know Owen by reading the Washington-based *National Interest* magazine that Owen co-founded and edited from 1985-2001, and in the mid-1990s they bonded over a mutual dislike of American over-reach in the aftermath of the Cold War. Tom's enthusiasm, and his role at the American Enterprise Institute (1995-1998) in Washington, led to a strong friendship, further strengthened after Owen and his wife Dorothy returned to Australia in retirement in 2001. Owen became a Senior Fellow at the Centre for Independent Studies (CIS) in Sydney, and Tom and Owen sometimes collaborated in writing. Sue Windybank, as CIS publications editor, got to know Owen, published some of his articles, and conducted a memorable interview that distilled Owen's thinking.

When Owen died in June 2020, we knew what we had to do – assist each other, especially Tom, in gathering his best articles for a book, develop a definitive bibliography, and decide how to best convey the importance of this man to those who knew his writings, and the wider universe of people who should. Hence this book.

We knew Owen had come a long way, intellectually. Born near the slag heaps of South Wales, he had not met a single conservative until he arrived at university. A man of conventional, Fabian-inspired leftish opinion, Australia changed him. A poster in the UK promoting migration to Australia, and an advertisement for a tutor's role at the Department of Adult Education at the University of Sydney, led to curiosity, application, success, and arrival in Sydney with Dorothy in 1955. What he saw "was immediately and gloriously attractive, a marvellous technicolour relief after a grey post-war decade: flawless blue skies, palm and flame trees, yellow beaches, and, not least, plenty of red meat and fruit." But he knew no one.

An early formidable intellectual influence was the John Anderson-inspired Harry Eddy (1913-1973), also in the Department. Harries recalled: "I can remember arguing with him during my first years in Sydney, and always having a sense of impending defeat." He went on to say that Eddy "took great pains to meet his opponent's case at its strongest and was never concerned simply with winning. Indeed, it was the combination of power and fairness which stayed in the mind as an object lesson of what academic work could and should be." Eddy was the example Owen aspired to and surpassed. Owen edited a festschrift in honour of Eddy, *Liberty and Politics: Studies in Social Theory*, 1976, and encouraged the publication of W.H.C. Eddy, *Understanding Marxism*, Edward Arnold, 1979.

Harries learnt to debate, inspire, and win with the best. He gravitated to the circle around *Quadrant* magazine and its founder Richard Krygier (1917-1986): The magazine "... became a rallying point for Australian intellectuals who rejected the prevailing leftism and the perverse but comfortable notion that principled liberalism required an anti-anti-communist posture."

Peter Edwards and Geoffrey Pemberton, in their 1992 history of Australia's Vietnam engagement (*Crises & Commitments: The*

Politics and Diplomacy of Australia's Involvement in Southeast Asian Conflicts 1948-1965), tribute Harries along with Geoffrey Fairbairn (1924-1980) at the ANU, as *the* leading intellectuals in Australia publicly articulating the defence of Australia's participation in the war in support of the independence of South Vietnam. Their arguments were more compelling and interesting than what the government ministers and spokespersons said. Owen was never just a tough Cold War warrior. Wit and iconoclastic insight were part of his inventiveness. It is why even serious ideological opponents often liked him personally. You knew he cared very much to win, but even more so to win you over, and he had a knack of listening like you might have something interesting to say.

⚬⚬⚬

One regret is not seeing in this book more of Owen's writings. There was so much, however, from which to choose. For example, his articles in the early 1960s in the globally prestigious *Foreign Affairs* journal on "Faith in the Summit" and "Six Ways of Confusing Issues", written when he was 30 and 31. Apart from Julius Stone (1907-1985) who proposed in 1959 a "hot-line" – a dedicated telephone connection between the White House and the Kremlin (implemented in 1963) – in that period, besides the Prime Minister and Foreign Minister, there was no other Australian figure having as significant, considered and practical policy impact on the world stage. Needing to select from a vast output (as the bibliography at the end of this book shows), and knowing many of his earlier themes were revisited and sometimes repeated, led the editors to concentrate on more recent articles. That bias is justified. Owen's writings improved as he matured and refined his thinking.

Owen worried that he had never developed an overarching theory of international relations. But this was not his forte. Besides, there is merit in the argument by the realist policy thinker Martin Wight (1913-1972), who in the journal *International Relations* wrote on "Why There is No International Theory" (1960). Wight and Harries were sceptical of grand explanations. Discussing issues as important as the organisation of relations between nations requires nuance and a lively appreciation that neat and tidy first principles can be blind to the reality of history, individuals, and differing conceptions of national interest. In his sparkling essays, "The Dangers of Expansive Realism", "Fourteen Points for Realists", and others reproduced in this collection, Harries brought his scalpel to the table.

He urged caution, prudence, restraint, awareness of the fallibility and unpredictability of human beings, the ever-present risk of unintended consequences, to consideration of what can be accomplished. He wrote: "Resist the notion that we must now find a new, grand, elevating cause to perform the same function as anti-communism did until recently – that of providing coherence, unity, and high moral content to foreign policy. The Cold War was exceptional, not typical." Owen shifted his thinking as circumstances changed.

He contested the "sleep-walking" opinion that America should act as if the Cold War had never ended, cautioned that the United States' need for enemies and high purpose might lead to major strategic mistakes. With the ever-eastward expansion of NATO, he foresaw potential catastrophe. The Iraq adventure, also, its poor strategic objectives, and the extraordinarily utopian prognosis of "democracy-creation", blithely tossed around during the George W. Bush presidency, was a project bound to end in tears. Owen was alive to risks, his warnings unheeded. In one essay, "Realism in a New Era" (1995), extracted in the pages ahead, he opined: "Realism is an affront to liberalism in many ways ... It stresses conflict as a central and enduring fact of life, while liberalism asserts a true and peaceful harmony of interests, obscured only by temporary and removable ignorance and misunderstanding."

With Iraq, Owen saw the difference between liberals and neo-conservatives (whom he thought were "neo-liberals" on foreign policy), as opposed to conservative realists, was scepticism about the perfectibility of mankind. Alas, there is no white cocoon, silky chrysalis remedy. Never is it easy or quickly possible to transform whole societies, especially where tribal hatreds, long memories, and the honour of blood-vengeance are important, into sustainable, "end of history" liberal nations. The premature promise and the hasty actuality of majority rule in such cultures is certain to bring boiling feuds to the surface. This is not to advocate cynicism or indifference. Nobility of purpose, yes, but policymakers need always reckon with "the crooked timber of humanity", in Kant's phrase. It is not one or the other.

Turning his gaze to Australian policy, Owen urged that Australia need not share every burden and every engagement in lockstep with America. We had our own thinking to do and interests to protect. Yet he also insisted that the American alliance was the cornerstone to Australian policy, though nothing should be taken for granted. In correspondence published in the *Quarterly Essay*, No. 25, 2007, Harries observed:

> As statesmen as diverse as Bismarck, Gladstone and Teddy Roosevelt had cause to stress, the reserve *rebus sic stantibus* – "while the same conditions apply" – is always silently understood in every treaty. In other words, no firm and unconditional guarantees are ever available in international politics.

And, therefore, every important relationship, in particular Treaty relationships, need to be permanently cultivated and renewed. His Boyer Lectures (2003) convey the point and punch of his reasoning; the best of those lectures is reproduced here.

Owen, discussing "The False Choice Between Realism and Morality" in *The Interpreter*, the Lowy Institute's online publication, in February 2009, proffered:

> I suggest that instead of classifying people as either wholly realist or wholly moral, it might be better to acknowledge that both elements exist in most if not all of us, the nature of the mix depending partly on temperament, but also on experience and understanding of the facts of a particular situation, and of the nature of the international system in general.

He went on to say:

> In so far as realism stresses the importance of stability and order, it stands for the necessary (but far from sufficient) condition for a moral life; and in so far as it emphasises selfishness, secrecy, and mutual suspicion, it forewarns against unintended consequences (The road to hell is paved etc., etc. ...).

How best to grapple with the challenges of the times he lived, how to apply principle and realism to reach coherent outcomes, how best to attain plausible and compelling conclusions, discarding cant and woolly thinking, made Owen a fine writer on foreign policy.

More the applied strategist than a grand strategic theorist, what we have here is a rich harvest of writings by Owen written over a half century. A crop of the best lay before you. Read them and see how the art of substance married to fine rhetoric, spotlights issues, values, and pathways guided by a hardy realist outlook.

Congratulations Tom and Sue, you have done great honour to our wonderful, mutual friend.

Dr Michael Easson AM

Harries with wife Dorothy (left) and daughters Jane and Rowena
(front) in London in the early 1980s

SECTION ONE

General Writing

How to Win Arguments and Influence Debate

Australian Financial Review, 1 February 2002

Based on a September 1984 article – "A Primer for Polemicists" – in *Commentary* magazine, the article was reprinted as "12 Rules for Winning" in *Quadrant* (December 1984) and as "Tactical Notes No. 10" by the Libertarian Alliance in London. After returning from Washington to Australia in 2001, Harries revised and updated the article for the *AFR*. The then Governor of the Reserve Bank of Australia (RBA), Ian Macfarlane, subsequently invited him to address a RBA Board meeting about the piece.

Unlike its regional neighbours, and reflecting its Western origins, Australia has a political culture that revels in robust polemical exchange. But in an age when virtually every other area of human activity – from how to succeed in the boardroom, to how to succeed in bed, to how to live in perfect health till the day you die – has received saturation coverage, remarkably little attention has been given to the strategies and techniques of polemical debate.

In a modest attempt to repair the omission, and in particular to help beginners avoid a long and tedious process of reinventing the wheel, here are a few suggestions based on the trials and errors of my own experience.

Rule 1: Forget about trying to convert your adversary. In any serious polemical confrontation (as opposed to genuine intellectual discourse) the chances of success on this score are so remote as to exclude it as a rational objective. On the very rare occasions when it does happen, it will be because the person converted has already and independently come to harbour serious doubts concerning his existing position and is teetering on the edge of defection. This will be due, more often than not, to some outrageous action by his own side or some shocking revelation: Witness the effect on members of communist parties in the West of the Nazi-Soviet pact of 1939 and Khrushchev's 1956 speech denouncing Stalinism. Then, but only then, a particular argument or example may provide the catalyst to complete the process.

Rule 2: Pay great attention to the agenda of the debate. He who defines the issues, and determines their priority, is already well on the way to winning. That is why, to take a current example, there has been such a determined attempt since September 11 to contest the initial definition of the issue as one of terrorism and to make American arrogance or globalisation the issue. See also the continuing struggle to determine whether the *Tampa* issue is to be defined as a humanitarian refugee issue or in terms of the integrity of controls over borders and an orderly process of selection for entry. It is essential, too, to resist semantic aggression – to prevent your opponents from imposing their language and concepts on the debate, and always to use terms that reflect your own values, traditions and interests.

Again, consider the use of terms like "racist", "genocide" and "elite"; and the selective and asymmetrical use of labels like "conservative" and "right-wing" (try to remember the last time you heard someone described on the ABC as "socialist" or "left-wing"). Carelessness or misplaced tolerance in this respect can be enormously costly.

Rule 3: Preaching to the converted, far from being a superfluous activity, is vital. Preachers do it every Sunday. The strengthening of the commitment, intellectual performance and morale of those already on your side is an essential task, both in order to bind them more securely to the cause and to make them more effective exponents of it. As religious movements in earlier times, and the anti-Vietnam war and civil-rights movements more recently have shown, conviction and dedication are enormous assets, often more than compensating for lack of numbers. On the negative side, one of the most embarrassing experiences in a polemical exchange is to have one's case misrepresented and mangled by one's own supporters.

Rule 4: Never forget the uncommitted: almost invariably they constitute the vast majority. This may seem obvious, but in the excitement of combat and lust for polemical kill the uncommitted are often overlooked. The encounter becomes an end in itself rather than a means of influencing wider opinion. Yet what works best in throwing opponents off balance – cleverness, originality, pugnacity, ridicule – is often counterproductive with the neutral or undecided, who are more likely to be impressed by good sense, decency and fairness.

Rule 5: Be aware that, at least potentially, you are always addressing multiple audiences. Decide whether on a particular occasion, you want to make a broad appeal to many different groups, which will usually involve compromise and restraint in presentation, or to make a sharply-focused pitch to a particular audience, even at the risk of alienating others. Either decision – or one to strike some sort of balance between the two – may be right, depending on circumstances; the important thing is to know what you are about. Politicians understand this readily and usually sacrifice impact on a limited group for breadth of appeal, which is one reason their utterances so often appear anodyne and bland. On the other hand, intellectuals – who tend to regard all who are not intellectuals as unimportant, and to equate compromise with sin – are particularly bad in this respect. Which is why their victories are so often Pyrrhic in character.

Rule 6: Be prepared to go around the block many times. When you have a good point to make, keep repeating it. Success in ideological polemics is very much a matter of staying power and will. Communists used to understand this rule very well and practised it to excess.

Western politicians vary in respect to it – Tony Blair is always "on message" and John Howard is not afraid of being repetitious. Again, intellectuals, who put a high professional premium on novelty and originality and have a great fear of being thought boring by their peers, have greater difficulties. They might consider pinning on their study walls a passage from Saul Bellow's *Mr Sammler's Planet*: "It is sometimes necessary to repeat what all know. All mapmakers should place the Mississippi in the same location and avoid originality. It may be boring, but one has to know where it is. We cannot have the Mississippi flowing toward the Rockies, just for a change." They might also put up, alongside this, Wellington's remark at Waterloo: "Hard pounding this, gentlemen; let's see who will pound longest."

Rule 7: Shave with Occam's razor. Knowing what you can afford to give away is one of the great arts of polemics. It is truly astonishing how often experienced polemicists will expend time and energy defending what is irrelevant or peripheral to their case. Thus, if one wishes to defend the proposition that the US is the freest and most creative country in the world, there is no need to deny that it is also a violent society, any more than it was once necessary to contest that Hitler built good roads or that Mussolini made the trains run on time in order to establish their evilness. Practising polemical economy narrows the area you have to defend and gives you more time or space to concentrate on what is really essential to your case.

Rule 8: Be very careful in your use of examples and historical analogies. More often than not, their illustrative value is outweighed by their distracting effect. People will tend to concentrate on the factual content of the particular episode referred to, the validity of your account of it or the legitimacy of analogies in general, and ignore the original point you were trying to make.

Thus, any references to the appeasement policies of the 1930s in the context of a discussion, say, of American policy towards China is likely to bring progress to an end and precipitate a prolonged wrangle over the precise circumstances of the occupation of the Rhineland or the writings of Winston Churchill. Analogies are often a powerful and persuasive way of bringing a point home. But you should generally be economical in their use, careful in their choice and well-armed to defend the ones that you do choose.

Rule 9: Avoid trading in motives as an alternative to rebutting the opposing case. Or, in Sidney Hook's words, "Before impugning an opponent's motives, even when they may legitimately be impugned, answer his arguments." This admonition is routinely ignored by many

Australian opinion journalists and intellectuals, for whom recourse to attributing and attacking motive is often the first step in debate. (Witness the way that much-needed public discussion of Australia's Aboriginal and refugee policies, and of multiculturalism generally, is inhibited and poisoned by the charges of racism readily levelled against anyone critical of the liberal orthodoxy on these issues.)

Hook's advice is worth following for two reasons. First, it is the proper thing to do and you will feel better for doing it. Second, motives are irrelevant to the soundness of an argument. Anything that is said by someone whose motives are suspect or bad could equally well (and in all probability will) be uttered by someone whose motives are impeccable, and an answer will still be required. Motives can explain error, distortion and falsehood, but they cannot establish the existence of these things. The place to discuss them is not at the beginning but at the end, when the facts have been established and error exposed.

Rule 10: Emulate the iceberg. In any polemical exchange, make sure that you know several times more about a topic than you can conceivably use or show. This is important, for one thing, because you will not know in advance what precisely you will have to use on any given occasion. Even more important, the fact that you have much in reserve (which will usually become evident through an accumulation of small touches) will give a resonance and authority to what you do use. Witness the difference between the writing of the genuinely knowledgeable and the instant experts on the Taliban.

Rule 11: Know your opposition. Always bear in mind John Stuart Mill's observation that he who knows only his own position knows little of that. Understand the position of your adversary not in a caricatured or superficial form but at its strongest, for until you have rebutted it at its strongest you have not rebutted it at all. This is a necessary condition both for developing your own position fully and attacking your opponent successfully. It was no accident that many of the most effective anti-communists were people who at one stage of their lives had been either in or very close to a communist party.

Rule 12: Before employing these or any other debating stratagems, make every effort to ensure that the position you decide to defend is intellectually, morally and politically worthy of your efforts. Being on the side of the good and the true does not guarantee success, but, other things being equal, it certainly helps.

What Conservatism Means

The American Conservative, 17 November 2003

First published as "What It Means to be Conservative" in the Centre for Independent Studies (CIS)'s quarterly magazine *Policy* (Winter 2003) before being extracted in *TAC*, the original essay was an edited version of a talk Harries gave to the Blackheath Philosophy Forum in March 2003.

John Stuart Mill famously dubbed the Conservative Party the "stupid party". Mill was, of course, a liberal – but then so are most intellectuals. The English conservative, Roger Scruton, has recently written of his own experience growing up in the middle of the 20th century: "[A]lmost all English intellectuals regarded the term 'conservative' as a term of abuse ... [it was] to be on the side of age against youth, the past against the future, authority against innovation ... spontaneity and life."

As well as hostility, there is likely to be ignorance. Conservatism does not lend itself easily to schematic, didactic exposition, and conservatives do not readily engage in it. In introducing his anthology, *The Conservative Tradition*, R.J. White defensively (or perhaps smugly and archly) claims, "To put conservatism in a bottle with a label is like trying to liquefy the atmosphere or give an accurate description of the beliefs of a member of the Anglican Church. The difficulty arises from the nature of the thing. For conservatism is less a political doctrine than a habit of mind, a mode of feeling, a way of living."

Bearing this resistance to formal treatment in mind, it is perfectly in character that what is widely accepted as the ablest and most influential statement of conservative views – Edmund Burke's *Reflections on the Revolution in France* – is not a systematic statement of a position but a polemic reacting to a particular political situation: an unprecedented upheaval in the most illustrious and powerful country in Europe. Embedded therein, in unsystematic fashion, are the tenets of a political philosophy.

The Limits of Politics

Two initial points about Burke's *Reflections*: first, it was published in 1790, before the most violent manifestations of the revolution – before the terror, the regicide, the revolution devouring its own children, and the emergence of a military dictatorship. Therefore, Burke was writing with foresight, not hindsight.

Second, at the time it was published, the revolution was still seen in England as an immense liberating step forward. Most are familiar with Wordsworth's "Bliss was it in that dawn to be alive" reaction and that of Charles James Fox: "How much the greatest event it is that ever happened in the world! And how much the best!" In launching his denunciation of the revolution, Burke was not expressing a popular opinion among thinking Englishmen but rather going against the tide.

Central to his reaction was a profound hostility toward what he called variously "speculation", "metaphysics", or "theoretical reasoning" as applied to social and political questions and his conviction of the danger of such applications. He was writing at a time when the revolutionaries in France seriously believed that they could reconstruct the world from scratch by the application of general, abstract principles – to the point of introducing a new calendar to mark the beginning of that new world. In holding this belief, they were not exceptional but representative of the most sophisticated opinion of their time, putting into action belief about the power of reason that representatives of the Enlightenment had energetically propagated.

Burke rejected that belief for two reasons, the first having to do with the nature of society and politics, the second with the nature of human beings and their rational faculties.

When he wrote *Reflections*, Burke had been engaged in politics at a high level for three decades. He saw that activity as an infinitely complex, difficult, and delicate one. The factors at work were many, and the ways they interrelated were complex. Politicians had to act in concrete, discrete situations, not in general or abstract areas. He wrote:

> The science of constructing a Commonwealth, or renovating it, or reforming it, is, like every other experimental science, not to be taught *a priori*. It is a matter of the most delicate and complicated skill. ... A statesman differs from a professor at a university. The latter has only the general view of society; the former, the statesman, has a number of circumstances to combine with those general ideas, and to take into his consideration. Circumstances are infinite, and infinitely combined; are variable and transient; he who does not take them into consideration is not erroneous but stark mad – he is metaphysically mad.

In other words, discrimination in terms of circumstances trumps consistency in terms of principle and logic, and insistence on consistency regardless of circumstances and consequences is likely to be disastrous. Think of this the next time someone insists that because we act in one way toward Country X (say with respect to human rights) it would be hypocritical not to act in the same way to Country Y, regardless of the difference between the two countries or of the difference in our relationships. As Dean Acheson once put it, "I am not in the slightest bit worried because somebody can say, 'Well, you said so and so about Greece, why isn't all this true about China?' I will be polite, I will be patient, and I will try to explain why Greece is not China. But my heart will not be in the battle."

Society, for Burke, is neither a collection of loosely-related individuals nor a mechanism with interchangeable parts. It is a living organism, and anything that affects the well-being of any part of it will affect the whole. It is, therefore, he insists, "with infinite caution that any man ought to venture on pulling down an edifice which has answered in any tolerable degree for ages the common purpose of society."

There are two problems of which Burke, and conservatives after him, have been acutely aware. The first is that of unintended consequences – that because of the complexity and interconnectedness of things, in initiating change on an ambitious scale, more is almost invariably set in motion than the initiator had in mind, and the result may be quite different from the intended one. Thus, in Burke's words, "[V]ery plausible schemes with very pleasing commencements have often shameful and lamentable consequences." To stop elephants from being killed, the ivory trade was banned. This made ivory scarce. Prices went up, and the rewards for poaching became greater. More people engaged in it, and more elephants were killed than before the ban was introduced.

The second problem is that of latent function. As well as their apparent functions, institutions often perform other, hidden functions of a very important nature – something that may not become apparent until those institutions have been dismantled.

In his 1959 book, *Political Man*, widely regarded as a classic of its kind, the sociologist Seymour Martin Lipset observes the apparently "absurd fact" that 10 out of the 12 stable European and English-speaking democracies are monarchies. This, to Lipset's mind, could not be an accident. He suggests that during the rapid and profound social and economic changes of the last 100 years, which apparently were making monarchy increasingly irrelevant, the institution played a crucial role in retaining the loyalty of those groups that were losing as a result of the changes: the aristocracy, the traditionalists, the clerical and rural sectors. The persistence of the central institution provided reassurance that the world they knew was not totally lost, that the new social and political order could be adapted to. On the other hand, in countries that dispensed with monarchy (e.g., France, Germany, and the Habsburg empire after World War I), reconciliation and stability proved much scarcer commodities. Therefore, concludes Lipset, the changes that apparently made monarchy more anachronistic actually increased its importance as an "important traditional integrative institution during a transitional period."

Conservatives may be more attuned to the appreciation of latent function than liberals precisely because they tend to be more concerned with stability and what might disturb it and because they have an organic view of society. If one's focus is on individual rights and needs, and if one thinks in terms of rational patterns, then one may be less alert to latent functions.

The Denial of Human Nature

If the complexity of society and the political order was one reason Burke feared radical and rapid change, a second and just as powerful reason was his reservation about the proposed engine of change: the role of reason in human affairs. Burke rejected the Enlightenment view of man as a predominantly rational, calculating, logical being. His rational side exists, but it is a small part of his total make-up. "We are afraid," said Burke, "to put men to live and trade each on his own private stock of reason, because we suspect that this stock in each man is small." Habit, instinct, custom, faith, reverence, prejudice – the accumulated practical knowledge acquired through experience – all this was more important than abstract reasoning. Collectively, and for better or worse, it constituted man's nature.

Burke was not alone in expressing these views. The great Scottish philosopher David Hume had insisted on the importance of habit and custom a generation earlier. And a year or two before Burke wrote, across the Atlantic the shapers of the American constitution and authors of *The Federalist Papers* were insisting that in constructing a political order, the aggressive, selfish, acquisitive aspects of man's nature must be taken fully into account. "A man must be far gone in Utopian speculation," thought Hamilton, "to forget that men are ambitious, vindictive and rapacious."

But they were all arguing against the prevailing intellectual tide of the times – the Age of Enlightenment – which saw customs and habits and prejudice as impediments that could be swept aside to restore the human mind to its pristine state as a clean slate on which reason could then write its message. For the French revolutionaries, what passed for human nature was not something to be accommodated or curbed, as the authors of *The Federalist Papers* believed, but rather to be altered.

One might see this as the crucial difference between the French, with their notion of restarting history and creating an entirely new set of perfectly rational political institutions, and the Americans, who when it came to framing a constitution, put their faith in checks and balances and the separation of powers to keep in control the effects of what Christians would term original sin. This conflict between the *tabula rasa* school and the human-nature school has continued and has been central to many debates about social and political policy.

In contrast to what was happening in France, where everything was concentrated in Paris, Burke put great emphasis on the local, the proximate, and particular. "To be attached to the subdivision, to love the little platoon we belong to in society, is the first principle (the germ as it were) of public affections." Here Burke may be seen as anticipating Tocqueville in stressing the importance of civil society and intermediate, participatory associations, as against the state; the actual particular wills of people going about their particular lives, as against the abstract General Will espoused by the revolution.

As opposed to the abstract Rights of Man, Burke spoke of the existing rights that man actually possessed and enjoyed. He sometimes used the term natural rights but meant by it the historical, prescriptive rights inherited within the context of particular societies and legal systems: the rights of Englishmen, or Americans, or Indians or Frenchmen – not of "man" in the abstract. Again, the particular is contrasted to the general and the historical to the abstract.

For Burke, historical continuity was central to his understanding of society. In one of his most quoted phrases, he described it as a "partnership ... between those who are living, those who are dead and those who are yet to be born." That is, the present is not the property of the living, to make of it whatever they will. It is an estate held in trust. Those who hold it have a fiduciary responsibility to hand it on in good condition. This trust the revolutionaries were in the process of betraying. In the name of reason, liberty, and equality they were destroying all the historical institutions of legitimate authority.

With authority gone, the result would be not liberty but increasing dependence on naked force to compel obedience and maintain order. With extraordinary insight, and no historical precedent to guide him (the concept of totalitarianism was still to be invented), at the outset of the revolution, when optimism and idealism reigned, Burke intuited that it must end in terror and dictatorship.

Burke has frequently been represented as a reactionary. But Burke was not defending or advocating a return to an aristocratic or monarchic order. He was defending the mixed system that existed in the Britain of his day – a combination of aristocratic, commercial, oligarchic, and democratic elements. Far from opposing all reform, Burke insisted, "A state without the means of some change is without the means of its conservation." The issue was not reform versus no reform; it was between the view that reform was a simple matter that could be engaged in sweepingly and the view that it required prudence and was best approached incrementally.

That Burke sometimes sided with those in authority, and sometimes with those resisting it, has led to the charge that he was inconsistent and opportunistic. But Burke was perfectly consistent in that he opposed the abuse of power, whoever was abusing it – king, corrupt company, intellectuals, or mob.

Conservatism and Neoconservatism

When, then, do his ideas become relevant and attractive? Michael Oakeshott gives the obvious answer: when there is much to be enjoyed and when that enjoyment is combined with a sense that what is enjoyed is in danger of being lost. It is the combination of enjoyment and fear that stimulates conservatism.

That seems convincing until one considers: if one is living in and enjoying, say, a liberal or a social democratic or a capitalist society; and if that society suddenly comes under threat, why can't one defend it with liberal arguments, or social democratic, or capitalist arguments? Why does one need conservative arguments?

In an article called "Conservatism as an Ideology", published in 1957, Samuel Huntington observes that unlike nearly every other ideology, conservatism offers no vision of an ideal society. There is no conservative Utopia. Indeed, conservatism has no substantive institutional content. It has been used to defend all sorts of different institutional arrangements, from traditional to feudal to liberal to capitalist to social democratic. Because it is concerned not with content but with process, with change and stability, its true opposite is not liberalism but radicalism. Conservatism advances arguments that stress the difficulty and danger of rapid change and the importance of stability and continuity and prudence; radicalism expresses enthusiasm concerning innovation and boldness in embracing change.

Conservatism, Huntington maintains, is the product of intense ideological and social conflict when consensus breaks down and when an existing institutional order can no longer be defended in its own terms. "When the challengers fundamentally disagree with the ideology of the existing society ... and affirm a basically different set of values, the common framework of discussion is destroyed." When it is precisely liberal values and institutions that are being rejected, there is no point in appealing to those values to defend them. It is then that conservative arguments become indispensable: arguments that defend the established institutions precisely because they are established. When radicalism prevails, conservative arguments must be resorted to in order to counter it.

Particularly intriguing about Huntington's argument is that it perfectly predicted what was to happen in the 1960s. In that decade, there was a powerful upsurge of radicalism, associated initially with the civil rights movement and protest against the Vietnam War but quickly going beyond that to reject the whole fabric of American society. New Deal liberalism was denounced and rejected as "Cold War liberalism" or worse, and the radicals began their long march through our institutions.

It was in these circumstances that a group of liberal intellectuals – almost all of them members of the Democratic Party, many of them prominent members of the New York intellectual community – began to oppose the radical movement, to defend American institutions and values with classic conservative arguments. They were attacked from the left and derisively labelled "neoconservatives". It was meant as an insult but readily accepted by Irving Kristol – the godfather of neoconservatism – and his colleagues.

They became an important force in American politics and have remained so. Many joined the Republican Party. They brought with them intellectual and polemical skills that had been in scarce supply on the right, and by the 1980s they had seized the intellectual initiative from the left.

Under the neoconservatives' guidance, we now have an American president committed not only to nation-building in Iraq but also to region-building throughout the Middle East. The belief that democratic institutions, behaviour, and ways of thought can be exported and transplanted to societies that have no traditions of them is a profoundly unconservative, indeed a radical, belief. Conservatives traditionally have believed in the slow, organic growth of political institutions, not their imposition from without. Yet the most enthusiastic advocates of exporting democracy are American neoconservatives, which perhaps suggests that their break with their earlier modes of thought has been less than complete.

In the 1770s, when Britain had recently added North America and India to its empire, when its economy was the strongest in the world, when it ruled the seas, it occupied a position not too different from the one occupied by the United States today. Contemplating all this power, Burke uttered a warning that seems to be pertinent in our present circumstances:

> Among precautions against ambition, it may not be amiss to take precautions against our own. I must fairly say, I dread our own power and our own ambition: I dread our being too much dreaded … We may say that we shall not abuse this astonishing and hitherto unheard of power. But every other nation will think we shall abuse it. It is impossible but that, sooner or later, this state of things must produce a combination against us which may end in our ruin.

It Pays to be Prudent When It Comes to Morality in World Politics

Sydney Morning Herald, 21 February 2005

This article was based on the Occasional Paper, *Morality and Foreign Policy*. Published by the Centre for Independent Studies in February 2005, the paper was an extended version of the first George Shipp Memorial Lecture delivered by Harries to the Workers' Educational Association in Sydney on 29 October 2004. Mr Shipp was an old and very close friend. Edited versions were published in *Policy* (Sydney), *Prospect* (London) and *Orbis* (Philadelphia). Extracts also ran in *The Age* and the *Australian Financial Review*.

To a remarkable degree, the debate over Iraq has been conducted in moral terms. President Bush has justified his policies in terms of implementing God's will, of "freedom on the march", and conferring the gift of democracy on those unable to achieve it for themselves. His liberal critics have condemned him for, among other things, flouting the alleged moral authority of the United Nations and "the international community", the improper pre-emptive use of force, and deliberately lying about the evidence used to justify going to war.

All this raises an important and difficult question: what is – what can be – the role of morality in international politics? Over the years there have been two diametrically opposed views on the subject. Each has a long and distinguished intellectual pedigree, but simpler versions of both can be heard in any bar, common room, board room or dinner party.

The first holds that in the realm of international politics, power and self-interest must prevail, and all the rest is decoration. "The strong do what they can and the weak suffer what they must," wrote Thucydides 2500 years ago, and, given the state of anarchy, distrust and chronic insecurity in which states continue to exist, that remains true today. At best, there is only room for a little altruism and disinterestedness at the margins.

The second view, usually associated with liberalism, is that there is not, or need not be, any problem in applying moral criteria to the conduct of foreign policy. As John Bright, the great 19th-century English radical, put it, "the moral law was not written for men alone in their individual character ... it was written as well for nations." That this truth is not understood and acted upon is due to ignorance and the influence exerted by special interests of a selfish and bellicose kind. But these impediments can be removed by a combination of education, democracy, the spread of commerce, and the creation of international institutions. This view was propagated vigorously by Woodrow Wilson, the 28th president of the United States.

Both these positions seem to me to be seriously flawed. The first – which usually invites the cynical conclusion that "they're all the same" – is wrong because, even though all states do pursue their own interests, the nature and quality of those interests differ greatly, often in morally significant ways. Britain and Germany were both selfishly pursuing their own interests in World War II, and both did terrible things in the process, but it did not follow that it was a matter of moral indifference who won the war – democratic Britain or Nazi Germany. The same was true of the Cold War.

As for the second position, I believe it is profoundly mistaken in its belief that states can realistically be held to the same moral standards as individuals. Individuals, if they choose, can be as self-sacrificing, generous and compassionate as they like, even to the point of self-destruction. They can be saints or martyrs, putting virtue before everything, even survival. States, and those who act in their name, cannot properly be or do any of those things.

☙☙☙

Where, then, does this leave the matter? I am not a believer that the truth is usually or always somewhere in the middle, but in this instance I think it is. Moral standards can and should be applied to foreign policy, but the morality that is appropriate to, and that can be sustained in, the soiled, selfish and dangerous world of power politics is a modest one. Its goal is not perfection – not utopian bliss – but decency. It is, more often than not, a morality of the lesser evil, of prudence.

In a system composed of a large number of independent and conflicting wills, uncertain intelligence, deadly weapons, different cultures, and no universally recognised and enforceable authority, a prudent morality requires modesty – modesty of ends, of means, and not least of rhetoric.

A prudential ethic places importance on those most mundane of virtues – order and stability. These do not, of course, constitute a sufficient condition for anything. But they are a necessary condition for everything whose achievement and smooth functioning require a degree of predictability and continuity: a system of justice, for example, or genuine democracy, or sustainable commercial relations.

Prudence requires that one is often prepared to settle for half a loaf, rather than making the best the enemy of the good. Compromise is usually an intellectual vice, muddle masquerading as tolerance; but, except in the most extreme cases of dealing with outright and threatening evil, it is a political necessity and virtue, especially in conditions in which the alternative is usually a resort to force.

Prudence requires doing everything one can to anticipate the possibility of unintended consequences. It requires care in the setting of precedents that may come home to haunt one, and an appreciation of why some rules and conventions that may seem redundant have withstood the test of time so well.

Prudence requires resisting the impulse to claim the right to double standards – one for other people, a different and more permissive one for oneself, usually on the grounds that one represents higher values or has special responsibilities. There is something intrinsically nutty about using one's claimed moral superiority to justify the adoption of lower ethical standards.

A prudential ethic requires that, in making policy, discrimination takes precedence over consistency. This is because a country may pursue a number of goals that have moral worth: among them justice, peace, freedom, security, prosperity, stability. Sometimes these compete or conflict and which should be given preference will vary. In other words, judgement is involved, not merely the automatic application of general principles.

It is in terms of such a morality of prudence that I believe that the Bush administration has seriously failed in Iraq. Its policy has been rich in unintended consequences (a global wave of intense anti-Americanism, the strong opposition of some of America's most important allies, the indefinite tying down of a third of a million military personnel, disgusting images of torture, the killing of large numbers of civilians) and dangerous precedents that may be exploited by others.

Those who criticise American policy are often criticised for being insensitive to the importance of freedom as a foreign policy goal. It might therefore be appropriate to end with a contribution from John Stuart Mill, a pre-eminent liberal philosopher and the author of a classic treatise, *On Liberty*:

> We have heard something lately about being willing to go to war for an idea. To go to war for an idea, if the war is aggressive, not defensive, is as criminal as to go to war for territory or revenue; for it is as little justified to force our ideas on other people, as to compel them to submit to our will in other respects.

These words were published in 1859 in an essay on the subject of non-intervention. At a time when we have been hearing much about "exporting democracy", they are worth a moment's consideration.

Irving Kristol – The Australian Connection

Quadrant, November 2009

Irving Kristol – the New York intellectual, writer, editor and publisher – died on 19 September 2009. This essay first appeared in *The New Conservative Imagination: Essays in Honor of Irving Kristol*, edited by Christopher DeMuth and William Kristol, Washington, AEI Press, 1995.

The connection between Australia and Irving Kristol, "the godfather of neoconservatism", is not obvious. Having politely but firmly rejected repeated invitations to do so, he has never visited the country. He has never written about it. Australia – along with a great deal of the rest of the Earth's surface, including Asia, Latin America, Africa and Canada – does not claim his serious attention, which is reserved for what goes on in the United States, Europe and Israel. I am the only Australian who has had a sustained working relationship with Irving, but he has shown a warmer interest in my original Welshness than in my acquired Australianness. (Not that Wales has a vital grip on his imagination either. True, he and Bea [the distinguished historian Gertrude Himmelfarb, Irving Kristol's wife] did visit the country once, when they were based in London in the 1950s. But when they got there, they managed to stay in the least Welsh place it was possible to find in the principality: the eccentric Italianate "village" created by Clough Williams-Ellis at Portmeirion, a location where one was more likely to meet Noel Coward than the Reverend Eli Jenkins.)

Still, a Kristol-Australian connection has existed for the past four decades, and it has had a significant effect on Australia's intellectual and cultural life. It should surprise no one that it has to do with magazines. Irving's working life has centred on magazines – creating them, publishing and raising money for them, editing them, and writing for them. A strong belief in their efficacy as instruments for furthering a cause and propagating a position is almost certainly the only belief that he has shared with the late Vladimir Ilyich Lenin.

In Irving's own writing, the polemical magazine essay has been his weapon of choice, and he has become one of the acknowledged masters of the form in our time.

Except for a short break in the 1960s, he has been continuously involved with intellectual magazines from the time he became assistant editor of *Commentary* in 1947 until now, when he easily (and from my point of view, embarrassingly) combines being editor of *The Public Interest* and publisher of *The National Interest* with a variety of other activities. In between, Irving launched *Encounter*, in the opinion of many the single most important journal of ideas to appear during the Cold War period; in his six years as its nominal co-editor but real editor (1953–58) he gave the magazine its definitive character. (His partner, Stephen Spender, while distinguished and well-connected, was too impractical and vacillating to be effective. Not long after the Russian repression of the Hungarian Revolution, Spender was still feebly objecting to the term "Soviet empire" as unduly provocative.) Irving was also editor of Max Ascoli's lively magazine, *The Reporter*, for a short period in the late 1950s.

Like many others, I first got to know about – and, in a sense, to know – Irving by reading *Encounter*. That began in Sydney in 1955, shortly after I had arrived in Australia. I was a bit slow off the mark because I'd spent the previous two years doing my national service in the rural depths of Somerset, and new intellectual magazines were hard to come by in Royal Air Force messes. Then I got a job at Sydney University (advertised in the back of another magazine, the leftist *New Statesman and Nation*, which had a circulation of around 90,000 at that time and *was* to be found in the mess).

Recently married, my wife Dorothy and I made the long four-and-a-half-week journey from London in the P&O liner, the *SS Strathmore*, travelling the great British imperial route – Gibraltar, Port Said, Aden, Bombay, Colombo, Singapore, Perth – in its last days, just a year before the Suez crisis. (This may be as good a place as any to note that Irving is a great admirer of the British empire.

Kipling is one of his favourite poets, and *Zulu* – depicting the epic of Rorke's Drift, where a handful of redcoats fought off a Zulu army – his all-time favourite movie. One of his few disappointments with the United States, I suspect, is that it is constitutionally and temperamentally unsuited to sustaining the burdens of an imperial mission.)

Sydney was immediately and gloriously attractive, a marvellous technicolour relief after a grey postwar decade: flawless blue skies, palm and flame trees, yellow beaches, and, not least, plenty of red meat and fruit. But initially it was also lonely, isolated and strange. We knew no one. The landscape was utterly different from anything we were accustomed to. There was not another country within 1200 miles, and not even another sizable city within 600. The politics were strange and harsh, involving Catholics and communists as major actors in a way that was more European than British. (The Australian Labor Party had spilt along these lines the previous year, which was to keep it out of power for nearly two decades.) The newspapers were dull and parochial. Literary-political magazines were few and hardly readable. The most conspicuous of them was the antediluvian and xenophobic *Bulletin*, a survivor from the late 19th century that still carried the slogan "Australia for the White People" on its masthead.

Despite *The Bulletin* and the fact that Robert Menzies's conservative party was in office, the country's intellectual and cultural life was dominated by the pro-communist left, and a shallow, reflexive, progressive orthodoxy prevailed. A man widely regarded as Australia's leading historian – Manning Clark – went to the Soviet Union at this time and wrote a glowing book called *Meeting Soviet Man*. He singled out for special praise – a "very great man", one of "earthy images and folk wisdom" – none other than Alex Surkov, the thuggish secretary of the Soviet Writers' Union. The Fellowship of Australian Writers was so impressed that, shortly after the Hungarian Revolution, it invited that tormentor of Russian writers to Australia as its guest. And so it went.

Such behaviour will not strike American intellectuals of a certain vintage as particularly unusual. There was a lot of it about in the 1950s in all parts of the West, and indeed to an extent Australian academics and intellectuals were only mimicking admired overseas models. But there was a difference. In a much smaller and more isolated cultural community – one characterised simultaneously by an aggressive commitment to an egalitarian ethos and by desperate concern to distinguish itself from the surrounding philistinism – there was much less diversity and pluralism, less in the way of countervailing challenges to this orthodoxy, than in either America or Europe. To the untutored eye, at least, the Australian cultural landscape seemed as flat and unvaried as an Australian sheep station.

Although my own views at the time were leftish (I had, after all, grown up in a South Wales mining valley), I found all this depressing. It was, for one thing, a coarse-grained radicalism, unadorned by any of the (in retrospect, perhaps spurious) sophistication and glamour that the Bevans and the Crossmans brought to the British version. For another, it was much more uncritically pro-Soviet than I was used to – for, Kingsley Martin notwithstanding, the British left as a whole was not fellow-travelling. But there was another reason: once in Sydney, I began that important process of self-education that is involved in preparing lectures, in my case lectures on international affairs and on totalitarianism. Once engaged in a close study of these matters (something that I had managed to avoid at Oxford) and having to declare myself in public on them, I quickly came to doubt and to move away from the prevailing leftist interpretations.

🚲🚲🚲

In these circumstances I discovered *Encounter*, and its effect was exhilarating. I had never before heard the political and cultural case for the West argued with such assurance, style and intellectual force. This was not surprising because for at least 20 years no one else had heard it either – the initiative had been entirely with the left. What celebration there had been of the West – mostly during the war – had been left in the inadequate hands of the likes of Sir Arthur Bryant. Otherwise, all had been denigration, or at best gloom, of the sort expressed by Cyril Connolly in his notorious sentence declaring that it was "closing time in the gardens of the West."

Now Irving Kristol and *Encounter* appeared, combining the panache and aggression that used to be the birthright of New York intellectuals with the style and self-possession of the English man of letters, to make an unapologetic case for the West. It was all enormously liberating, as well as being a splendid read. (One remembers articles like Leslie Fiedler's "McCarthy and the Intellectuals", with its lines: "From one end of the country to another rings the cry, 'I am cowed! I am afraid to speak out!' and the even louder response, 'Look, he is cowed! He is afraid to speak out!'" And there was Nancy Mitford's famous essay on U and Non-U.)

One of the interesting things about little magazines is that while they are produced in the great metropolitan centres with the readers of those cities principally in mind, they often have their greatest impact in the provinces and on the periphery. At the centre, the magazines represent merely one form in a dense complex of activities (public meetings, debates, clubs, cafes, dinner and cocktail parties, many other readily available magazines and newspapers); on the periphery, a good magazine may be the only thing that effectively and regularly links someone to the larger issues and intellectual community, and it can assume an inordinate importance in a life. At least, that was substantially the case 40 years ago, when communications were much more primitive – and Sydney was very much on the periphery.

But it didn't take long to find out what should have been obvious from the start (I was very young at the time): there were others, native-born Australians, who were roughly in the same predicament and who had the same concerns, often in a much more developed form. They included some distinguished and interesting men: Sir John Latham (a former chief justice of the Australian High Court); John Kerr QC (later to be the governor general who dismissed Prime

Minister Gough Whitlam in controversial circumstances); James McAuley (one of Australia's best poets, and co-perpetrator of the famous anti-modernist Ern Malley hoax); Peter Coleman (writer and editor and politician-to-be, who would one day write the history of the Congress for Cultural Freedom); Donald Horne (author, later, of *The Lucky Country*); and a bunch of academics including Richard Spann, Doug McCallum and David Armstrong.

And there was one other who was of outstanding importance: Richard Krygier, a Pole by origin, who in 1941 had, along with his wife Roma, found his way to Australia via Lithuania, Siberia, Tokyo and Shanghai. Arriving broke and with little English, he started by taking a job as a waiter in one of Sydney's nightclubs. By the 1950s, Krygier had a successful book-importing business. He was passionately, knowledgeably, uncompromisingly, and effectively anti-communist. When the Congress for Cultural Freedom was formed, Krygier was determined that Australia should participate in it. Despite initial indifference in Paris, he succeeded: in 1954, a small Australian committee was formed.

How was that committee to be most effective in an environment made up, in more or less equal parts, of indifference and hostility? The answer was given to Richard Krygier by – Irving Kristol. And it was, in retrospect at least, a predictable answer, as well as being right on the mark. Peter Coleman has described the episode:

> Krygier's great achievement was the founding of *Quadrant*. Its conception was in 1955 in the Russian Tea Room on West 57th Street, Manhattan, where he met with Irving Kristol, the editor of *Encounter*, to discuss the Australian situation. "You should start a magazine!", Kristol said. "Like *Encounter*!" Krygier wrote to the Paris office of the Congress for Cultural Freedom and asked for a subsidy. Malcolm Muggeridge, who had returned from his first visit to Australia, supported Krygier and told the Congress executive that this was an idea whose time had come.

ॐ ॐ ॐ

Thus did Irving contribute to the founding of *Quadrant*, probably the most important and successful magazine of ideas in Australia's history. (Its only significant rival in recent decades has been the leftist *Meanjin*, but it has not been a serious one. The Australian writer Frank Moorhouse once explained that "meanjin" was an Aboriginal word meaning "rejected by *The New Yorker*".) Indeed, *Quadrant* was destined to outlast *Encounter*; 40 years after that conversation in the Russian Tea Room – a long time for a little magazine – it is still a lively and substantial monthly, capable of starting a vigorous controversy and frequently quoted in the national media. It has even acquired a small but devoted following in the United States. William F. Buckley Jr was once generous enough to describe an issue of the magazine (a special one on China, put together by Simon Leys) as "the single most liberating issue of any magazine I can remember."

More generally, *Quadrant* became a rallying point for Australian intellectuals who rejected the prevailing leftism and the perverse but comfortable notion that principled liberalism required an anti-anti-communist posture. Around it grew a pattern of activity involving seminars and lectures and dinners and committee meetings – as well as close friendships and intense rivalries. (When it was eventually disclosed in the 1960s that the Paris congress, and through it the Australian association of *Quadrant*, had been funded secretly by the CIA, our general inclination was not to condemn but to congratulate the CIA for having been smart enough to give us the wherewithal to do what we wanted to do in any case – and then not to interfere or to impose conditions. The secrecy was regrettable, but we didn't live in a perfect world and it had been a condition for the thing being done at all.)

In due course, air travel became cheaper and quicker, and the tyranny of distance over Australian life slackened. In the 1960s, visits to the United States became less rare. When anyone from the *Quadrant* circle made it to New York, the preferred way of coping with the initial overwhelming impact of the city was to ring Irving Kristol. It must have become tiresome for him after a while, but he bore it with good grace, and some lucky Australians enjoyed lunch in the agreeable setting of the Century Club as one of their first meals in the city.

My own first meeting with Irving was in 1968, when I spent part of a sabbatical in America. My initial impression, strengthened rather than changed over the years, was of how comfortably high intelligence and good nature – two qualities that are not habitually found together (or even separately) in intellectuals – were combined in him. The intelligence was evident in the way the conversation seemed to be happening in a higher gear than I was accustomed to: the sharpness of the wit, the speed in anticipating one's point, the shorthand in stating his own. (The latter was easy to mistake initially for off-the-cuff dogmatism, until one probed and found that the arguments were all in place and that it was just a case of dispensing with the recitative. When, say, Irving pronounced flatly that NATO should be abolished, it was after he had thought hard and carefully worked out his position.)

At the same time, there seemed to be none of the insecurity or vanity that is commonly part of the make-up of intellectuals, no urge simply to score points or put down or claim credit. The wit was funny – very funny – but not vicious, and the gossip was affectionate and tolerant. Irving was, and remains, a kind man: what he does not like he usually prefers to dismiss rather than attack. As it happened, when we met we had both just had articles published in *Foreign Affairs*,[*] and Irving helped put me at ease by adopting the flattering fiction that the two articles were equally vital contributions to the intellectual life of Manhattan. Shortly after, he invited me to a dinner party at his home at Riverside Drive, and I met Bea. Before the evening was over, an enduring and, to me, greatly-valued friendship had begun.

In the mid-1970s, I left academic life – left with no regrets whatsoever, for the foolishness and cowardice of the American

[*] *Editors' note*: The article – Owen Harries, "Should the US Withdraw from Asia?", *Foreign Affairs*, October 1968 – was reprinted in *Quadrant* (Sydney), November-December 1968, and *Survival* (London), December 1968.

university scene had been faithfully copied in Australia. For the next seven and a half years, I worked for the Australian government. As part of my job was to help interpret the political culture of the United States, and as the tide of neoconservatism was running strong in those years, Irving Kristol continued to figure prominently in my thought and work. As a self-conscious position, neoconservatism was to all intents and purposes his creation, and in explaining the phenomenon to my political masters, I drew heavily on his ideas. (Our professional diplomats, like their counterparts elsewhere, spoke mainly to other professional diplomats and officials and were slow to recognise and to appreciate the significance of intellectual innovations.) In explaining the significance of the sudden appearance of numerous conservative think-tanks – a startling and unsettling new form of institution for many Australians, who had been schooled to believe that conservatives didn't think – one also had to talk about Irving. His belief in the importance of the struggle of ideas in determining who would own the future meant that his ramifying practical activities – particularly in encouraging young talent – were shaped by a determination that it would be right-thinking conservatives who would do so.

When I had to help write a major speech outlining Prime Minister Malcolm Fraser's political philosophy – not the easiest of tasks, given that Fraser, though gifted with a strong intelligence, was not comfortable expressing himself in terms of abstract ideas and principles – I did so with Irving's *Two Cheers for Capitalism* open at my elbow. The speech was later published as a definitive statement of Fraser's beliefs, and I wish I had a copy on hand to find out how much I had plagiarised.

Fraser's period in office came to an end when he lost an election to Bob Hawke in early 1983. This also brought to an end my spell in Paris as ambassador to UNESCO (a personal highlight of which had been a dinner I hosted at which a group of Parisian intellectuals led by Raymond Aron – ailing, but still with a hearty appetite for both conversation and food – met a group of New York intellectuals led by Irving who happened to be passing through on their way to a conference). I retired to Washington and spent a productive year at the Heritage Foundation, writing and helping to get the United States and Britain to leave UNESCO.

℮℮℮

But what to do next? Irving Kristol had the answer ready, and it had a familiar ring: "Why not start a magazine! Like *Encounter*, but mostly about foreign policy!" Irving's friend Michael Joyce was thinking along the same lines and was in a position to help make it happen. So *The National Interest* was conceived, and in 1985, exactly 30 years after first reading Irving Kristol, I began to work with him.

Irving was to be the publisher, and Robert Tucker, of Johns Hopkins, and I the co-editors. Bob and I had never met, but any worries we might have had about each other were overshadowed by our shared uncertainty about how Irving might interpret his role as publisher. He was, after all, one of the great editors of his day and a man of forceful opinion. Would he not want to have his say, and would not a triumvirate of editors, each with firm views, be disastrous? Our concern was strengthened by Irving's opinion, freely offered, that one didn't actually need to *know* anything to write about foreign policy, it was only a matter of applying common sense. This was a view of things that left me uneasy, but Tucker, who had devoted his whole working life to an exhaustive study of the subject and was one of the country's leading scholars of foreign policy, found it positively alarming.

In the event, all our worries were misplaced. Bob and I got on famously, and Irving, perhaps remembering the trouble that he himself had experienced with interference from the Paris office of the Congress for Cultural Freedom during his *Encounter* editorship, performed immaculately as publisher: always interested and supportive, always respectful of editorial autonomy, ready with praise and tactful with advice and criticism, taking on himself the onerous but crucial responsibility of looking after the funding. On one thing

Irving was firm: *The National Interest* would not be a "journal", it would be a magazine. It would be concerned about reaching the educated general reader, not the specialist; it would give attention to ideas and arguments and policy, rather than emphasise scholarship; it would put a premium on decent writing.

After a quiet start, *The National Interest* steadily gained prestige and influence. Oddly, though we could be fairly characterised as a "Cold War magazine" when we began (in our first issue, we asserted quite firmly that "the Soviet Union constitutes the greatest single threat to America's interests, and will continue to do so for the foreseeable future"), we performed rather better after the collapse of communism and the Soviet Union. We took up the questions of the nature of the post-Cold War era, and of the appropriate American foreign policy for it, more quickly and in more lively fashion than most others. Francis Fukuyama's "The End of History?" (1989) gave us a flying start, and we have continued to be pace-setters in the discussion of the character of the new era.

While the magazine has always welcomed a variety of conservative and centrist views, the prevailing editorial position, or disposition, has been one of realism. Initially, this was something that Irving – a New York intellectual accustomed to focusing on the role of ideas – did not altogether share. In the lead piece that he contributed to our first issue – "Foreign Policy in an Age of Ideology" – he declared the traditional conception of national interest to be "dead beyond resurrection", thereby directly challenging the validity of the new magazine's name! But over time *The National Interest* has succeeded in converting its publisher, and he has now sometimes taken to describing himself as a neoconservative neorealist when the subject of foreign policy comes up.

One of the great pleasures of going to work as editor of *The National Interest* is that one gets to meet Irving, sitting just across the room as editor of *The Public Interest*, every day. As befits a New York intellectual, he is rarely to be caught without firm – or at least definite – opinions on both current issues and editorial matters, and listening to them is a stimulating way of starting the day. (On the editorial questions he is tough-minded, and he quotes with relish Cyril Connolly's response to an author complaining about the non-appearance of his article: "Well, it was good enough to accept, and it was good enough to set in type, but it wasn't good enough to publish.") As is much rarer in the case of intellectuals, Irving is also an exceptionally good and responsive listener.

Another major advantage of working with him is that one gets to meet a lot of bright and nice young people. Irving is a great believer in, and practitioner of, the intern system; there has been a flow of such young talents through both our offices during the ten years I have been there. More often than not, he and I have been the only people over 30 on the premises.

This commitment to the young is a matter of affinity as well as policy: he *likes* the company of young people. When I was beginning to write this piece in the fall of 1994, Irving and Bea gave a party for those who had worked on the two magazines as interns over the past 25 years. Nearly 50 men and women turned up, a fair sample of Irving's young people over three decades and with an age range from the early 20s to the early 50s. They included many who now hold prominent positions in government, universities, think tanks, newspapers, foundations – as well as some editors of magazines. These are all people who, at a crucial stage of their lives, benefited greatly from exposure to Irving: from his instruction, his advice, his encouragement and care and friendship – and most of all from his example of how to live honestly and creatively on that uncertain ground where the worlds of ideas and of public policy meet. At that party, affection for him radiated through the company. Brilliant writer though he is, and enormously influential though he has been, I suspect that Irving might regard the people in that room as his most satisfying achievement.

Don't Panic. It's Only Prophecy

The Spectator Australia, 24 April 2010

Based on remarks Harries made to graduating students after being presented
with an honorary Doctor of Letters at Sydney University on 9 April 2010, this
op-ed revised and updated a September 2005 article from the inaugural issue
of *The American Interest*, "Suffer the Intellectuals". The article was extracted
as "The Parochialism of the Present" in the *Australian Financial Review* (16
September 2005), and was also later reprinted in CIS's quarterly magazine
Policy (Autumn 2008).

Today's university graduates are going out into the world in
less than optimistic circumstances, with not one but several
predictions of doom hovering over their heads and the world at
large. Among them are global warming, the collapse of capitalism,
the prospect of more terrorism and further nuclear proliferation.

It seems to me that in the circumstances, they could do with a
bit of cheering up. I recently turned 80 and one of the few benefits
of growing old can be that, while one's short-term memory may
be pathetic, one retains a functioning and commodious long-term
memory. This can provide context and a sense of proportion. It
can do something to rescue one from what has been well termed
the "parochialism of the present" – the tendency to believe that
what is happening now, and to us, must be of unprecedented and
transcendent significance.

Bearing that in mind, let me briefly recall some of the things that
many of the best minds have predicted during my lifetime.

In the 1940s, most of the leading intellectuals in Britain believed,
as many do now, that capitalism was a failed system, one which
had "manifestly no future", to quote George Orwell's words on the
subject. An up-and-coming historian, A.J.P. Taylor, agreed, declaring:
"Nobody in Europe believes in the American way of life – that is
in private enterprise." A leading man-of-letters, Cyril Connolly,
expressed the prevailing mood more melodramatically: "It is closing

time in the gardens of the West, and from now on an artist will be judged only by the resonance of his solitude or the quality of his despair."

Splendid words. But what actually followed these declarations was not collapse and despair, but the most successful era in the history of capitalism. Output in Western countries rapidly doubled and redoubled. And, for the first time in their lives, millions of ordinary people enjoyed a taste of affluence – home ownership, automobiles, labour-saving white goods, proper vacations, and so on.

A second memory: during most of the Cold War many leading scientists and intellectuals – men of the calibre of Albert Einstein and Bertrand Russell no less – insisted that the world was poised on the knife-edge of a nuclear disaster, one that would certainly occur unless there was prompt nuclear disarmament. The *Bulletin of the Atomic Scientists* had as its logo a clock set permanently at five minutes to midnight. No issue was given higher priority by intellectuals than "banning the bomb".

In the event, of course, nothing happened – no nuclear disarmament and no war. As far as the superpowers were concerned, the Cold War turned out to be an exceptionally stable state of affairs. Over four decades not a shot was fired in anger between them. This, not despite nuclear weapons but precisely because of the fear and caution they generated. In Winston Churchill's words, "by a process of sublime irony", safety would turn out to be "the sturdy child of terror".

My third and final example: in the mid-1970s, after the turmoil of the 1960s, with its assassinations, violent street politics, and the scandal of Watergate, some prominent thinkers began to deny the viability of liberal democracy as a political system. As the one-time Harvard professor and future US senator Daniel Patrick Moynihan put it: "Liberal democracy on the American model ... has simply no relevance to the future. It is where the world was, not where it is going." The prominent French commentator Jean-François Revel concurred, declaring that "democracy ... may be an historical accident, a brief parenthesis that is closing before our eyes."

But even as the ink was drying on their writing, the number of democracies in the world was rapidly increasing, not decreasing: first in Europe (Spain, Portugal and Greece), then in Asia (South Korea, Taiwan, the Philippines), then other parts of the world (including much of the disintegrating Soviet empire). By the end of the century the number had increased threefold and Francis Fukuyama had published his famous article, "The End of History?", pronouncing not the death but the universal triumph of liberal democracy.

What is one to make of this record? The predictions that I refer to were all made by men of repute, all were taken very seriously, all were very pessimistic, and they all turned out to be wrong. This does not, of course, point to the conclusion that all other predictions of disaster must be false. As the old fable taught us, however many times the cry of "Wolf!" has been raised misleadingly, one day the beast may really come.

But what these examples do surely justify is the rather reassuring conclusion that, in human affairs, prediction is far from being an exact science even when it is engaged in by the most eminent minds. Given their track record, there will be a much better than even chance that they will have misunderstood or overlooked something crucial. There are no experts on predicting the future. All too often, events confirm the experience of the English Prime Minister Lord Melbourne: "What all the wise men promised has not happened, and what all the damned fools said would happen has come to pass."

Beyond that, and more important, the future is not to be seen as something preordained, not something already existing and impatiently waiting in the wings for its turn on the stage of history. The future does not exist, is not something already there to be discovered, like an island or a mountain. It is something which is still to be made. And how it is made, and what it will become, will depend on tomorrow's leaders, here and throughout the world.

Photographed at his home in Sydney for a profile by Geoffrey Barker, "The Long Journey of an Australian Conservative", *Australian Financial Review*, 22 May 2004

With Tom Switzer in Sydney in 2009

GEOFF HENDERSON, *SYDNEY MORNING HERALD*

Harries (left) at a Forum on Vietnam in St Ives with W. C. Wentworth, Ald. R. S. Turner, Senator L. Murphy (standing) and Dr I. V. Newman, September 1965

(Left) Remembering Richard Krygier at *Quadrant*'s 30th Anniversary Dinner in 1986, with Christopher Koch looking on and (right) Author photo from *Strategy and the Southwest Pacific*, 1989

SECTION TWO

Australian Foreign Policy

The Menzies Foreign Policy: A Study in Realism

Quadrant, December 1983 [extract]

Harries published this major study of Menzies – Australia's longest-serving prime minister – when he was the John M. Olin Visiting Fellow at the Heritage Foundation in Washington, having recently resigned as the Australian Ambassador to UNESCO (1982-83) following a change of government in Canberra.

In the 1940s Robert Menzies developed a position on the United Nations which reflected very accurately the classical realist critique of utopianism in international affairs. He did so with considerable cogency, force, and – given the expectations of the time – political courage. No doubt his enthusiasm for the task was greatly increased by H.V. Evatt's vulnerability to such a critique, but it is worth noting that he began to sound sceptical warnings ("we may be too tempted to try to solve [the problem of maintaining peace] by some rather superficial formula ... we may unduly pin our faith in some particular word or phrase") before Evatt had shown any particularly strong commitment on the question. Some of the key arguments he used were ones he had already advanced in relation to the League of Nations in the 1930s. There is no reason to doubt that the position he developed represented his genuine views.

Menzies did not denounce or oppose the United Nations outright. He specifically dissociated himself from the "extremely pessimistic" view which regarded the organisation as representing a hopeless dream. But his main concern was to expose the fallacies and dangers contained in the other extreme view, the "unduly rosy and optimistic" one, which maintained that the organisation was the means by which international politics could be transformed, with justice replacing power as the operative principle. His position was that of someone wanting to save the organisation from both its enemies and its misguided friends, by directing attention away from appearances – constitutions, formulae, procedures – to its "real" nature, thus making it possible to recognise what could and could not be reasonably expected of it.

In his massive realist tome, *Power Politics,* Georg Schwarzenberger headed a chapter on "The Phenomenon of Power Politics in Disguise" with a remark by Menzies: "We have to face many dangers, and I am not at all sure that the greatest is not one we have suffered from frequently – which is to say 'Let's pretend.'" While the remark itself falls somewhat short of being scintillating, the choice of a Menzies quotation for a chapter with such a title was appropriate. For the whole thrust of his comments on the United Nations was to establish that the organisation did not and could not replace power politics, but could only provide it with a different façade. In doing so it altered the nature of the game somewhat – not necessarily for the better – but it remained essentially the same game. He vehemently and repeatedly rejected the drawing of a sharp distinction between power politics and collective security as "the most unreal antithesis that was ever put in the history of the world."

His analysis of the United Nations was based on the fundamental observation that it left the sovereignty of its members undiminished. It was founded on a contract of fully sovereign states and therefore faced all the difficulties inherent in such a contract, including, crucially, the fact that it was unenforceable except by war. What the Charter really amounted to was "a provision for a species of alliance" between the great powers, "to which there is attached for many useful purposes of discussion and co-operation a great number of smaller powers"; and the Security Council was in reality a kind of conference, with facilities for discussion but with no major obligations or commitments on the part of its members. Menzies rightly saw that the veto power, the subject of so much controversy at the time and which Evatt had elevated into a major issue, merely recognised these facts and was a necessary condition for the acceptance of the organisation by the great powers. It was "just a waste of time to argue about the veto in the Charter as if it were a special artifice that some obliging draftsman could remove", for it was "completely in line with the real facts of international life."

All this means that the United Nations could do little more than reflect the realities of the political situation. Far from being able to determine or to transform the behaviour of the great powers, its own character would be determined by the relationships existing among them – and, as always, those relationships would be shaped by the prevailing configuration of power and interests. To think otherwise was to see the organisation as "a house fully constructed which in due course, by some miracle, would be able to build its own foundations." Only if the great powers reached a state of harmony could the United Nations function effectively as a peace-keeping body; if they did not, it could only be a "forum for international debate and a vehicle for international propaganda", and the decisive actions would have to be taken outside it. That is, in the event of great power conflict and aggression, the United Nations would be virtually irrelevant, and peace would depend, as it always had done, on those states which wanted to preserve it having more power than those which did not.

All this was developed with the inexorable logic of a theorem and given the premise on which it was based it was irrefutable. Certainly, it was much more intellectually coherent than the case put forward by Evatt. It is precisely because it was such a thoroughgoing and typical realist analysis that Menzies' treatment of the United Nations issue is interesting, because it brings out very clearly some of the main features of the realist position.

ॐ ॐ ॐ

One of the things it illuminates is the harmony between realism and conservatism. "The antithesis of utopia and reality", E.H. Carr maintains, "reproduces itself in the antithesis of radical and conservative, of Left and Right … The radical is necessarily utopian, and the conservative realist." Here, as elsewhere, Carr overstates his point – sometimes radicalism is purely destructive and nihilistic, and sometimes conservatism is romantic – but he is right in pointing to a general affinity between realism and conservatism. Both stress the extent to which situations are determined and intractable, and accord a limited role to individual will and reason in shaping events; both value prudence highly and are sceptical of abstract, general theories; both look to interest rather than principle as the motive for action, and to history or experience rather than to "philosophy" for the basis of sound judgement.

Certainly, this affinity existed in Menzies' case. He was concerned to stress the "experimental", untested character of the UN and the consequent unwisdom of placing all one's faith in it at the expense of more securely grounded institutions. In Burkeman terms, he maintained that

> Whilst a new world charter may have a value which is as yet untried, our relationship with the British Empire has a value which has been proved in circumstances of very great trial over many generations.

In similar terms, he counselled against haste and over-ambitiousness:

> In all matters of government ... it is good to take one step at a time and learn to walk before we try to run ... I would say that the history of failure is based not upon attempting too little, but usually upon attempting too much.

The sound procedure was that of building progressively on "natural foundations".

The conservative nature of the analysis was also apparent in that his whole emphasis was on the immutable character of the long-established factors in the situation – sovereignty, national power, the self-interest of states and so on. The new factors – the hopes and aspirations for a new order in Western countries, the reaction against power politics – were treated as illusions to be exposed or utopian schemes to be refuted, rather than as data whose political significance would have to be explored and taken into account in formulating policy. It is true that Menzies occasionally referred to the effect which the United Nations had on the conduct of foreign policy – he was sometimes eloquent on its effects as a "forcing house" in which publicity quickly transformed small disputes into big ones – but he did so in the context of exposing error rather than suggesting adjustment to new circumstances. Yet these effects were part of the new reality.

This brings out a general dilemma of realism: that standing opposed to utopianism, it cannot easily encompass the presence and consequences of utopianism in its account of reality. The practical effects of this were to be clearly evident in Australia's dealings with the United Nations during the Menzies period in office, when the style adopted was a defensive, resistant one, generally unsuited to exploiting the possibilities offered by the ethos of the United Nations.

Another feature of Menzies' position was the sharp distinction it made between form and substance. One of his major themes was that attention was directed much too much to questions of procedures and forms and not enough to substantive questions. He quoted Carr about the danger of putting one's faith in "some neat paper construction". He accused Evatt of "occupying too much time on shadows and too little on substance, of occupying too much time on questions of procedure and too little time on matters which will really affect the world's peace." Here, again, Menzies was making a characteristic realist point. In his celebrated attack on legalism in American foreign policy, George Kennan points to the emphasis on institutional frameworks ("All that was needed was a framework") which characterises such an approach and speaks of "a cast of thought which holds the form in higher esteem than the substance."

As against Evatt, who often seemed to proceed on the assumption that if the appropriate changes in machinery were implemented a change in the behaviour and attitude of states would automatically follow, the point was effective and justified. But Menzies, and most other realists, tended to go too far in the other direction and to maintain that forms could only reflect the substance of international politics and that they had no independent force. The truth is, surely, that there is an interaction between form and substance, and that while the influence of the latter on the former is normally by far the greater, it is still true that forms can and frequently do have some influence on behaviour and hence on the substance of international politics. To dismiss questions of form as "the artificial problems of the superstructure" is to expose oneself to precisely the same criterion as the Marxist model of base and superstructure is vulnerable to.

♋♋♋

Before leaving the question of Menzies' attitude towards the United Nations, it is worth observing that in one important respect he deviated from the realist position. As I have pointed out, he rejected the antithesis between power politics and collective security. Such a rejection is entirely justified in so far as it is based on the recognition that collective security will depend on the mobilisation of sufficient power to create a balance unfavourable to a potential aggressor. But in his search for a permanent system of collective security Menzies went much further than that. When he talked of giving power politics a "collective quality", he spoke not of conventional balance of power strategy, but of

> an alliance not on lines which are based on mere self-interest to preserve or gain territory, but on lines which represent a real consensus of thought among peace-loving people that between them will, at all times, have enough strength to keep the peace.

The state of affairs thus envisaged, with its stress on permanent consensus and the subordination of self-interest, deviated very significantly from the classic Hobbesian model of the realists.

The same quest also led Menzies to stress the importance of "spirit" as a decisive factor, as when he spoke of "the true and tenacious existence of an international spirit which alone can make any 'new order' succeed." While it is true that he emphasised "spirit" in opposition to the tendency to focus on forms and procedures, it still represented a move away from the characteristic determinism of realism which tends to interpret "spirit" as a function of structure, rather than as an independent variable. To pin one's faith on the possibility of a new "spirit" emerging to transform international politics was, after all, tantamount to expecting "a home to build its own foundations", and it vitiated his own criticism of Evatt, who could reply that the fostering of a new "spirit" was precisely what he was engaged in. More generally, this appeal to a structurally disembodied "spirit" suggests that, even here, at its toughest and most consistent, there was something of a soft underbelly to Menzies' realism.

The Clash of Civilisations

The Weekend Australian, 3-4 April 1993

Published when Harries was based in Washington as Editor of *The National Interest*, the article led to a spirited exchange with *The Australian*'s Foreign Editor, Greg Sheridan, and former Australian diplomat Richard Woolcott in the letters page. He later wrote that it "elicited the most violent response of anything that I have ever published in Australia or anywhere else."[*]

Since the end of the Cold War, much of the discussion about Australia's place in the world and its foreign policy has been shaped by two assumptions: first, that in the new era economic considerations are going to be the decisive ones; second, that Australia's future lies with Asia.

The first assumption reflects both a proper concern about Australia's declining economic position and the now fashionable view that, in international affairs, economic power is displacing military power as the decisive indicator of status and influence – that geoeconomics is replacing geopolitics.

The second assumption has many components: the changed pattern of Australia's trade; admiration for the fantastic economic progress made by much of Asia; a sense of freedom from Cold War dependence on the United States; resentment of Europe's exclusionary policies and of abandonment by Britain; and, not least, a need to demonstrate national independence and renewal by breaking with established historical patterns and striking out in new directions.

Given these two assumptions, it should be of considerable interest to Australians that the US's leading political scientist, Professor Samuel Huntington at Harvard University, has recently propounded a thesis that directly challenges the first and implicitly challenges the second. This article will appear under the title "The Clash of Civilisations?" in the Summer issue of *Foreign Affairs*.

---

[*] *Editors' note*: See "Power and Civilisation", *The National Interest*, Spring 1994, p. 109.

Huntington's thesis is this: the fundamental source of conflict in the new post-Cold War world will not be primarily ideological or economic, but cultural. A "clash of civilisations" will now dominate global politics, and the fault lines between civilisations will constitute the principal battle lines. It is a thesis pregnant with implications for Australia.

As Huntington sees it, mankind is divided into nine civilisations: the two variants of Western civilisation – European and North American – Confucian, Japanese, Islamic, Hindu, Slavic-Orthodox, Latin American, and African. While conceding that these are not entirely tidy entities – that there is a blurring and overlap at the edges, and some room for debate about definitions – Huntington insists they are real and meaningful.

The differences between civilisations are fundamental. Instead of the positional ideological question, "Which side are you on?", they raise the more fundamental one: "What are you?".

As the world shrinks and interaction increases, the result is not, as has been widely assumed, universal harmony, but increased awareness of differences and friction at the interface. And as modernisation severs people from their traditional local identities, culture generally and religion in particular assume greater importance in filling the gap – witness the spread or revival of religious fundamentalism, not only in Islam but in Hindu India, Latin America and indeed in much of the West.

In current relationships among civilisations, the West occupies a special place. It is the dominant civilisation economically, techno-logically, militarily and culturally. Its popular culture, particularly that of the North American branch, is spreading throughout the world, threatening the autonomy of other cultures.

Because of this, Huntington maintains, a powerful reaction is setting in among the elites of other civilisations in the form of de-Westernising, return-to-roots movements. And as their economic strength increases, particularly in Asia and the Middle East, both the material means and the pride to drive such movements grow. Thus, "the West at the peak of its power confronts the non-Wests that increasingly have the desire, the will and the resources to shape the world in non-Western ways."

Of all the clashes of civilisation, the most acrimonious are going to be those between the West and those other civilisations (acting either alone or in de facto alliances) who feel that their fundamental character is threatened by the impact and incursions of the West.

♋♋♋

Why should this thesis be of particular concern to Australians?

First, because Australia, with New Zealand, is the most isolated fragment of Western civilisation in the world. If international politics is to be dominated by such a clash, with the hostility of other civilisations to the West its central theme, Australia's location makes it particularly vulnerable.

Second, and even more ominous from Australia's point of view, Huntington identifies as the main challenge to the West a de facto anti-Western co-operation between the Confucian and Islamic civilisations of Asia. The most striking present manifestation of this is China's readiness to supply arms and weapons technology to Islamic states: material for nerve gas to Libya and Iraq; help in building a nuclear reactor in Algeria; nuclear technology to Iran.

Now, if Huntington is right in identifying such an emerging Confucian-Islamic challenge to the West as a central fact of the new era, it means Australia is living on the edge of the most dangerous "fault-line" in the world – and is the softest Western target on that line.

Third, Huntington's thesis should encourage Australia to think more carefully (as thoughtful Australians have already been urging us to do) about the nature of the "Asia" that it is proposed we should join. Leaving aside the more distant parts of that continent, the Asia that is closest to Australia encompasses three distinct civilisations: the Confucian, the Islamic, and the Japanese.

Of these, Japan – the one most Australians probably have in mind when they talk of "joining Asia" – is a society and civilisation unique to itself. No other country or society in Asia identifies with it, many are extremely suspicious of it, and it is itself characterised by a conspicuous level of xenophobia and racism.

This, maintains Huntington, is important not only in cultural and political terms, but in economic ones. He argues that the "economic regionalism", which is widely thought to be a growing trend in the world of the 1990s (and which is one of the principal reasons given for Australian association with Asia), "may succeed only when it is rooted in a common civilisation" – just as the European community rests in a shared foundation of European culture and Western Christianity, and just as the North American Free Trade Association is based implicitly on the successful Americanisation of the whole region.

If this hypothesis is sound, then any principal East Asian economic bloc that emerges will be centred not on a Japan that stands culturally alone, but on China, which shares a common culture with a number of countries and has substantial cultural presence in others. In fact, such a "Greater China" is already emerging as Taiwan, Hong Kong and South Korea shift production of labour-intensive manufacturing to factories on the Chinese mainland and as the economic weight of China increases rapidly.

The last reason why Australians should ponder Huntington's thesis is perhaps the most compelling of all. In the course of his analysis, he identifies an important category of states that he labels "torn countries".

What he has in mind here is not ethnically- and religiously-divided countries such as Yugoslavia, but something more subtle and interesting – countries that have a considerable degree of cultural homogeneity but which have become seriously divided over whether their society should belong to one civilisation or another.

Most usually, this occurs when leaders and elites want to make their countries members of the West, but whose history, culture and traditions are non-Western. The examples he gives are Turkey (Turkic-Islamic but wanting to be European), Mexico (Latin American but wanting to be American), and Russia (long torn between full membership of the West and leadership of a distinct Slavic-Orthodox civilisation).

In these terms, Australia looks like providing a historic first – that is, the first known example of what might be called a "reverse torn country"; historically a fully Western country in which a significant section of the elite now advocates a move to membership of another, non-Western civilisation.

To the extent that this is true, Huntington's identification of the three requirements a torn country must meet in order to redefine its civilisational identity successfully should be of great interest to Australians.

These are: first, that its political and economic elite has to be generally supportive and enthusiastic about the move; second, that its public has to be willing to acquiesce in the redefinition; third, that the dominant group in the recipient civilisation has to be willing to embrace the convert.

Those who have lived in Australia while this "let's become part of Asia" thinking has been gathering strength will be better qualified to judge to what extent Australia meets the first two of these requirements. My impression from a distance is that while a significant part of Australia's elite has bought the idea (without having thought very seriously about either the condition for its successful implementation or its consequences), the public at large is not enthusiastic, and is unlikely to acquiesce in it once its implications become clear.

In any case, the wishes and desires of Australians are not the decisive factors in the equation. For there can be no doubt about Australia's inability to meet the vital third requirement: there is no evidence at all that any of the available civilisations of Asia – the Confucian, the Japanese, the Malay-Islamic – show any inclination whatsoever to accept Australia as a new member. Indeed, if civilisation and culture provide the test, how could they?

Australia's credentials for acceptance by any of the Asian civilisations are in fact much weaker than are those of Turkey to become part of the European community, and Europe, which has tolerance as one of its cultural values, refuses to accept Turkey. Why on earth should we expect civilisations that have no tradition of tolerating and embracing outsiders, and which are today reacting strongly against Western domination, to accept an Australia that shares few of their values and traditions and which represents an outpost of the West?

To the extent that Huntington's thesis is valid and civilisational frontiers represent the vital cleavages and lines of tension, Australians will have to accept that the only choice they have is the limited one between the two branches – European and North American – of Western civilisation. It would be evidence of emerging realism if they began to address themselves to that question instead of indulging in the fantasy of shedding their past like a skin and becoming "Asian". Culture is more than a skin.

To avoid misunderstanding, I should make it clear that Huntington's paper does not deal with Australia's predicament: the version I have seen does not even mention it. I have merely extrapolated his arguments to the Australian case. And, of course, the fact that Huntington advances a thesis does not mean that it is necessarily true.

Still, his track record as a leading thinker in the field suggests his views should be taken seriously. Even more important, so does what has been happening in the world since the end of the Cold War. When we look around, what we see increasingly – in the Balkans, along the southern rim of Russia, in India, in the Middle East – is evidence that the clash of civilisations is indeed setting the agenda of the post-Cold War era. When confronted with airy proposals about "making Australia part of Asia", Australians would do well to ponder that evidence.

Time to Reconsider Our US Ties

Australian Financial Review, 10 September 2001

Written shortly after Harries returned to Australia from Washington and joined the Centre for Independent Studies as a Senior Fellow, this op-ed was published the day before the 9/11 terrorist attacks in America.

You win one, you lose one. Immediately after coming out of the *Tampa* affair well ahead politically, John Howard found that the main purpose of his trip to Washington – the negotiation of an agreement on a bilateral trade deal – had been aborted even before he had fastened his seat belt.

Frustrating as this certainly was, it may also have been salutary – a healthy reminder that however sweet the rhetoric and however warm the hugging, the priorities of the two countries are likely to differ at least as often as they coincide.

This is a reminder that some Australians seem to need. Since returning here two months ago after 18 years in Washington, I have been struck by how criticisms of US policy that would be considered routine by many American conservatives are characterised as anti-American by some of their Australian counterparts. And by the praise lavished on the policies of the Bush administration by some commentators here, praise that would make even a loyal Republican blush.

Many things conspire to make it difficult to think realistically about Australia's relationship with the superpower. For one thing, there is the grip of habit, the result of cleaving closely and pretty uncritically for 60 years to what Robert Menzies used to delight in calling "our great and powerful friend". That policy served us well in World War II and during the Cold War, when there were credible threats to our security, but times change.

The English statesman Lord Salisbury once warned that "the commonest error in politics is sticking to the carcass of dead policies." While the US-Australian alliance is anything but dead, habitual ways of thinking and behaving can obscure the extent to which different circumstances have altered the nature of the alliance and the way it fits Australian needs. It is necessary to cultivate the habit of breaking habits.

There are other obstacles to clear thinking about our relations with America: the fascination that enormous power exercises, especially on politicians who are occupationally conditioned to be power-worshippers; the desire to be liked and approved of by others, still not a negligible factor in the Australian make-up, as demonstrated by the recent consternation at being lectured by a Norwegian sea captain, and by European countries that have made a dreadful mess of their own immigration policies.

And, of course, on the other side of the ledger there is the persistence of that unlovely cultural ambivalence that causes Australian elites to denigrate and reject things American even as they borrow and imitate.

As these things are easily misrepresented, let it be clear that my point is certainly not that the US alliance should be dispensed with. And, equally certainly, it is not that we should relapse into a region-first policy.

But Australia should proceed carefully and without illusion in dealing with its powerful ally. For one thing, post-Cold War American foreign policy is still, in some respects, a work in progress, and those who get too close to it run the danger that a piece of the scaffolding might fall off and hit them. That is certainly so in the case of America's China policy, as powerful domestic forces still contend to determine its ultimate shape and direction.

Even more important, while the US is by historical standards a benevolent hegemon, a hegemon is what it is. Not only is its power vast, but it is concerned to use that power – economic, military, "soft" – to create a world in its own image, with institutions and rules determined by Washington (though Washington sometimes insists on excluding itself from its own rules).

While such a world would have many attractions, the attempt to bring it into being will inevitably generate serious opposition and involve a great deal of strife and conflict. It would be inappropriate and dangerous for a country of Australia's limited means and interests to associate itself closely with such an enterprise.

Above all, Australia should not put its trust in a "special relationship". Such relationships usually exist principally in the imagination of the weaker parties and, even when they have some limited reality, they are incapable of bearing the weight of a serious clash of interests.

Witness how, only a decade after the closest of partnerships during World War II, the US had no compunction in cutting Britain off at the knees during the 1956 Suez crisis.

Or for a contemporary example, consider the current treatment of Pakistan. In recent decades, it has had a close relationship with the US. But now, with Washington concerned to improve its relationship with India for geopolitical reasons, Pakistan has been unceremoniously dumped. The ubiquitous and loquacious Richard Armitage has recently characterised it as a "rogue state" and dismissed the past US-Pakistan amity as a "false relationship".

Can we assume that Australia will always be an exception in this respect? Not really. Those with good memories will remember that, even at the height of the Cold War, when it came to the choice between supporting Indonesia – then under the rule of the ultra-radical, anti-Western Sukarno – or Australia over the future of the Western half of New Guinea, the US supported Indonesia.

Nothing wrong with that (except, of course, for the poor people of West Irian). It is the way international politics works. A troublesome Indonesia outweighed a compliant Australia in American calculations.

Rather than engaging in a futile effort to change it, or proceeding on the assumption that we are a special case, the sensible thing is to come to terms with it and act accordingly.

Who Says We Are in the Doghouse?
The Australian, 4 February 2002

In the eyes of much of the world, the Australians of today are a relaxed, self-confident people, at ease with themselves. Which makes it very strange that many Australians – and in particular those who take it upon themselves to represent the country's conscience – spend much of their time agonising over what the world thinks about us, and convincing themselves that we are in the doghouse.

Recently, this aspect of the national psyche has been having a field day as editorial writers, columnists and sundry intellectuals fret and wail about what is happening to our reputation because of what has been happening here concerning refugees. A recent editorial in Sydney's *Sun Herald* was expressing the current orthodoxy in those circles when it declared: "Once again, we are being condemned at the court of world opinion as callous and inhumane." (Note, by the way, that "once again", making it clear that this has not been seen as an isolated act of delinquency.)

At one level, this sort of obsession may represent a form of vanity, in that it assumes that the world is constantly scrutinising and reacting to events in Australia. As anyone who has lived abroad knows, this isn't so. Indeed, in many parts of the world for long stretches of time, good peripheral vision is required to be aware of Australia at all. When the country does get attention, as often as not it is either to record some natural event (bushfires, most recently), or in the form of glowing praise in the travel, sports, cinema, or food and wine sections of newspapers.

Has the refugee issue really changed all this? Who is it exactly who regards us as "callous and inhumane"? Who is it who sits in that "court of world opinion"? Is it perhaps Japan, which is notoriously hostile to accepting immigrants? Or is it China, with its improving but still very bad record on human rights? Or India, which operates an informal caste system and has made a practice of burning villages in Kashmir? Or again, it might be Indonesia's shock at our behaviour that we have to worry about, now that it has stopped killing people in Timor and only occasionally indulges in assassination.

Add to these four countries an Africa soaked in its own blood, a Middle East that contains no democracy other than Israel and Turkey, and a Latin America that has still not completely kicked the habits of dictatorship and torture, and one has accounted for more than three-quarters of the world's population.

But, of course, these are not really the countries that Australia's intellectuals have in mind when they talk of "world opinion". In so far as they have countries in mind, they are talking about those of the West, that is of Europe and North America, which together account for only about 13% of the world's population. It is before the West, in particular, that Australia should feel ashamed.

Or should it? As far as Britain is concerned, we have heard of the violent riots in its northern towns last year. The United Nations High Commissioner for Refugees (UNHCR) has talked of a "climate of vilification" in Britain, and of a racist press and a complacent police force. After pointing this out in a recent lead review article in *The Times Literary Supplement*, biographer and broadcaster Caroline Moorehead sums up the situation in and around Europe: "Everywhere, from Spain to Germany, France to Egypt, refugees and those seeking asylum are hounded and reviled."

She also informs us that in 1999 Canada, that paradigm of political correctness, spent $300 million – 10 times what it contributed to the UNHCR that year – on erecting tough barriers against refugees.

So, it appears that Europe and Canada are not particularly well-placed to pass stern judgment on Australia. Which leaves the US. But we can be as sure as we are of anything that it is not judgment by that country that our liberal intellectuals have in mind. The US is a country to be criticised and condemned, not one to be accepted as arbiter or judge.

෨෨෨

What then actually constitutes the court of world opinion? It is difficult to resist the conclusion that its principal and regular members, in the eyes of the Australians who so readily appeal to it, are a few left-liberal newspapers such as Britain's *The Guardian* and *The Observer*, a legion of non-government organisations, and the bureaucrats of the UNHCR and some other UN bodies. In other words, "people like us".

Others will be recruited on an ad-hoc basis when their views happen to serve the right ends on a particular issue. Thus, the conservative *Wall Street Journal*, usually anathema to liberals, is useful on the refugee issue because of its commitment, based essentially on economic grounds, to open borders.

Especially prominent in the context of refugee matters is, of course, the UNHCR, represented widely as an objective, dedicated and expert source of enlightenment on these matters. This is not the picture that Moorehead presents. She speaks of the agency in terms of an "inflexible bureaucracy, resentful of criticism, run by people more interested in protecting their turf than in devising workable solutions." She also mentions in passing that not long ago a number of UNHCR employees were sacked for selling refugee status for vast sums of money. Nobody's perfect these days.

The truth is that there is no such thing as "world opinion", let alone a "court" of the same. What we have is a variety of contending and shifting opinions, reflecting different values, interests and states of knowledge. To try to elevate one, or some combination, of these to the status of "world opinion" simply represents an attempt to gain advantage in debate on the cheap. It clarifies nothing and validates nothing. And note that those who appeal most readily to its supposed moral authority, as representing a sort of global majority verdict, are the same people who are most reluctant to grant any such authority to the expressed views of a real majority in their own country.

The moral and political problems posed by illegal immigrants and detention centres are real and extremely difficult ones, and there is much to be said on both sides of the matter. They are issues that exemplify very well the central belief of political philosopher Isaiah Berlin, that the values human beings hold are not mutually compatible and in harmony; that choices have to be made, not only between good and evil but between conflicting goods; and that such choices inevitably involve loss and often involve conflict. This, in Berlin's view, is the tragedy of the human condition.

Humanitarian care, alleviation of human suffering, and tolerance are important human values; but so are security, civil order, and fairness and consistency in the application of laws and rules – even if their appeal is less obvious until such time as they are not available. Public discussion would gain immeasurably if it proceeded from a recognition of this.

Unfortunately, "world opinion" is no help in this respect.

Hearts, Minds and Immigration

Quadrant, October 2002

Harries initially presented this essay as a talk to the Boston-Oxford-Melbourne Conversazione on immigration, held in Melbourne in September 2002. It was reprinted in 2003 in *The Multi-Cultural Experiment*, editor Leonie Kramer.

Let me begin by declaring an interest. I am myself an immigrant. Forty-seven years ago, I came as a young man to take up my first ever job, at Sydney University. I came from a monochrome, austere Britain, where rationing had only ended the previous year, to a gloriously technicolour Sydney – blue skies, golden beaches, palm and flame trees, and, not least, more red meat than I had seen since 1939.

I came entirely on Australia's terms. Multiculturalism had not been invented and the human rights industry was in its infancy. It did not occur to me that I could make demands on Australia. If I wanted to stay, it was up to me to fit in. This did not involve shedding my past loyalties and affections. They were my business. True to the affinities of my youth, I continued to support Wales in rugby, as I do to this day (and given their recent success rate, a dismal duty it is). But Australia didn't owe me anything; on the contrary, I owed Australia.

I lived in this country for the next 26 years. Then I went abroad, first as an employee of the country that had adopted me and then as an editor in Washington DC. Altogether I was overseas for 20 years. Then I came back again last year to live the rest of my life in Australia.

So, in a sense, I am twice an immigrant. But the conditions of my second arrival were rather different. Multiculturalism was now settled bipartisan policy. The culture of human rights – and, it sometimes seemed, of any other rights you could think of – was thriving. Within two months of my arriving home a major political quarrel had broken out over an immigration issue, and while the rest of the world – certainly the Western world – was preoccupied with the terrible drama of September 11, Australia's political and intellectual classes were even more preoccupied and even more emotional over the *Tampa* affair.

Two things are true about immigration, two things that don't sit particularly well together. First, it is a topic that is capable of generating enormous heat. Sensible and normally civil people can and do divide violently on the subject. It is one that taps deep, visceral feelings – feelings, among others, of possession, identity, solidarity, violation, rejection, exclusion, discrimination, and regeneration. In Australia we witnessed the emotive force of the issue some years ago in the reaction to some measured comments by Geoffrey Blainey; and we have witnessed it again in the last year, with extravagant claims of being ashamed to be Australian and a ready resort to charges of racism and concentration camps. But this is by no means an Australian peculiarity. In Washington DC we had highly-sophisticated friends who were prepared to argue in a civilised fashion about virtually anything, but who broke off relations with each other because of differences on the subject of immigration.

All the more remarkable, then, that a second thing that is true about immigration is that, in itself, it doesn't make much sense to see it as good or bad. It is surely true that, intrinsically, migration – the process of moving people from one society to another – has no moral quality. Everything depends on the circumstances.

Edmund Burke once insisted that "[c]ircumstances are what render every civil and political scheme either beneficial or noxious to mankind." That is certainly true of immigration. The term can cover everything from tribal wandering, to invasion, to economically-driven movement, to the humane acceptance of refugees, to entry by a process of moral blackmail. The trans-Atlantic slave trade was a kind of immigration program, as was the involuntary transportation of convicts from England to Australia. Circumstances count: who comes, why they come, how they are chosen, the conditions of their arrival, and the conditions of their settlement.

The European Experience: Identity and Control

What I want to talk about are the respective recent immigration experiences of Western Europe and Australia. And I do so because I believe that the European experience can help us in evaluating our own performance.

By common consent, Europe now has a major immigration problem. Indeed, some serious people would say that immigration and its consequences are destined to become the continent's most serious problem – which, considering the competition, is a bold prediction. To a large extent it is a problem of Europe's own making, brought about by sins of both omission and commission over the last half-century.

Until the Second World War nearly all the countries of Europe had very homogeneous populations and very little recent experience of immigration. Overwhelmingly, it was a place people went from – to America, Canada, Australia, South Africa, New Zealand, and dozens of colonies – rather than came to. All this was to change rapidly and dramatically after 1945.

A number of factors were at work. One was the abrupt ending of the age of European imperialism and the rapid dismantling of empires, as a result of which the combination of a residual sense of responsibility, guilt, and a desire to maintain the advantages of at least the vestiges of the old order (in the British case in the form of the Commonwealth) led to the granting of immigration rights to the peoples of the old empires. (Incidentally, it seems to me that guilt is almost always an unsound guide to policy, because its focus of attention is not the world but the state of one's own conscience and one's own peace of mind.)

Andrew Roberts has written brilliantly about how this happened in postwar Britain, and the consequences that followed, in his book *Eminent Churchillians*. Sufficient now to say that over the decades immediately following the war, hundreds of thousands poured in from the West Indies, India, Pakistan, Bangladesh, Sri Lanka, Uganda, and various other parts of Africa.

In the case of France, there was to be substantial and sustained movement from North Africa into metropolitan France, as well as a significant intake from Indo-China. Smaller but still substantial numbers came from Indonesia to the Netherlands, and from various colonies into Portugal. Once started, family reunion and other rights ensured that the flow never stopped.

As the European economies recovered from the devastation of war in the 1950s and entered a period of sustained growth and prosperity, the need for cheap labour became another major motive for encouraging immigrants. Germany now has several million resident Turks who originally came as "guest workers". In Britain, there are large numbers of people from the Indian subcontinent who were brought in to work in the textile industry of northern England, an industry that no longer exists.

More recently, the collapse of the Soviet Union and empire, and the disorder and violence that followed, particularly in the Caucasus and Balkans, set in motion another movement of large numbers of people westward and northward into the countries of the European Union – 700,000 from Bosnia alone.

But the problem has not been, and is not, only or even primarily, one of numbers. In fact, many insist that there is *no* problem of numbers, that with a rapidly ageing population Europe needs more rather than fewer immigrants if it is to sustain economic growth and current living standards. It has been claimed, for example, that Germany will soon need as many as 450,000 migrants each year merely to be able to support its growing army of pensioners and the rapidly increasing welfare burden that involves. Others disagree, and given that during the last decade Europe has suffered serious unemployment rates – as high as 12% in some years, and still over 7% for the EU as a whole – and that most European countries already have rapidly growing under-classes, a non-economist might find it hard to follow that argument. But there it is.

In any case, the real issue is not primarily one of numbers but of identity and of control, both of which have been progressively undermined by forces that initially did not derive primarily from immigration itself. As far as a sense of distinct national identity is concerned, until quite recently most European nations had it in abundance. For many it was badly shaken by the humiliation of defeat and occupation in the Second World War, by the rapid loss of imperial status, and then by a long sense of impotence as, sandwiched between two superpowers, European countries lost control over their own destiny and depended on America for security. The one European statesman who fully understood the significance of this for national identity and shaped a national policy accordingly was Charles de Gaulle.

But it was partly to compensate for that dependence, and partly to free themselves from their own disastrous recent history, that the Europeans embarked on the bold but uncertain enterprise of creating a European Union, for a long time modestly and dishonestly described as merely an economic arrangement. In terms of the problem of identity, however, the European venture has not been able to provide a satisfactory solution. For while it has progressively required the subordination, if not the abandonment, of a sense of national identity and sovereignty to the greater cause of Europe, that cause cannot yet – and perhaps never will – provide a satisfying substitute identity. The EU, sponsored by political elites, run by bureaucrats, is a matter of innumerable committees and acronyms. It has no sustaining myths or symbols, no hold on the imagination or loyalties of ordinary European people, not even a common language.

The result of all this? According to Roger Boyes, writing in *The Times* earlier this year, "The problem is Europe ... is marooned between increasingly enfeebled nation states and an incomplete European Union." And he adds, "Native Europeans, confused about their identity, are thus unable to embrace outsiders." (Others might have phrased that last sentence differently. Perhaps: "Native Europeans, confused about their identity, are unable to deal with the immigration problem resolutely.") At the time of the elections earlier this year, *The Economist* spoke of the French people in very similar terms, as suffering from "a perceived loss of national identity between the twin fears of America-led globalisation and the homogenising forces of the European Union."

Raymond Seitz, a recent US Ambassador to London, described the consequence of this eroded sense of self with some wit in a recent speech:

> For Europeans, there is something vaguely embarrassing or even dangerous about sovereignty, except perhaps in the football stadium or the Eurovision Song Contest. And the phrase 'national interest' should never be mentioned in polite society.

As that last remark of Seitz's about national interest suggests, as well as the problem of identity, and partly related to it, there is the problem of diminished control, and this bears directly on the immigration issue. Most obvious in this respect is the matter of control of borders, of entry. In their different ways, the processes of Europeanisation and of globalisation both downgrade and undermine the integrity of borders. According to the logic of these processes, borders are *meant* to be insubstantial and porous, both globally and, especially, within the European Union itself; otherwise they frustrate interdependence and homogenisation.

☙☙☙

The effects of the resulting loss of control did not became fully evident until the last decades of the 20th century, when in depressed economies the demand for cheap labour tapered off and European countries started to become seriously concerned at the numbers flowing in – now not only from the Third World but from the collapsed and conflict-torn Soviet empire. Belated attempts to limit immigration simply had the effect that people declared themselves to be asylum-seekers or resorted to the rapidly growing people-smuggling business, or both. By 1992 the level of asylum-seekers in Western Europe had reached 700,000 per annum. Of these, an official publication of the UNHCR itself – *The State of the World's Refugees 2000* – says, "Most did not have a well-founded fear of persecution" – which should, of course, be the test for qualifying the asylum.

In the same way that water will run downhill, people will move from poor, backward, overcrowded, often corrupt and disorderly countries to wealthy, prosperous ones with generous welfare provisions, unless there are effective impediments to their doing so. In Europe there have been no effective impediments. And once inside the European Union, ease of movement from one country to another has made "asylum shopping" – looking around for the country that offered the easiest acceptance and best conditions – common practice.

A combination of lack of political will, genuine compassion, and pervasive political correctness has made it virtually impossible to exercise firm control over the situation. "Human rights" override EU and national rules and regulations. In Britain, more than 47,000 illegal immigrants were detected in the year 2000. Only 6,000 – about 13% – were sent home.

European governments have made belated efforts to harmonise and strengthen policies to control the inflow, and to encourage burden-sharing. The Schengen Convention, the Dublin Convention, the Treaty of Amsterdam – there have been many meetings, many agreements, but so far with very limited results. Different governments interpret and implement the measures differently. They often play the game of "pass the parcel", moving asylum-seekers from one country to another. Northern governments suspect that the southern, Mediterranean ones are lax in letting people in as long as they will then move north. More basically, the will for firm action still seems to be lacking.

In any case, it is largely a matter of trying to wind up the draw-bridge after the invader is inside the fort. By now, nobody knows exactly how many immigrants have settled in Europe legally and illegally. When it ran a survey article on the question last April, *The New York Times*, usually meticulous in these matters, threw in its hand and settled for "untold millions". But the scale is indicated by the fact that Germany alone is reckoned to have at least seven million immigrants (9% of its total population and with much higher birth rates than the native-born); and that it is estimated that something of the order of 15 million Muslims now live in Western Europe. And there is no sign of the process coming to an end.

All this has happened – is happening – in countries which, as we have seen, are experiencing a crisis of identity, whose sense of themselves has already been attenuated significantly for other reasons, who feel that the world and the inherited culture they know are under threat. In these circumstances, the urge to explain and blame one's predicament in terms of an alien, recently arrived, conspicuously different element in one's society will be strong in many and irresistible in some. It will be strengthened by the belief – unfortunately not altogether unfounded – that many in that group will have arrived by dubious-to-illegitimate means (people-smuggling, destruction of documents), that they are disproportionate consumers of welfare, that they commit more than their share of crime – and, more than anything, that they are conspicuously different and that many of them show little inclination to be less so, thus complicating the matter of national identity even more.

These feelings are likely to be strongest in the losers of Western societies – who are also the ones who live closest to the immigrant communities, who share the streets and the schools with them, and who compete for jobs with them – rather in the way that recently arrived Irish peasants competed with free Negroes for jobs in mid-19th-century America, a competition that led to bloody riots in most American cities.

To preach tolerance and multiculturalism to that segment of society from a safe distance (both geographically and socially) seems not only futile but presumptuous. One can only deny the reality and gravity of the problem that exists if one is prepared to maintain either that a sense of national identity and cohesion is unimportant, or that the identity is so tough and resilient a thing that it can withstand virtually any assault.

The Europe of today has its riots. It has its growing number of extreme right-wing parties, exploiting genuine grievances and anxieties for racist and xenophobic ends. In these circumstances, to stake out grounds for a firm, controlled, effective, non-racist policy on immigration is a difficult challenge – one which Europe's conservative parties have not yet been very successful in meeting, and one which the parties of the left have so far barely acknowledged as existing. (David Blunkett, the British Home Secretary, was considered to be unusually brave, or foolish, when he recently used the word *swamping* to describe the effect of migrant numbers on British institutions.)

Australia: Effectiveness and Compassion

I've taken this extended look at the European scene because I believe that it helps to get the Australian situation and record into perspective, and because so many of Australia's *bien-pensants* have been so vexed about what the so-called "world community", of which Europe seems to be the main component, thinks about Australia's performance in the realm of immigration and asylum-seekers.

The first thing to be said is that Australia is very much in better shape than Europe on this issue. Unlike European countries, and like the United States, Canada and New Zealand, Australia is overwhelmingly a country of immigrants, accustomed to receiving, settling, and integrating a continuous flow of arrivals. At least as yet, Australians do not suffer from a serious problem of identity, though one sometimes gets the impression that purposeful work is in progress to change that.

Again, Australia has maintained pretty effective control over its immigration policy for the last half-century. During that time it has taken in six million immigrants – a number equal to nearly a third of its current total population. Ten percent of these – 600,000 – entered under humanitarian programs.

During that time, too, Australia moved successfully and without trauma from a White Australia policy to a multi-ethnic one. In the year 1999-2000, a third of Australia's migrant intake of 92,000 came from Asia, and another 16% – altogether making up almost half the total – came from the Middle East and Africa. Bear these figures in mind when assessing charges of racism against the Australian government.

Australia is one of only ten countries in the world that accepts an annual quota of refugees. (Britain, France, Germany and Italy are not included in the ten.) It has the third-highest annual intake of refugees – averaging about 12,000 – and ranks only behind Canada in terms of the proportion accepted relative to population. Bear this in mind when assessing charges that Australia is callous and inhumane in its treatment of refugees, and that it stands condemned before the court of world public opinion for that treatment.

Unlike Europe, Australia has a substantial body of water between it and potential sources of illegal immigrants. This makes the control of borders considerably easier, though the coastline and water to be kept under surveillance are extensive.

In comparison with Europe, then, and as far as the near future is concerned, Australia's circumstances look pretty good. But there are some other facts to consider.

Australia is an attractive country to live in, and the Olympic Games, a vigorous promotion of tourism, television generally and cheaper travel are making that fact much better known. It has a modest population with a high standard of living in a very large country. Programs focusing on cities, beaches and sport do not convey the fact that much of the country is arid.

As far as the longer, but not *very* much longer, term is concerned, Australia lives adjacent to very heavily populated parts of the world. While some scepticism is always appropriate when presented with population projections, we cannot do without them when considering the future. According to the estimates of the US Bureau of the Census, which are probably as good as any, by the year 2050 – that is, by the time that a child born today will have entered early middle age – the population of the world will have increased by over 50%: from its present six billion to about 9.3 billion. Of that increase of 3.3 billion, it is projected that well over a third of it – something of the order of 1.4 billion – will occur in nine countries stretching from Pakistan to China. The population of Indonesia alone is projected to increase by 120 million in the next 50 years.

All that does not, of course, mean the guaranteed down-pouring of the infamous "yellow hordes" of yore. But taken together with the fact that people-smuggling is already a highly-developed business to our immediate north, it does suggest that the control of borders is going to be a matter that will preoccupy Australia increasingly in coming years.

Bear in mind too that while these formidable population increases are happening to our north, Australia itself has a lower fertility rate than at any time in the last 100 years, except for the Great Depression. Indeed, immigrants apart, the birth rate of native-born Australians is lower than it was in the 1930s.

There are some other circumstances that qualify optimism, such as the evidence provided during the last year of the potential that the issue of illegal immigrants or asylum-seekers has to divide, embitter and polarise opinion in Australia – which must leave one wondering about the country's ability to handle more severe tests when they come, as come they will.

As I indicated at the beginning, one of the things that struck me most about the *Tampa* debate was its vicious, violent nature, particularly on the part of those who claimed the moral high ground. Words like *racist, brutal, savage, politics of fear, pariah state* were tossed about freely and with little in the way of supporting argument. The racist charges against John Howard, for example, seemed perfectly circular: "Why does Howard pursue the policy he does? Because he is a racist. How do you know that he is a racist? Because he pursues the policy that he does."

Another striking feature of the debate has been its parochialism – evident in the frequent claims that the world was appalled at what Australia was doing, and that we stood condemned before something called the Court of World Public Opinion. The truth was, of course, that the world, preoccupied with its own affairs, was paying little attention; that many Western countries were in the process of considering or adopting much tougher measures of their own; and that in so far as they were paying attention at all, they were probably looking to see whether there were any tips they could pick up from Australia in terms of effective control.

There are other interesting features of the *Tampa* debate that might be mentioned. There is the fact that while the captain of the ship was much-lauded for respecting the traditional law of the sea in turning to pick up the boat people, nothing much was said of that other law of the sea – that the captain's will should prevail, and that any attempt to override it – to disobey or intimidate the captain – is the most serious of crimes (known as mutiny when it is engaged in by a crew). Yet the *Tampa* captain made it clear that he had only turned away from Indonesia and towards Christmas Island because he had been intimidated by a group of those he had saved, who had come up to the bridge of the ship to confront him.

If this was mentioned at all it was excused because of the alleged "desperation" of the boat people, though why they should have felt desperate at being returned to Indonesia, a lax and in this respect tolerant Islamic state, was not clear.

Again, while there have been frequent references to the 1951 Convention on the Status of Refugees, the fact that the convention requires refugees to seek refuge in the first safe country they come to was not often referred to. The asylum-seekers on the *Tampa* had almost certainly already passed through two, three or more such countries, Muslim countries, before getting on their boat to Australia.

⚜⚜⚜

I would not want to make too much of these points. They are the sort of lapses that people have when they are making a case, especially when strong emotions are involved.

More important, central and interesting, it seems to me, has been the sustained attack on the government – and particularly on John Howard and Philip Ruddock – for being morally callous, harsh, insensitive, lacking in compassion, even brutal. They have been depicted as failing as human beings, as moral beings, in these respects. These charges are interesting in what they indicate about expectations concerning the way those conducting the affairs of government should behave – to wit, that what they should do is consult their best moral impulses and then be guided by them.

There are three responses that can be made to such a view. One is to deny that any harshness has been involved. I personally do not find that convincing. The measures taken have been pretty severe, if not harsh.

A second possible response was indicated brutally by the late Martin Wight, probably the most respected English thinker on international politics of the last 50 years: "A foreign minister is chosen and paid to look after the interests of his country, and not to be a delegate for the human race."

The same point can be made a little less abrasively. In their conduct of foreign affairs, ministers are in the position of agents, not principals. They are in the position of trustees whose first and overriding duty, just like legal trustees, is not to give expression to their own moral views or preferences but to secure the interests of those they serve. In so far as deterring any further violation of the integrity of the country's border is seen as the overriding interest, deterrence requires firmness and, if necessary, harshness. You do not deter by being gentle and compassionate.

On the subject of compassion and of the difference between one's private and public roles, let me quote my friend and colleague Irving Kristol:

> Compassion organised into a political movement is a very dangerous thing and, I think, a wicked thing. If you want to be compassionate, go out and be compassionate to people. If you want to give people money, go out and give people money. If you want to work with poor people, go out and work with poor people. I have great respect for people who do that. But when people start becoming bureaucrats of compassion and start making careers out of compassion – whether political, journalistic or public entertainment careers – then I must suspect their good faith.

That is one kind of response, phrased in the typically abrasive style of a New York intellectual. But there is another, more sombre one that meets moral condemnation with a moral counter-argument. It was put most eloquently perhaps by Isaiah Berlin in his celebrated essay *Two Concepts of Liberty*:

> If, as I believe, the ends of men are many, and not all of them are in principle compatible with each other, then the possibility of conflict – and of tragedy – can never be wholly eliminated from human life, either personal or social. The necessity of choosing between absolute claims is then an inescapable characteristic of the human condition.

What Berlin is saying is that, contrary to the assumption often made in liberal and progressive circles, all good things are not in harmony, are not mutually reinforcing. There is not a unity of goods. Often the hardest and most unpleasant choices have to be made, not between good and bad things, but between desirable things – between freedom and order; between generosity and justice; between peace and human rights – and making them is not a matter of hypocrisy or double standards, as it is regularly accused of being, but, in Berlin's words "an inescapable characteristic of the human condition."

What does all this point to with respect to policy for Australia? To me it points to three things.

First, at the very least maintaining the present level of immigration, and preferably increasing it significantly – say by a third – with the emphasis heavily on skilled immigrants. I am persuaded that this is desirable for economic reasons; and I believe that, in an increasingly crowded world, it will also make Australia's international position more secure.

Second, playing down multiculturalism and playing up integration and assimilation as policy goals. If it is not possible to reverse multiculturalism, then at least as much support and encouragement should be given to those who prefer to aim for complete assimilation as is given to the cause of diversity.

Third and last, holding firm on the strong policy that has been adopted on border control, because if Australia loses control over its borders in the next half-century it will be in dire trouble, and other aspects of policy will become largely irrelevant.

Punching Above Our Weight?

In *Benign or Imperial? Reflections on American Hegemony* [2003 Boyer Lectures], ABC Books, February 2004

In November-December 2003, Harries delivered the Australian Broadcasting Corporation (ABC)'s annual Boyer Lectures. This chapter was the last of six lectures. Extracted in *The Australian* as "The Men Who Shaped Our Place in the World" (16 January 2004), it also formed part of a chapter, "Australia and the Bush Doctrine: Punching Above Our Weight?", in the 2005 book *Confronting the Bush Doctrine: Critical Views from the Asia Pacific*, editors Mel Gurtov and Peter Van Ness.

A couple of years ago, Walter Russell Mead, a Fellow of the Council on Foreign Relations in New York, wrote a book identifying four traditions of American foreign policy, each one represented by a leading American statesman.

- The Hamiltonian tradition consists of a combination of commercialism and realism.

- The Jeffersonian tradition is apprehensive of the corrupting influence of the outside world and therefore sceptical about international commitments and what Thomas Jefferson referred to as "entangling alliances".

- The Jacksonian tradition is populist, patriotic, pugnacious, and ultra-sensitive concerning any slight to the country's honour.

- And last there is the Wilsonian tradition of crusading liberal internationalism.

Throughout the country's history, Mead maintains, these four traditions have interacted: sometimes mutually supporting each other, sometimes competing and conflicting, always overlapping, the mix changing as both domestic and international circumstances change.

Reading Mead's book encourages reflection as to what a similar exercise concerning Australia's foreign policy traditions would yield. It seems to me that here there have been three main traditions.

❧❧❧

First, there is the Menzies tradition. This is a thoroughly realist, power-and-interest-based tradition, though in Menzies own case it was sometimes obscured by his taste for sentimental declarations of attachment to Britain and the Queen, which misled some into thinking that he was merely a romantic loyalist.

As a realist and a conservative, Menzies was sceptical of abstract, general schemes. He looked to interest rather than principle as the motive for action; to history and experience rather than abstract reasoning for the basis of sound judgement.

Menzies' central assumption was that in an international environment that was inherently dangerous – and which in his day contained predators like Nazi Germany, a militarised Japan, and later the Soviet Union – it was vital for a large, sparsely populated and geographically isolated Western country like Australia that the global balance of power should favour the leading democratic powers. And it was also vital that Australia should have close, friendly relations with those powers. In order to ensure that state of affairs, Australia must be prepared to support the United States and Britain politically and, when necessary, militarily. Such support was our insurance policy.

It was also highly congenial to Menzies personally, since it was a policy which enabled Australia – and Menzies himself – to be wired in to the main game of global power politics in a way that was otherwise impossible.

National interest and personal ambition, then, were both served by such a policy. But inherent in it was the risk of losing sight of a distinctive Australian identity and of exaggerating the cohesion and solidarity represented by the larger concept, whether it be the British Commonwealth, "the West", or "the Free World".

The Menzies tradition is sceptical of most international institutions, including the United Nations, which, it claims should be seen not as an alternative to power politics, but as power politics with a different façade – a different way for sovereign states to play essentially the same game. The Security Council is in reality no more than a kind of permanent conference of the great powers, where important and contentious issues can be discussed. Every member votes according to how it sees its own interests. To think otherwise, Menzies once argued, was to see the organisation as a "house fully constructed which in due course, by some miracle, would be able to build its own foundations." The UN reflects the realities of international politics, but it does not and cannot change them significantly. The UN had no particular moral authority, and to make one's response to a course of action depend on whether or not it is sanctioned by the UN is more a way of evading than of making moral choice.

The Menzies tradition is, of course, strongest on the conservative side of politics, though it has its representatives across the spectrum. John Howard is probably the tradition's purest representative since Menzies himself.

The second tradition is, I think, best identified as the Evatt tradition. It is both strongly nationalist and internationalist. No contradiction is involved here, since internationalism is favoured, not only on principle, but because international organisations are regarded as the most congenial and effective forums for a middle power like Australia to register its presence and extend its influence.

This tradition is assertive and energetic. It is concerned to give Australia a high profile as a country capable of making a distinctive contribution to international affairs. Sometimes it leads to hyperactivity and attention-seeking. At the Paris Peace Conference of 1946, to take an extreme example, Dr Evatt, as leader of the Australian delegation, managed to table no fewer than 400 amendments. Sadly, only one of them was adopted.

The Evatt tradition is concerned to establish Australia's independence, is sensitive to slights, and is concerned with status. It is suspicious of great powers, and will go out of its way to assert its independence of them, both in order to preserve its freedom of action and to strengthen its own sense of identity. It is inclined to believe that lesser powers like itself, being more detached, are better able than great powers to assess the morality and justice of an issue objectively. Power politics tends to be seen as a chosen mode of behaviour, rather than something inherent in a system of sovereign states and necessary for survival.

One of Evatt's favourite words was "machinery", by which he meant organisational and institutional frameworks, procedures and rules. In his view, getting the machinery right was the secret of progress, for he believed that, to a great extent, form determines substance. Those of this persuasion tend to subscribe to the dictum "build and they will come".

They also attach great importance to international law. Thus in Evatt's first ministerial statement to Parliament, only a few days before Pearl Harbour and in an atmosphere of impending crisis, he found time to express concern that Australia was not legally at war with Finland, Hungary and Romania, explaining that if this was not rectified the consequences "might well be disastrous to Russian morale." In somewhat the same spirit, three decades later, another eminent representative of the tradition, Gough Whitlam, was to feel compelled to recognise formally the incorporation of the Baltic States into the Soviet Union, in order to clarify the legal situation. Realists, on the other hand, tend to be sceptical about the claims made for a system of law that lacks any coercive power to enforce itself.

Unlike the Menzies tradition, the Evatt tradition draws a sharp distinction between power politics and the United Nations, seeing the latter as laying a foundation for an entirely different international order and norms of behaviour. Action that is sanctioned by the UN has a legitimacy and moral quality that is otherwise lacking. For, whatever its shortcomings, the organisation represents an ideal to be striven for. A typical realist reaction to the stress on machinery and forms is that of Nicholas Mansergh in his magisterial *Survey of British*

Commonwealth Affairs, "Dr Evatt did not appear to understand …
that no elaboration of machinery could sensibly modify a relationship
determined by relative power."

This is a tradition represented mostly clearly on the Labor side
of politics and, as well as Evatt himself, Gough Whitlam and Gareth
Evans have embodied much of what it stands for.

The distinguishing mark of the third tradition – call it the
Spender-Casey tradition, or, if you prefer, the Keating tradition – is
the importance it attaches to regional affairs. The nature and content
of that concern has varied over the decades: strategic and security
matters during and immediately after World War II; support for
Indonesian independence by the Chifley government in the late 1940s;
the Colombo Plan and other aid to the newly independent states
of the region in the 1950s; concern over the increasing instability,
violence and radicalisation of the region in the 1960s, leading to
military involvement in Malaya and Vietnam; and, increasingly from
then on, a concern to develop relations, and to integrate with a region
that had become economically dynamic and significant.

As Ministers for External Affairs, both Percy Spender and Richard
Gardiner Casey represented this tradition early on, creating and
extending the Colombo Plan, and developing diplomatic relations
with the region's new states. All this in the face of considerable
indifference on Menzies' part. According to Spender, Menzies viewed
his preoccupation with the region as a "hobby horse" and was given
to saying patronisingly, "Come on Percy, let's have your thesis about
Southeast Asia."

Menzies' power-centred outlook made him a big-picture man,
inclined to play down a regional approach. "Regionalism", he once
reflected, "is open to the view that it may involve nothing more
than a slightly enlarged form of isolationism – a collective form of
isolationism, if I may use a curious phrase." He tended to regard the
parochial affairs of weak, inexperienced regional states as low on
the agenda. Like many conservative realists, he was slow to identify,

and to react to, significant forces of change. As time passed, such an attitude toward the region became increasingly unsustainable. By the 1990s, Paul Keating was giving priority to regional relationships.

In contemplating these three traditions, the question is not which one of them is the right one for Australia to adopt in perpetuity, but what balance or mix of them is appropriate at any given time, as circumstances, and the priorities of our interests, change.

⛪⛪⛪

Against this background, what can be said about the policy of the Howard government since 2001? That has been a policy of unhesitating, unqualified and – given the attitude of many other states – conspicuous support for the United States in its wars against terrorism and against Iraq. As such, it is a policy that can be and has been defended both on Menziean grounds – that is, protecting one's own security and paying one's insurance premium to a great and powerful friend – and in terms of our values, given that it was tyranny and terror that were being combatted.

Many people whom I respect have found this combination of arguments a compelling one, demanding support for the policy of the Howard government. I would like to explain why, on realist grounds, I have not.

First, a bit of self-protective ground-clearing. As things have not exactly gone according to plan in Iraq since Saddam Hussein was overthrown, and as a favourable outcome seems less than certain, it might seem that I'm simply being wise after the event and second-guessing the government. This isn't so. As it happens, I published a relevant piece on Australian-US relations in the *Australian Financial Review* on 10 September 2001; that is, precisely one day *before* the terrorist attacks on New York and Washington. In it, I argued that:

> Australia should proceed carefully and without illusion in dealing with its powerful ally. For one thing, post-Cold War American foreign policy is still, in some respects, a work in progress, and those who get too close to it run the risk

that a piece of the scaffolding might fall off and hit them
... Even more important, while the United States is by
historical standards a benevolent hegemon, a hegemon is
what it is. Not only is its power vast, but it is concerned to
use that power ... to create a world in its own image with
institutions and rules determined by Washington ... While
such a world would have many attractions, the attempt
to bring it into being will inevitably generate serious
opposition and a great deal of strife and conflict. It would
be inappropriate and dangerous for a country of Australia's
limited means and interests to associate itself closely with
such an enterprise.

I went on to maintain that "however sweet the rhetoric and
however warm the hugging, the priorities of the two countries are
likely to differ at least as often as they coincide."

I believe that, while these arguments had validity before
September 11 and the Iraq War, they, and some additional ones,
have even more validity today. Let me enumerate.

First, concerning terrorism, the first and overriding responsibility
of an Australian government is not to combat global terrorism
generally, but to protect this country from terrorism. The two ends
are not necessarily identical. By being an early, unqualified and
high-profile supporter of American policy, when so many others
– including longstanding allies of the United States and some of
our neighbours – were expressing serious reservations about both
the legitimacy and the effectiveness of that policy, Australia may
well have increased rather than decreased its chances of becoming
a terrorist target.

Second, the course Australia has followed since September 11 is
open to the charge that it has got the balance between alliance policy
and regional policy wrong. We are living in the same region as the
most populous Muslim state in the world, a state that is less than
a model of stability and order, and which is a breeding ground for
terror. As well, we are in close proximity to some failed or failing
states which are potential hosts for terrorists.

Looking ahead, by the year 2050 – that is, by the time someone born now will be entering middle age – the population of the nine countries extending from Pakistan to China will have increased by something in the order of 1.4 billion. That of Indonesia alone is projected to increase by 120 million in that period.

While all this does not mean that the region is inevitably going to be more unstable or threatening than it is now, it does suggest that its importance is going to loom larger rather than smaller in our strategic calculations, and that anything that can justify distracting our attention and resources from it must be of a compelling nature.

But, third, the case made by the Bush administration for the Iraq War was not compelling. Indeed, it was inconsistent and surprisingly incompetent, with dubious and shifting rationales being offered: one day, weapons of mass destruction; the next day, links with al-Qaeda; after that, the cruelty of the regime and the liberation of the Iraqi people; and then Saddam's alleged reckless, unpredictable nature, which, it was claimed, ruled out deterrence and required pre-emption. As well as all that, the case for overthrowing Saddam Hussein was made against the background of a proclaimed new strategic doctrine aimed at nothing less than remaking the world in America's image.

Given all this, restraint, some deep reflection and a request for clarification, rather than eager and unqualified support, would have been an appropriate Australian response; appropriate not only in terms of Australia's own interests but that of its great ally. And it could have been accompanied by a clear statement of our need to give priority to dealing with terror where it was most likely to impinge on us; that is, not in the Middle East but in Southeast Asia.

Supporters of the policy might respond to such criticism by saying that, however things turn out in Iraq, Australia has built up a lot of credit in Washington and with the American people, and that this on its own justifies the policy followed by Prime Minister Howard. Perhaps so. But – and this is my fourth point – in international politics, expectations of gratitude rest on shaky foundations. As Charles de Gaulle once remarked, great powers are "cold monsters", and gratitude is not one of their stronger motivators. When, in 1848, Czarist Russia intervened to put down an insurrection in Hungary, thus saving the Habsburg empire, which was then in deep trouble, the Habsburg Prime Minister commented that, "We shall astonish the world with our ingratitude." Sure enough, half a dozen years later when Britain and France went to war with Russia in the Crimea, the Habsburgs studiously stayed on the sidelines. But the world was not very astonished.

Now you may think that this example, like de Gaulle's remark, represents the cynicism of Old Europe. However, it was not de Gaulle but George Washington who observed that "no nation can be entrusted further than it is bound by its interests" and that "there can be no greater error than to expect or calculate on real favours from nation to nation."

Fifth, these words of Washington's are just as relevant and carry just as much weight when considering another assumption that many Australians, including John Howard, make concerning our American connection, which is that a great deal of weight should be attached to cultural affinity. Listen to Mr Howard in a 2GB radio interview, expressing a conviction about Australian-US relations that he has repeated many times: "… they do have a lot of values and attitudes that we share, and I'm a great believer that you should have close relations with the countries whose way of life is closest to your own."

Mr Howard is not alone in this belief. In recent years, there has been renewed support for an old idea – that English-speaking nations with cultural affinities should draw together and form some kind of political and economic union, what has been termed an "Anglosphere".

The whole notion that cultural affinity can be the solid foundation of a relationship needs to be treated very warily. Consider this:

Great Britain and the United States fought World War II together in an extraordinarily close alliance. One million American troops were stationed in Britain before D-Day. British soldiers fought under American generals, and American soldiers under British generals. President Roosevelt and Prime Minister Churchill were in constant touch and there was extraordinary intimacy between the top people on both sides. The American establishment at the time was very Anglophile and much more WASP (White, Anglo-Saxon, Protestant) than it is now. Yet as soon as the war was over, the United States cut off Lend-Lease aid to a virtually bankrupt Britain and imposed very harsh terms on the loan it negotiated with the Attlee government.

And only a decade after that close partnership, when Dwight D. Eisenhower and Anthony Eden, two wartime colleagues, were leading their respective governments, the United States publicly humiliated their British and French allies at the time of the Suez crisis, forcing them to climb down and leave the Canal in Egyptian President Nasser's hands. From this episode the British and the French drew opposite conclusions: the British, that they should never again cross the United States; the French, that they should never again depend on the United States.

Coming nearer to home, all Australian Prime Ministers should bear in mind the American handling of the Dutch New Guinea question in the early 1960s. Despite the ANZUS alliance, and despite the fact that Robert Menzies was a great "Western values" man whose standing in Washington was high, the Kennedy administration chose to try to placate a radical, anti-Western Sukarno over the issue, rather than support either Australia or America's NATO ally, the Netherlands.

None of this is meant as a criticism of the United States, which just behaved as great powers normally behave – quite properly putting their own interests ahead of everything else, and giving less weight to the views of those whose support can be taken for granted than to those whose support they wish to gain. Most people who follow international politics are familiar with a version of Lord Palmerston's dictum: "We have no eternal allies, and we have no perpetual enemies. Our interests are eternal and perpetual, and those interests it is our duty to follow." But again, George Washington had said it more crisply 50 years earlier: "Permanent, inveterate antipathies against particular nations, and passionate attachments to others, should be avoided."

Sixth, for the internationalists of the Evatt tradition, one of the drawbacks of this policy followed by the Australian government is that it has weakened Australia's position in the UN, by associating conspicuously with a course of action that, in the eyes of most members, lacked UN authority. Normally, this would be a matter of little concern to realists, but at a time when much of the serious diplomatic power game is likely to be played in the UN, as the other permanent members of the Security Council use it to try to restrain the United States, this has more significance than it would normally have.

My seventh and last point concerns ends and means. Australia is a large continent to defend. It exists in a region characterised by a great deal of turbulence. As by far the most populous, powerful and wealthy country in the south-west Pacific, it properly assumes responsibility for stability in some of the smaller countries of the region which have serious problems.

To meet these commitments, Australia spends under 2% of its gross national product on defence. It has an army of only 25,000 personnel. In these circumstances, for it to engage in serious military campaigns beyond its region as well, and to do so pre-emptively and when it is not directly threatened, is to leave itself open to the charge of being a cheap hawk, which is a dangerous and irresponsible thing to be. Punching above one's weight may be a source of pride, but it is also hazardous and a form of activity best avoided.

Back in the 1940s, Walter Lippmann wrote a sentence which has a claim to be one of the most important ever written about foreign policy. It reads as follows:

> Without the controlling principle that the nation must maintain its objectives and its power in equilibrium, its purposes within its means and its means equal to its purposes, its commitments related to its resources and its resources adequate to its commitments, it is impossible to think at all about foreign affairs.

Those responsible for Australian foreign policy could do worse than have that sentence framed and hung prominently on their office walls.

Loyal to a Fault

With Tom Switzer, *The American Interest*, 1 June 2006 [extract]

The Washington-based journal invited a "distinguished group of international observers" to provide perspectives from around the world on the US and the Iraq War. At the time, Harries was a Fellow at both the Centre for Independent Studies and the Lowy Institute in Sydney, while Switzer was Opinion Editor at The Australian.

Whatever course events in Iraq take from here on, two things may be said with confidence about the US-Australian alliance: first, it will endure; but, second, it will change.

It will endure not only because the advantages that accrue from it are real and substantial, but because the need for "great and powerful friends" (to use Sir Robert Menzies' favourite phrase) is deeply embedded in the Australian psyche. From its birth as a state a century ago – and indeed before that when it was still a collection of colonies far removed from the rest of the Western world – Australia has always sought a close association with a great power with which it shares values and interests. For the first decades of its existence, a declining but still formidable Britain filled that role. Then for a decade or two it was shared by Britain and America. For the last half century, it has been performed by the United States alone. On the American side, the alliance is of value because Australia is a stable, reliable and significant presence (the 14th largest economy in the world) in the international system – and in a part of the world where such partners do not exist in abundance.

The nature of the alliance will change for two reasons. First it will do so because the nature of American foreign policy has changed. When Australia first entered into alliance with the United States, both countries were concerned to protect an existing state of affairs against those – first Japan and Germany, then the Soviet Union and Mao's China – who were determined to transform it radically. That compatibility lasted for several decades.

Recently, things have altered. Australia is still the epitome of a satisfied, status-quo state – well-endowed, stable, not very powerful, but with its modest population enjoying an enviable share of the world's wealth and advantages. It has every reason to assume that any radical change in the existing state of affairs will diminish rather than enhance its position. But since becoming the sole remaining superpower, and especially since 9/11, the foreign policy of the United States has changed. Far from being the principal defender of the existing order, it has become, according to its own rhetoric and recent behaviour, a revolutionary force determined to use its great power – including, conspicuously, its military power – to reshape the world.

No doubt part of this can be put down to rhetoric, and no doubt after Iraq there will be some adjustments and modifications. But it would be a serious error to doubt the momentum created by a combination of hegemonic power and the powerful sense of an historic – indeed, for many Americans, divine – mission (a sense that is entirely absent in the Australian people, who are by nature sceptical, modest and pragmatic, more inclined to settle for decency than to strive for the sublime). All of which means that reconciling Australian and American views of the world and finding mutually-agreeable policies are likely to become increasingly difficult projects.

The second factor that will change the nature of the alliance is China. For the United States and Australia, the spectacular rise of that country means different things. For the former its main significance is the emergence of a potent geopolitical rival; for the latter it is the opportunity for a rewarding partnership, and that opportunity is being eagerly seized by Australia. China has recently overtaken the United States as Australia's second largest trading partner after Japan. With Australian exports to and imports from China both growing at well over 20% a year, with negotiations for a free trade agreement about to begin, and with the compatibility that exists between Australia's vast mineral and energy resources and the needs of the Chinese economy, it does not seem improbable that China will become Australia's leading trading partner sooner rather than later. There are, of course, risks and uncertainties involved. But as China approaches the completion of three decades of growth at an annual rate of over 9%, these appear progressively less formidable than they once did.

Politically and strategically, fear of "the downward thrust of communist China", which for decades provided the unspoken rationale for the ANZUS alliance, no longer constitutes a major motivating force. One of Australia's leading strategic thinkers, Hugh White, has recently observed that

> China has had great success in converting economic opportunities into regional political influence ... It has adopted a moderate and reasonable tone and deftly exploited its substantial soft-power assets ... As a result, most of its neighbours are now more comfortable with the idea of China's growing power – and so feel less dependent on America. This has deprived the US of an important political asset.

The recent creation of a new piece of regional diplomatic architecture, the East Asia Summit, of which China and Australia are members but the United States is not, may be a significant sign of change to come.

None of this means that Australia is faced with a hard, stark choice between the United States and China – not, at least, unless one or the other of them insists that such a choice be made. But it does mean that Australia must learn to play a more demanding diplomatic game than ever before, one that will on occasion involve the difficult feat of riding two horses simultaneously. And instead of the sturdy, straightforward virtues of dependability and unconditional loyalty that have served it well until recently, it will need to acquire and cultivate a range of new skills: discrimination, agility, qualified commitment, ambiguity.

There is nothing strange about these skills; they are among the basic tools of diplomacy. But the special conditions that have for much of its existence allowed Australia to dispense with their regular use are now ending. From now on, given the change, Australia will need to regard alliances not as a test of character ("Australia will be there!") or a union of souls ("the Anglosphere"), but as pragmatic devices to be adjusted to changing conditions. Yes, Australia will stay on the American Bandwagon, but instead of always leading the cheer squad it will need to cultivate some of the skills of the helpful passenger. These include the encouraging of careful steering, some timely map reading, a judicious use of the brakes, and – not least – better road manners. As with all efforts at back-seat driving, it is unlikely that such advice will be gratefully received. But it would serve the best interests of both countries.

Different Battles, Different Response

The Australian, 5 July 2006

This op-ed drew the ire of the late British-American writer, Christopher Hitchens – one of the Iraq War's most enthusiastic supporters – in the rejoinder "Vietnam was Appalling, Iraq's Ideal", *The Australian*, 7 July 2006.

R ecently, someone with a long memory asked me when and why my views on foreign policy had changed so radically. In the 1960s, he reminded me, I had invested a lot of time and energy in teach-ins, conferences, television debates and articles, defending US policy on Vietnam and Australia's support for that policy. But in the years since 9/11, I have spent almost as much effort opposing US policy in Iraq and Australia's undeviating support for it.

Why the change, he asked. Surely the two situations are very similar? A harsh local dictatorship behaves atrociously, abusing the people under its control and threatening the local balance of power. The US intervenes to stop it. While most US allies stay on the sidelines, the Australian government gives its wholehearted support (Harold Holt's "All the way with LBJ" in the 1960s; John Howard's unqualified commitment on the day after 9/11, even before he knew what form the US response would take). Things do not go very well in either instance, but in both cases Australians are urged by their government to "stay the course" and not "cut and run".

Why then, I was asked, if US policy and Australia's support for it were right in the 1960s, are they not right today? The short answer consists of two words: different circumstances. The longer answer can be summarised in seven points.

First, the Vietnam War occurred in Australia's region while the Iraq War is occurring thousands of miles further away. Despite foolish claims to the contrary, geographic proximity still counts in all but the most dangerous and general of global great-power conflicts, especially for a country of quite limited security resources. Australia intervenes in East Timor and the Solomon Islands; it does not intervene in Zambia or Chile.

Second, as well as its proximity, in the 1960s Southeast Asia was the most unstable and violent region in the world. The historian Arthur Schlesinger Jr, fresh from serving in the Kennedy administration, described it pretty accurately as "an underdeveloped subcontinent filled with fictitious states in vague, chaotic and unpredictable revolutionary ferment."

In these circumstances, Australia had a compelling interest in keeping the US interested in and committed to the region, which meant actively supporting its involvement there. We do not have a comparable interest in the case of Iraq. Indeed, if anything the US involvement in Iraq is causing it to neglect the part of the world of most concern to us.

Third, the Vietnam War occurred in the middle of the Cold War, a global geopolitical struggle between two superpowers. The communist government of North Vietnam was actively supported by the Soviet Union and China. In the mid-1960s, Indonesia – the largest state in the region and Australia's nearest neighbour – had the third largest Communist Party in the world, and in 1965 it only narrowly avoided succumbing to a communist coup.

In these circumstances, and given the general disorder and weakness of the region, fear of the downward thrust of communism was based on something more substantial than paranoia. A quick and easy communist victory in Vietnam, unopposed by the US, would have altered the whole character of Australia's strategic environment. Nothing comparable in terms of Australian interests is at stake in the case of Iraq.

Fourth, although today we speak of the "war on terror", there is nothing comparable to the Cold War in existence today. Osama bin Laden in his cave is not the Soviet Union of the 1960s. The use of the term "war" with respect to terror is metaphorical, as in the "war" on drugs or crime. Despite lurid and absurd comparisons with

Hitler's Germany, Iraq did not, and terrorism does not, constitute an existential threat.

Fifth, US action in Vietnam was based on sound intelligence. Despite strenuous denials at the time, North Vietnam did control the Vietcong and the conflict was not a civil war in South Vietnam. In the case of Iraq, US policy was based on hopelessly flawed – or, worse, cynically faked – intelligence.

Sixth, US policy in Vietnam was essentially defensive, reactive and limited by a healthy respect for Soviet power. Its Iraq policy was preventive, pre-emptive, and couched in unlimited and messianic terms. A revolutionary foreign policy does not serve the interests of a satisfied status-quo state such as Australia.

Seventh and last, while the US ultimately lost the Vietnam War, the time it bought in doing so enabled the region to convert itself from the dangerous shambles described by Schlesinger into the most prosperous and stable part of the Third World. In Iraq, on the other hand, the US (and Australian) "war on terror" has only succeeded in producing more terrorists by the day.

Those, in sum, are the reasons why I supported Australia's involvement in one war but have opposed it in the other. Circumstances alter cases, and as the great Edmund Burke observed: "He who does not take them into consideration is not erroneous but stark mad." Holt was right in giving full support to the US in the 1960s; Howard has been wrong in giving full support to the US in the very different conditions prevailing in the 2000s.

Speaking at the Kennedy Centre in Washington, C-SPAN, 19 February 1989 and (right)
At a viewer call-in program on global affairs, C-SPAN, 17 July 1989

Discussing the United Nations with Walter Hoffman, C-SPAN Live, 30 August 1990

With Richard Perle (left), Thomas Friedman, Alton Frye and Joshua
Muravchik (right) at an American Enterprise Institute panel on the US role
in world affairs, Washington, 19 April 1996

With Robert Kagan at a Brookings Institution panel on US foreign policy
after the Cold War, Washington, C-SPAN, 10 October 1997

With founding co-editor of *The National Interest*, Robert Tucker (right), ahead of the magazine's debut. From "A New Voice in Foreign Affairs", *The Washington Times*, 3 October 1985

With philanthropist Michael Joyce (centre) and Irving Kristol in Washington, 1996

With *National Interest* editorial staff Erica Tuttle (left), Alexandra Parent and Kristen Yessayan in 1996

With friend and historian, Gertrude Himmelfarb, in Washington, 1997

With Henry Kissinger (left) and Samuel Huntington at *The National Interest* editorial board drinks in Washington, 1998

With *Commentary* editor Norman Podhoretz (left) and *National Review* editor John O'Sullivan in Washington, 1997

Photographed at his office on 16th Street in Washington overlooking the Soviet embassy for a profile by Don Kowet, "In the National Interest", *The Washington Times*, 5 November 1991

Preparing speech notes in Washington, 1996

SECTION THREE

American Foreign Policy

Neoconservatism and Realpolitik

The National Interest, Fall 1985

Harries was Editor of the influential, Washington-based quarterly magazine, *The National Interest*, from its inception in September 1985 until June 2001. This piece featured in the inaugural issue.

One of the most interesting features of American neo-conservatism is its firm rejection of realism or realpolitik as an acceptable basis for US foreign policy. Interesting because, until now, it has been widely accepted that there is an affinity between conservatism and realism. When Hans Morgenthau wanted to give an example of realism in action, more often than not he referred to the performance of a conservative statesman – a Hamilton, Pitt, Disraeli, Bismarck, or Salisbury. Indeed, that other leading realist, E. H. Carr, characteristically pushing a sound point too far, maintained that, "The radical is essentially utopian, and the conservative realist." Unless one makes it so by the manipulation of definitions, there is no necessity involved (radicals are sometimes purely destructive, conservatives sometimes hopelessly romantic).

But the weaker claim of a compatibility and attraction between conservatism and realism seems sound enough: both put their stress on what *is*, rather than on what should or might be; both emphasise the importance of circumstance and are suspicious of abstract theory and general principles as bases for action; both are aware of the intractability of things and the difficulties and dangers involved in attempting sweeping changes.

Why, then, do neoconservatives oppose a foreign policy based on realpolitik for the United States? One answer is given by Irving Kristol in this issue. He maintains that such an approach is inappropriate in an age of ideological politics, when the major actors have universal aspirations. It properly belonged, he argues, to that earlier system of international relations associated with the nation-states of the 19th century, in which the actors did not contest each other's right to exist and were content to jockey for position to gain marginal advantages.

Norman Podhoretz, on the other hand, bases his rejection of realpolitik principally on the character of the American people. He maintains that if American foreign policy is not infused with "some higher purpose", if it (and particularly that part of it which is concerned with the Soviet-American conflict) is robbed of its moral significance – as he believes it will be if realism prevails – then the popular support necessary to sustain that policy will not be forthcoming. Kristol and Podhoretz both reject realpolitik in the name of the primacy of ideology; they differ only on why ideology must be primary.

Both also agree that the main danger associated with realpolitik is not (as most liberals would claim) that it would result in too harsh, abrasive, and selfish a policy, but in one that would be too accommodating and compromising. Kristol is concerned that the result would be an inappropriate policy of "live and let live" – inappropriate because America's main adversary would not be operating on that premise. Podhoretz is deeply impressed that the last serious effort to apply the principles of realism – by Nixon and Kissinger – led to a policy of detente with the Soviet Union and to the opening of relations with China, thus clouding the moral and ideological nature of the issues.

ԽԽԽ

Kristol and Podhoretz state their case against realpolitik in general terms and at no great length. As things stand, several questions – some genuine, some rhetorical – suggest themselves: Is it really the case that realpolitik points to compromise and accommodation in all circumstances, and that it is necessarily inadequate or inappropriate for coping with an ideological adversary? Does not the concept encompass just as comfortably the notion of unyielding opposition to states that attempt to achieve dominance as it does the virtue of compromise in dealing with less ambitious states? Are Podhoretz's views about the character of the American people and its implications for foreign policy sound and adequate as far as foreign policy is concerned? Does not the answer to this question turn on detailed analyses of some very complex episodes in America's history, some of which at least provide plausible evidence to support different conclusions? And even if it should emerge that a clear and unadorned realpolitik is alien to the American spirit, is it equally clear that the same is true of what might be described as an *adorned* version, in which an awareness of the demands imposed on all policy-makers by a system of international anarchy is combined with a sensitivity to the moral and ideological requirements of the American people?

The fact that confident conclusions have been reached without confronting such questions may partly be explained by considering together the two outstanding features of the neoconservative approach to foreign policy: one, that it is based on an extremely gloomy view of the world as a hostile and threatening place; and two, that at the same time it is concerned to advocate a strong, confident, and active American role in the world – all that is summed up in the phrase "walking tall".

As to neoconservative gloom, the sense of threat and danger, there can be no serious dispute. Consider their world picture: give or take a mini-state or two, there are some 165 countries in the world. Of these, 20 or so are communist and, whatever distinctions conservatives may draw between them, all are seen, rightly, as repugnant and basically hostile to democracy and freedom. Moreover, the military power of the most formidable of them has been increasing ominously in recent years. Another two dozen or so constitute "the West", the democratic and, for the most part, industrially-developed countries of the world. Most of these are America's allies. But in the eyes of neoconservatives nearly all of them are unsatisfactory allies: irresolute, irresponsible, selfish, and, more often than not, resentful toward and unsupportive of the United States, on whom they ultimately depend for their security. Virtually all the remaining countries belong to that phenomenon known as "the Third World" (or, to neoconservatives, as "the so-called Third World"). With few exceptions neoconservatives have little time for the Third World. It is widely seen as a source of disruption, violence, crises, and largely self-inflicted suffering; as constitutionally incapable of dealing constructively with its own economic and social problems; as addicted to authoritarian and tyrannical rule; and as congenitally anti-American. Adding all this up, neoconservatives typically see the world as one in which about 95% of states range from very hostile to unreliable.

Clearly, then, that sense of threat and danger which is usually taken to be a necessary condition for the rise of a strong conservative movement has been abundantly present. (It is not beside the point that two of Podhoretz's most powerful and influential pieces have been titled "The Present Danger" and "The Future Danger".) But equally clearly, it has been accompanied by something that is very *uncharacteristic* of conservatives: an assertive spirit of optimism and confidence and a propensity for bold risk-taking. One might say that the pessimistic view of the world that has sustained the rise of conservatism, and continues to do so, is at odds with the substantive content of what it is concerned to conserve: traditions and institutions that embody and celebrate confidence in the human spirit, freedom, and enterprise. In the realm of foreign policy this translates into a tension between, on the one hand, a rather beleaguered, view-from-the-bunker assessment of how the world is and, on the other, a confident determination to "walk tall". The problem being that walking tall in a bunker is a difficult feat.

⬳ ⬳ ⬳

One way of dealing with this problem is simply to redefine the world in more optimistic terms. A spectacular recent example of such an approach is provided by Secretary of State George P. Shultz in his article in the Spring 1985 issue of *Foreign Affairs*, entitled "New Realities and New Ways of Thinking". Secretary Shultz detects novelty all around him. We face a "new era" in arms control and exhibit a "new awareness" of the importance of conventional defence. In Europe, no less, he sees "new and creative thinking" about political unity. In the Middle East there are signs of "a new realism and a new commitment". The Pacific is even more remarkable: there, a "new reality", accompanied by a "new movement" towards collaboration, points to another "new era". In the Third World as a whole there is the "significant new phenomenon" of popular insurgencies against communist regimes. Newness is just as evident in the international economic sphere, where there are "world-wide revolutions" in economic thought, economic policy, and technology.

Secretary Shultz is concerned not merely to identify all this novelty, but to celebrate it and present it as a call to action. While he acknowledges some worrisome side-effects of change and makes a particular point of emphasising the seriousness of terrorism, overall the trends are very "positive". The West has been through a difficult period but things are now changing. The "correlation of forces" is shifting in our favour. We are faced with fresh opportunities and challenges that we are "well poised to master". The values of political and economic freedom are triumphant. History, he concludes, is on freedom's side.

It seems hardly appropriate to subject this picture of the world to exhaustive critical scrutiny. If Secretary Shultz, with all the information-gathering and evaluative resources available to him, really believes that "our key alliances are more united than ever before", mere argument is unlikely to change his mind. If he is convinced that what we are seeing in Latin America is "the steady advance of democracy", as opposed to some very unsteady, piecemeal, and fragile improvements, one can only wonder at his confidence. (As I write, *The New York Times* reports that inflation in Bolivia, one of the countries that sustains Shultz's optimism, is running at 15,000% a year and rumours of a military coup are strong.)

Again if, in his *tour d'horizon*, he thinks it unnecessary to take into account such matters as the attitude of our European allies toward American policy in Central America and the Strategic Defence Initiative; the crisis in the Philippines (one of those key allies, be it noted); the debt crisis; in the Middle East the assumption of a leading role by Syria and signs of weakening Israeli confidence; the problems with ANZUS (another "key alliance"); the significance of the Soviet base at Cam Ranh Bay; the growing dimensions of the refugee problem and the collapse of agriculture in huge areas of Africa – well, it is difficult to escape the conclusion that what Secretary Shultz is engaged in is not a serious analysis that leads naturally to optimistic conclusions, but rather merely the talking up of America's prospects in the world in order to promote optimism and confidence.

⁖⁖⁖

Neoconservatives are too wedded to their basic pessimism to follow Shultz. So the problem remains: How to reconcile an extremely pessimistic view of the world with the desire for a strong and effective foreign policy?

In confronting this problem, what they see as "realism" is no help to those whose impulse to prevail is strong. For, emphasising the obligation to see things as they really are and to subordinate the wish to the fact, purpose to the intractability of the world, realism plays down the importance of one's own will as part of the reality that is being considered. When it leads to conclusions that depict one's position as objectively unfavourable, this kind of realism tends to be immobilising. The point has frequently been acknowledged. Thus the younger, pre-detente Kissinger:

> The overemphasis on "realism" and the definition of "reality" as being outside the observer may produce a certain passivity and a tendency to adapt to circumstance rather than to master it. It may also produce a gross underestimation of the ability to change, indeed to create, reality.

And, again, E. H. Carr:

> In the field of action, realism tends to emphasise the irresistible character of existing tendencies, and to insist that the highest wisdom lies in accepting, and adapting oneself to, these forces and these tendencies.

To the extent that realism is seen in this way, it may seem that those conservatives who want, above everything, a forceful and effective American foreign policy – and who see their mission as being precisely to deny the irresistible character of existing tendencies – are displaying a sound instinct in rejecting it, regardless of whether the particular reasons they may give for doing so are or are not adequate.

The neoconservative way of resolving the tension is to put an enormous emphasis on the importance of *will* in confronting and changing the world. America is currently in as unfavourable a position as it is because, more than anything, of a failure of will, particularly on the part of its elites; it can overcome adverse circumstances and prevail again by the mobilisation and determined exercise of will.

This is not an absurd view and only those whose capacity to understand the world has been badly damaged by "scientific" teaching stressing the primacy of impersonal "forces" will think it so. In this century, the impact on events of Lenin, Hitler, Mao, Gandhi, Churchill, and the founders of the state of Israel – to take only some of the most obvious examples – testifies to the crucial role of will, particularly when it is harnessed to and sustained by ideological conviction.

It is true that a radical voluntarism sits oddly with the claim to be conservative – not because conservatives deny the capacity of will but because they distrust it profoundly and fear the unintended consequences that are likely to follow from its uninhibited exercise. In so far as neoconservatives have merely accepted a label originally applied to them by ideological opponents and do not really consider themselves conservative, this point need not concern them. (But those who do believe themselves to be conservative should bear it in mind.)

The basic objection to the position taken by Kristol and Podhoretz is, I believe, that it is based on an extremely circumscribed and limited notion of realpolitik. In their account, realpolitik seems to amount to no more than an intelligent and amoral cutting of deals, a sort of superior and systematised pragmatism that pays little regard to ideas or ideology. It is realism as practised by Neville Chamberlain rather than by Winston Churchill – an accountant's version, not that of a statesman. The example of Churchill is very pertinent. He surely demonstrated the way in which traditional statecraft, designed to cope with the unchanging conditions governing relations among sovereign states, can be combined with the mobilisation of the ideology of a free people to imbue foreign policy with that "higher purpose" that Podhoretz calls for and to make it appropriate for countering the challenge of a totalitarian adversary, as Kristol demands. Before advocating the abandonment of realpolitik, his example should be pondered.

The Day of the Fox

The National Interest, Fall 1992

"The fox knows many things, but the hedgehog knows one big thing." In his essay on Leo Tolstoy, Isaiah Berlin took this sentence by the obscure Greek poet Archilochus, and used it to identify

> one of the deepest differences which divide writers and thinkers, and, it may be, human beings in general. For there exists a great chasm between those, on one side, who relate everything to a single central vision, one system ... in terms of which they understand, think and feel ... and, on the other side, those who pursue many ends, often unrelated and even contradictory, connected, if at all, only in some *de facto* way ...

Berlin was concerned to use the distinction between the centripetal and monist hedgehog and the centrifugal and pluralist fox to illuminate two different intellectual and artistic styles, and the examples he gives are of thinkers and writers: Plato, Dante, Hegel, Dostoevsky, and Nietzsche among the hedgehogs; Aristotle, Erasmus, Shakespeare, Goethe, and Balzac the foxes. But, as Berlin acknowledges, the distinction can be given a wider application, and it works well with political leaders. First, some examples.

Two of the dominating democratic statesmen of the first half of this century – David Lloyd George in Britain and Franklin Delano Roosevelt in the United States – provide outstanding specimens of political foxes. They were complicated and devious men (though capable of inspiring multitudes) who certainly pursued many ends, "connected, if at all, only in some *de facto* way". Neither was unduly encumbered with beliefs, certainly not with one central, dominating belief, and both were regarded as unprincipled and without substance by those whose taste was for straightforwardness and consistency. Both were magnificently resourceful improvisers, comfortable with change and complexity, virtuosos in the use of power, prepared to shift directions and vary their methods without inhibition as circumstances required. The word "pragmatic" seems too banal and inadequate to describe either man; it was rather that the combination of an exceptional ability to see the full range of possibilities in a situation and a powerful will to prevail gave them an unusual flexibility, both in formulating and pursuing their various goals. Both testify to how impressive the fox can be at his best.

The second half of the century – the second two-thirds, really – yields many examples of outstanding hedgehogs, among them Churchill, Adenauer, de Gaulle, Reagan, and Thatcher. With each of these, it is possible to sum up almost in a sentence his or her central conviction and purpose as a political leader. In the case of several of them this has been acknowledged by the use of their name as a label for an easily recognised doctrine: Gaullism, Thatcherism, Reaganism. The case of Churchill is a little different from the others, partly because of his extraordinarily long and varied political career; but it was only with the coming of World War II, when circumstances permitted him to behave as a hedgehog – gave his pudding its theme, to use one of his own phrases – that he acquired greatness.

♾♾♾

As Churchill's case indicates, the prevalence and success of hedgehogs or foxes at any given time is not merely a matter of chance or personal ability. Some political circumstances favour one type rather than the other. Most obviously, when political life is more or less objectively dominated by one great issue, about the importance of which there is general agreement, conditions will favour hedgehogs.

This was very much the case over the recent decades of the Cold War. Taken seriously as a fight for survival against a formidable and ruthless enemy, the Cold War demanded leaders who were single-mindedly committed to that fight, had no doubt as to its reality, and were prepared to subordinate everything else to it. The struggle was inhospitable to foxes. Thus Lyndon Johnson, a man who, in another time, might have ranked with Lloyd George and Roosevelt as one of the great foxes, was broken by circumstances that were utterly alien to his talents.

An even more recent and dramatic example of the discord between circumstances and talent is provided by Mikhail Gorbachev, a man who set himself a great central task – that of fundamentally reforming the Soviet system – and then completely lost his way, the prisoner of his own brilliant talents as an improviser, compromiser, manoeuvrer, and risk-taker. Those who have set themselves hedgehog-like tasks cannot make it up as they go along.

Circumstances are not everything. The nature of a particular political culture – the extent to which it may favour one style as against the other – is also important, and that may work against what circumstances would otherwise seem to require.

The political history of post-World War II Britain is a case in point. Immediately after emerging from the war as a great and victorious power, Britain began to experience one of the most precipitate declines in history. Objectively, her situation surely called for highly-focused leadership that would give overriding priority to stemming that decline and dealing with its root causes. But during the 25 years between Churchill and Thatcher the system did not produce such leadership. Instead, the period was dominated by two second-rate foxes, Harolds MacMillan and Wilson, men of considerable tactical skill and a kind of sophistication who did everything but address in a serious way the reality of their country's predicament and the choices it necessitated. As they prevaricated, manoeuvred, and compromised, the deterioration continued.

It was not until very late in the day, after things had reached crisis point, that Thatcher came to office, fully equipped with what Berlin describes as the hallmark of the hedgehog – "one unchanging, all-embracing, sometimes self-contradictory and incomplete, at times fanatical, unitary inner vision." Until then, the political culture's hostility toward intellectualised politics, strong convictions, and single-mindedness, its preference for urbanity, moderation, and fudge, more than offset the way that other circumstances favoured the hedgehog. The strong distaste for Thatcher in office, manifested both in elite cultural circles and in her own party, testified to continuing discomfort with the type in anything but the most extreme circumstances, and contributed substantially to her ultimate downfall.

Though – as with writers – one or the other style may be more to an individual's taste, it would be a mistake to think of either the fox or the hedgehog as being intrinsically superior to the other. For one thing, in politics it is always a case of horses for courses. (It was, I believe, of Bakunin that it was said that he was indispensable at the barricades, but should be shot the morning after the Revolution succeeded.) Apart from this, representatives of both types range from the brilliant to the mediocre and outright stupid. If Lloyd George and Roosevelt represent the fox at his best, Harold Wilson and George Bush provide examples at the other end of the spectrum, men seemingly without *any* purpose other than staying in power, and for whom *everything* is negotiable to that end. Mediocre examples of the hedgehog type – think of Yitzhak Shamir – tend to be rigid, narrow, and obsessive, without the compensating virtues of penetrating insight and the capacity to integrate disparate elements into a cohesive whole. Many such examples, it has to be said, were to be found in the ranks of dedicated Cold Warriors.

☙☙☙

An interesting phenomenon, very pertinent to current American politics, is that of a politician of one type attempting to make himself over to the other, for reasons of expediency. Given the nature of the two beasts, examples of foxes striving to become – or at least to appear to become – hedgehogs are much more common than the reverse process.

There are two outstanding cases of this in recent American politics: Richard Nixon and, again, George Bush. To the extent that he functioned as one, Nixon appears to have been a situational and opportunistic, rather than a temperamental, Cold War hedgehog. Initially, in the late 1940s, he took up anti-communism because it was the right career move for an ambitious young Republican at that time. Even as he assumed the role of anti-communist hard man in the Eisenhower administration, there was an air of detached calculation about Nixon's performance, a sense that in different circumstances he could just as happily have argued the opposing case. As president, he found it easy to do business with the Soviet and Chinese leaders, and the vulpine politics of detente was highly congenial to him. No doubt, the tension of playing the role of a "conviction" statesman while being in reality a political fox was only one of many tensions that contributed to Nixon's tragedy; but it played its part.

If Nixon's is a subtle and complicated example (surely nothing that he ever did was uncomplicated) of one of nature's foxes masquerading as a hedgehog, that of George Bush is an unusually blatant one. If ever there has been a natural fox – someone entirely devoid of a "central vision" and naturally constructed to pursue "many ends, often unrelated and even contradictory" – it is surely George Bush, and his mediocrity should not obscure his claim to archetypal status. Yet in 1980, in a supreme act of expediency, Bush decided to convert himself into a Reaganesque hedgehog, abandoning his set of thin centrist beliefs overnight and substituting the whole conservative bill of goods, virtually without qualification. He – and we – have been living with the consequences ever since.

In the short term these were favourable for him, gaining him first the vice-presidency and then the presidency. But in the longer term they have been disastrous, resulting in an identity crisis of paralysing proportions. Having shamelessly changed his beliefs and then half changed back after becoming president, George Bush now seems to have no idea who or what he is – and neither have we. Those who now urge him to project a "vision" fail to understand that it is not in his nature to do so, and that the attempt to fake it back in the 1980s is responsible for much of the trouble he is now in.

His critics are wrong in another and more fundamental sense. In demanding of him a "vision" and a central defining purpose, they are asking not only for something which he is constitutionally incapable of giving, but for something that is inappropriate for the times. Most commentators have responded to the end of the Cold War by proposing or demanding an alternative grand purpose or theme that will perform the same function as anti-communism did until very recently – that of providing coherence, unity, and high moral content to American foreign policy. After 40 years of Cold War, this is not surprising. A hedgehog foreign policy is the only kind that most of them have ever known. Another and perhaps more important reason is a peculiar split in American political culture: While politicians with "foxy" qualities are consistently favoured in domestic politics, it is a widely-held article of faith that a high-minded hedgehoggery is essential in foreign policy.

ڼ ڼ ڼ

So over the last three years Bush has been urged to respond to the fall of communism by expounding a new, grand, activist foreign policy – with the promotion of democracy being the most favoured central theme – and has been roundly condemned for not doing so (his brief espousal of a "New World Order", followed by his refusal or inability to give any content to that term, serves to emphasise rather than mitigate his delinquency).

But President Bush is surely right in this respect, and he deserves praise for resisting those who have been demanding "vision" as if it were an entitlement. The post-Cold War world is a pluralist one that does not allow for a monist foreign policy. There *is* no central, global issue, nor any overriding and threatened American interest, that can bind together disparate regions and causes in a convincing way, as until recently the Cold War did. Different policies have to be shaped and justified in terms of diverse forces and competing interests, rather than be subordinated to and subsumed in an overarching, transcendent Policy.

In the world of the Cold War and of clear American supremacy, foreign policy was a matter of aggregation: of adding this *and* that *and* that to a comprehensive global policy. It was also an activity in which the question "How?" was the most important one, as the answer to the prior "Why?" was regarded as settled by the compelling nature of the anticommunist struggle. (Old habits do not die easily; in discussing American intervention in Yugoslavia, commentators have given much more attention to how it should be done than to whether it should be done at all, despite the marginal importance of Yugoslavia to the United States in the absence of any other great power involvement.) In a diverse world in which American power is diminished, Americans will have to learn to substitute the conjunction "or" for "and" with increasing frequency, and once again to give serious consideration to the question "Why?" before proceeding to "How?".

Another way of saying all this is that the day of the fox has replaced the day of the hedgehog. George Bush's weakness has not been that he is a fox but that his ineptness has tended to give that political animal a bad name. It is worth bearing this in mind, as Bill Clinton – despite his routine espousal of the idea of a "global alliance for democracy" – is also clearly a fox, someone whose political performance is unlikely to give rise to the coinage "Clintonism". And we are going to live with one or the other for the next four years.

My So-Called Foreign Policy: The Case for Clinton's Diplomacy

The New Republic, 10 October 1994 [extract]

This essay by Harries led the cover of the leading progressive American journal of opinion. Owen was reliably informed that President Clinton's senior adviser, George Stephanopoulos, put the journal's cover on his White House office wall.

One way of interpreting what has gone wrong in America's post-Cold War performance involves seeing Clintonism, in its foreign policy form, not just as an aberration resulting from the shortcomings of a few individuals but as a precursor, a sign of things to come. For the incompetence, itself beyond question, works to obscure and disguise something much more serious: a combination of old habits and new inhibitions that, as long as it lasts, virtually guarantees the recurrence on a regular basis of the kind of fiascos and embarrassments (not necessarily terribly damaging ones) that we have experienced in the last year and a half. In this sense, it might be said, Clintonism preceded Clinton and was clearly evident during George Bush's last year. Unless there is a drastic change in the way Americans think about foreign policy, it is also likely to outlast Clinton.

What we are witnessing is, I believe, a structural – or cultural – incompetence, arising out of a flawed view of the world and of America's power and interests. American confidence and optimism are an invaluable source of strength in times of adversity. In times of triumph they can be a handicap. As the Soviet Union disintegrated, many normally thoughtful Americans, and not least conservatives, experienced a rush of blood to the head and entered a state of Wordsworthian bliss. They surrendered to the euphoria of victory, bereft of any protective imagination of disaster and impatient of any suggestion of limitation or caution.

An indication of the extent of this surrender is that two of the most striking examples of it were provided by the country's leading conservative columnists, George Will and William Safire. In the fall of 1989 Will scathingly dismissed those who argued the case for giving serious consideration to maintaining some stability in the midst of the turmoil of that year: "Enough of the worship of stability and of 'gradual' progress toward justice long denied." Only the Soviet Union had a stake in "stability", he insisted (though even that stake was not to last for long). Safire followed not long after with a piece titled "Hail to Unpredictability", asserting that "stability" had now replaced "peace" as the excuse of the appeasers of tyranny. These essays accurately reflected the excitement of the times, but they were strikingly free of that concern for the danger of unintended consequences that has traditionally characterised conservative thinking about turmoil.

The idea that best expressed this early euphoric sense of no limits was that of the universal triumph of liberal democracy. But as the deep troubles of the CIS states became evident, as disillusionment set in in Central Europe, as China and other Asian states resisted American urging to take the democratic path forthwith, and as even the established democracies of Western Europe began to look sickly and uncertain, the vision of a triumphant progress toward a democratic world faded. But "vision" has remained one of the key terms in discussion of America's foreign policy in the new era, along with "global leadership" and "sole remaining superpower". These three terms repay close examination.

◈ ◈ ◈

What is striking about the first two is the disembodied, contentless quality they have assumed. In the case of "vision", the demand has been not for this or that particular sense of purpose and destination but for vision in the abstract – for any grand picture of a future. Bush perfectly reflected the character of this American yearning by advancing the concept of a "New World Order" and then failing to give it any content whatsoever. The very notion of a vision-driven foreign policy, carrying the assumption of a grand end-state to be achieved – rather than the sense of an endless process driven only by proximate and provisional objectives – is questionable. Michael Oakeshott has given classic expression to that second approach in a celebrated passage:

> In political activity, then, men sail a boundless and bottomless sea; there is neither harbour for shelter nor floor for anchorage, neither starting-place nor appointed destination. The enterprise is to keep afloat on an even keel; the sea is both friend and enemy; and the seamanship consists in using the resources of a traditional manner of behaviour in order to make a friend of every hostile situation.

This may be too austere and bleak a view for most American tastes, but it should raise the question of whether something more modest and adaptable than a "vision" – say, a set of sensible middle-range objectives (call them interests) – might provide a more appropriate basis for policy in a fragmented and pluralist world.

Similarly, in the call for "leadership", what has been demanded is not American leadership to achieve this or that specific goal – as, say, it was exercised to achieve victory in World War II, or survival and containment of communism in the Cold War – but simply for the United States to demonstrate that it is in charge and running the show. This stress on being in charge, on behaving as if everyone's business is America's business and the world cannot go on without an assertion of US will, indicates how ingrained the Cold War habit of being out in front is by now. It suggests that, despite complaints about the burden it imposes and the freeloading of others, segments of the American elite have become more enamoured of their country's role as leader than they admit – or perhaps realise. Anyone who questions that role, or suggests that it need not involve intervention everywhere and always, runs a serious risk of being characterised as a neo-isolationist.

Such characterisations are often based on the belief – which I recently heard articulated by someone who held a responsible position in government in the 1980s – that the United States is only capable of functioning abroad in two modes, "full on" or "full off", so that any rejection of the former is taken as an endorsement of the latter. This is surely an utterly unjustified extrapolation of the experience of the interwar years, when the country was much less globally integrated (culturally and materially) than it is now. There is very little evidence in contemporary America of a desire to pull up the drawbridge and withdraw from the world. What there is – and it should surely be welcomed – is evidence of a re-ordering of priorities to require more deliberation and discrimination before becoming heavily engaged.

Like the first two terms, the third – "sole remaining superpower" – reflects a Cold War cast of mind. On the face of it, it may appear to be simply an unobjectionable description of fact. There were two superpowers during the Cold War, one of them collapsed, so there is one and only one remaining, right? Not really. For one thing, the phrase is rarely used as merely a flat statement of fact. Nearly always it is used in a prescriptive context, carrying with it the assumption of special prerogatives, special responsibilities and special interests. It is intimately linked with the whole global leadership business.

More important, the very idea of a "sole remaining superpower" amounts to a contradiction in terms. The superpower game is a relational one, not solitaire, and it takes at least two to play it. If you have two superpowers and you take one away, what is left is something less than a superpower. For being a superpower involves more than having certain capacities in the abstract, certain potentials (if it did not, after all, the United States would have been a superpower as long ago as the 1920s). It involves being fully-energised, motivated and focused to mobilise and deploy these capabilities and potentials – and it's very unlikely that a state can achieve that condition without the galvanising presence of at least one rival superpower to provide the needed sense of urgency and danger. The United States has ceased to be a superpower, not because it has "declined" but because its circumstances and its interests no longer require or permit it to be one.

To expect or demand that the same level of activism be maintained in the post-Cold War era is to doom oneself to disappointment and the kind of embarrassment resulting from the wide discrepancy between posture and performance – between old habits and new inhibitions— that has come to be associated with Clintonism. Patterns of thought and behaviour that developed over the four decades of the Cold War persist and are deeply ingrained. They involve basing policy on the assumptions that everything counts and nothing is irrelevant; that American leadership is always and everywhere required; that American institutions and ideas are universally valid. But these habits are now being challenged and balanced by countervailing concerns.

⚙ ⚙ ⚙

Several inhibitions now prevent the United States from behaving consistently in the manner of the sole superpower it believes itself to be. One is the political impossibility of subordinating domestic policy to foreign policy as was routine as long as we were confronting the evil empire. It is not only the so-called isolationists of left and right who have called for an alteration of priorities in favour of domestic affairs but also tough-minded foreign policy specialists such as Jeane Kirkpatrick ("The time when Americans should bear such unusual burdens is past. With 'normal' times, we can again become a normal nation") and William Hyland ("What is desperately required is a psychological turn inward").

A second inhibition operates against the resort to the unilateral use of force – *the* mark, one would have thought, of superpowerdom. Everything now, even the invasion of Haiti, requires multilateral cover, for democracy must be exported not only to individual countries but to the international state system itself. In the eyes of many Americans, the test of the virtue and legitimacy of a policy is no longer to be found in its substance but in the process by which it has been adopted – and, specifically, whether it has or has not been endorsed by a UN majority.

A third, and by far the most novel and limiting inhibition operating on the United States – and to varying degrees on most European countries, including Russia – is that against taking large numbers of casualties to further foreign policy objectives other than sheer survival. Perhaps, as Edward Luttwak has suggested, it is the result of the greater value placed on young lives in the West because of smaller families and the fewer early deaths that have followed the great medical advances of the past 50 years. Or perhaps it is because of the cumulative effect of the wars fought by Western countries in this century, the way they have progressively leached nationalism and patriotism of their appeal. James Kurth recently has related the reluctance to fight to the abandonment of loyalty to the Western civilisation of the Enlightenment:

> Among liberals, the political energy is now found among multicultural activists. Liberalism is ceasing to be modern and is becoming postmodern. Among conservatives, the political energy is now found among religious believers. Conservatism is ceasing to be modern and is becoming premodern. Neither these liberals nor these conservatives are believers in Western civilization ... A question thus arises about who, in the United States of the future, will still believe in Western civilization. Most practically, who will believe in it enough to fight, kill and die for it in a clash of civilizations?

Whatever the explanation, an extreme reluctance to take large casualties, and an unprecedented sensitivity to even very modest ones (as in Somalia), must be balanced against America's military might and must cast serious doubt on the validity of the concept of "sole remaining superpower" and many of the assumptions accompanying it.

ℋℋℋ

The most important and ironic consequence of Clintonism is that it has laid the ground for the reintroduction of a sense of realism in American foreign policy. For 40 years the Cold War imposed such a sense. When that struggle ended, so did the discipline it fostered. Now the President's indifference and inattentiveness, the fact that foreign policy is the only sphere of government in which he does not have large ambitions, and the blundering mediocrity of his foreign policy team, are combining to bring back a sense of limits and caution. It is overdue.

The American impulse to promote freedom and democracy in the world is a noble and powerful one, not to be casually ridiculed or dismissed. Acting on it is a complicated and delicate business. Success requires that this impulse be balanced against, and often circumscribed by, other interests that the United States must necessarily pursue – more mundane ones like security, order and prosperity. Success requires, too, an awareness of the intractability of a world that does not exist merely to satisfy American expectations – a world that for the most part cannot satisfy those expectations in the near future. While determination and purposefulness are important ingredients in any effective policy, the attempt to force history by an exercise of will is likely to produce more unintended than intended consequences.

Such observations and precepts may appear banal, and indeed in a sense they are. But politics, including international politics, is a banal business. When Walter Lippmann maintained that "without the controlling principle that the nation must maintain its objectives and its power in equilibrium, its purposes within its means and its means equal to its purposes, its commitments related to its resources and its resources adequate to its commitments, it is impossible to think about foreign policy," he was being banal.

Critics of realism claim that it is alien and inappropriate to the American tradition and temperament. It is neither. Far from realism's being alien, the United States was founded, initially led, and expanded to its full dimension by realists. And far from being inappropriate, the very strength of American idealism and optimism make it highly desirable that they be supplemented and balanced by the prudence and respect for what is the case that realism provides. This is especially true at a time when, superficially, anything looks possible for the United States. It was, after all, not Hans Morgenthau but George Washington who said, "No nation is to be trusted further than it is bound by its interests." It is on the basis of such banal truths that a sound foreign policy is constructed. Bereft of "vision", preoccupied with his domestic agenda, and equipped with too uncertain a trumpet for forceful international leadership, Bill Clinton may, however inelegantly and inadvertently, be performing the valuable service of backing the United States toward those banal truths.

The Anti-China Syndrome: How Not to Handle China

National Review, 5 May 1997

Reprinted in *Prospect* (London) and *Quadrant* (Sydney) in July 1997, the article led the *Review*'s cover. Shortly afterwards, former US Secretary of State, Henry Kissinger, wrote to Harries: "I have read your article in the *National Review* and can't remember when I have read an article in which I agreed with every word. I am only sorry I didn't write it myself, but I will plagiarise it liberally." The letter is displayed at the Sydney office of the Lowy Institute, which Owen joined as a Visiting Fellow in 2003.

Since the end of the Cold War, many Americans have been suffering from an enemy-deprivation syndrome. This is not surprising. After all, for 50 years they had experienced a clearly identified, formidable, and generally agreed upon enemy. That enemy provided a simply grasped organising principle for thinking about foreign policy, and its sudden disappearance threatened disorientation and discord. It imbued foreign policy with a sense of heroic moral purpose, and without it things seemed likely to become mundane and boring.

Whatever the mixture of motives, as soon as the initial euphoria over the Soviet Union's collapse had passed, most of the American foreign policy cognoscenti – and especially a large section of its conservative component – began to search for a substitute enemy. For a short while, Japan was favoured. Scores of authoritative books and hundreds of closely-argued articles were written about the impending "clash" between it and the United States. But then a Japan that had been presented as an irresistible juggernaut suddenly faltered. Its economy lost momentum, its politics became a shambles, and it was no longer a credible enemy.

Temporarily at a loss, some then tried to fill the gap by a process of aggregation. If a single powerful and convincing enemy was not available, then perhaps several small ones added together might do – North Korea, Iran, Iraq, Libya, Serbia, and so on. But it soon became clear that a lizard, a hyena and a couple of skunks did not add up to a dragon. Nor did Islamic fundamentalism really work, for, again, its multiple, divided agents lacked the heft and presence to be convincing rivals.

At this point some turned back to Russia as a dependable candidate for the role of principal enemy. True, its economy was in a pitiful state, its military performance in Chechnya was abysmal, and its whole social fabric was in tatters; but it certainly resonated, and if one was prepared to take the long view it still had adversarial potential. That, at least, seemed to be the assumption of those who took up the cause of the eastward expansion of NATO with enthusiasm. As one of the most honest of them – Peter Rodman – put it: "The only potential great-power security problem in central Europe is the lengthening shadow of Russian strength ... Russia is a force of nature; all this is inevitable."

But although Russia is potentially dangerous and needs careful handling, in the way that a wounded animal does, a declining former superpower making a serious stab at becoming a democracy is not really well suited to play the role of a principal enemy. Certainly it does not capture a combative imagination with the same conviction as a coming superpower that is performing spectacularly economically, that is still governed by an obnoxious regime, that frequently says nasty things about the United States, and that encompasses over one fifth of the earth's population – which is to say, China.

It is not surprising, then, that there is now widespread support for the view that China is America's main enemy, that the two countries are on a collision course, and that the only sensible policy for the US to follow is a tough and hostile one. In the words of *The New Republic*'s editors, we "must engage China adversarially". Anything else will amount to appeasement or "coddling".

Things may indeed turn out that way. Perhaps China really is evil, hostile and aggressive. But there is another possibility: that asserting these things will be self-fulfilling. If you insist on treating another country as an enemy, it is likely to become one. All the more reason, then, to look carefully at the arguments advanced for treating China in this way, and to consider what can be said against them.

1. **China as Aspiring Global Hegemon.** "Most experts agree," the editors of *The Weekly Standard* assure us, "that China aims … in the long term to challenge America's position as the dominant power in the world."

China's supposed appetite for global power is based on *no* empirical evidence whatsoever. China has been singularly unambitious beyond its region. Its most conspicuous venture in this respect was a half-hearted and incompetent effort to establish a presence in Africa more than three decades ago. True, in recent years China has sold arms to a number of countries outside the region, but if that is to be taken as evidence of hegemonic ambitions, then a number of Western powers – even Israel and Sweden – would qualify.

The global hegemony claim is based essentially not on empirical evidence but on a "logic of the system" argument, which maintains that rivalry is inevitable between the dominant power and the next strongest state, especially if the latter is an ascendant power. In their new book, *The Coming Conflict with China*, Richard Bernstein and Ross H. Munro set this out explicitly: "China, soon to be the globe's second most powerful nation, will be a predominating force as the world takes shape in the new millennium and, as such, it is bound to be no longer a strategic friend of the United States but a long-term adversary." The words "as such, it is bound to be" assume an ineluctable logic of cause and effect. Sometimes (though not by Bernstein and Munro) this claim is bolstered by reference to the notorious Anglo-German rivalry at the beginning of this century, when Britain as the dominant power was challenged by the German *arriviste*.

What is to be said about this systemic argument? First, it is true that a certain amount of friction between a hegemon in being and a rapidly rising state is virtually inevitable. Indeed, a certain amount of friction between *any* two powerful states that have regular intercourse is inevitable. But that by no means implies an unavoidable and continuing adversarial relationship. At the time of the Anglo-German rivalry there existed another – and, in the long run, more formidable – challenger to British supremacy, namely the United States. Yet Britain and the US did not become deadly enemies; on the contrary, they got on rather well and ultimately became allies. That relationship alone refutes the "inevitable" argument – and serves as a reminder that the Anglo-German rivalry required an exceptionally vain and foolish Kaiser Wilhelm in order to flourish.

One further point: Americans, more than any other people, should be wary of arguing that being or aspiring to be a global hegemon is necessary evidence of sin and sufficient cause for enmity. For were that so, every state in the world would have cause to regard the United States as its enemy.

2. China as Aspiring Regional Hegemon. The charge that China is set on becoming a regional hegemon *is* based on empirical evidence: on an alleged pattern of assertive, intimidatory and acquisitive behaviour, particularly towards Taiwan, Japan and certain islands in the South China Sea. What can be said about this evidence?

First, to the extent that China is assertive in its region, there is nothing peculiar or pathological in its behaviour. This is the way ascending powers – democratic as well as authoritarian – normally behave. If their efforts become egregious, they have to be checked; if they are reasonably modest and restrained, it is wise to cut them some slack.

Second, by historical standards, China's recent and current assertiveness *is* modest. Taiwan apart (of which more below), it has mainly manifested itself with respect to uninhabited or sparsely inhabited islands whose ownership is in dispute: the Senkaku Islands (claimed by China, Japan and Taiwan), the Paracel Islands (claimed by China and Vietnam) and Mischief Reef in the Spratly Islands (claimed by China and the Philippines).

Even if Chinese restraint does not necessarily reflect modest ambition, it does represent a rational and healthy sense of the power realities that will continue to exist well into the next century. We are, after all, talking about a country that, as Robert S. Ross pointed out in the March-April issue of *Foreign Affairs*, does not possess a single aircraft carrier, and will not possess one for a decade or so. The South China Sea is strategically important, and should the Chinese attempt to dominate it, they would have to be reminded of their limited capacity to project power. In the meantime, vigilance rather than enmity is required.

Third, Taiwan is a special case. Handling the issue has involved an implicit bargain: Peking will leave the island alone to enjoy de facto autonomy as long as Washington and Taipei do not force the issue of its ultimate status. When China mounted a show of force against Taiwan in March 1996, it was not in an effort to upset the balance represented by that bargain but as a reaction to its having been already upset by Taipei and Washington – by President Lee's campaign to have Taiwan readmitted to the United Nations (which would have been tantamount to recognising its independence), by the Clinton administration's allowing Lee to visit the US and so burnish Taiwan's independent image, and by a $6 billion sale of F-16 fighter planes to Taiwan. Ill-judged, ugly, and dangerous as was the Chinese intimidation, it was a *reaction*. It was not evidence of a determination to change the status quo. While the US has a political, moral and economic interest in safeguarding the de facto autonomy of Taiwan, there is ground for thinking long and hard – about the costs that would be involved and what American interests would be served – before assuming any obligation to support its formal independence.

One further point about Taiwan: While Americans tend to think of the issue primarily as a political question involving legal status and freedom from outside interference – and it is certainly that – for the Chinese it is also, and unavoidably, a major strategic issue. For, as Ross reminds us, the island is indeed the equivalent of an "unsinkable aircraft carrier", only 90 miles or so off China's coast. To the extent that Americans are sensitive about Castro's Cuba (which is badly armed compared to Taiwan, and which has had no superpower patron for the last six years), they should be able to appreciate China's apprehension about Taiwan.

3. The Chinese Arms Buildup. Much is made of what *The New Republic* calls China's "program of massive militarization", a program it is alleged to be implementing "frantically". *The Weekly Standard* emphasises that "China is the only major world power increasing rather than decreasing its defence spending." Arthur Waldron, writing in *Commentary*, sees this as "part and parcel of the regime's major shift ... toward repression and irredentism."

China certainly has increased its defence budget, although how much of that increase reflects inflation and the need to keep the military content through increased pay is in dispute among specialists. Certainly, too, there have been serious and successful efforts to acquire modern weaponry from Russia and Europe: SU-27 fighter aircraft, quiet submarines, destroyers equipped with cruise missiles, and so on.

That said, these points are relevant: 1) The increases have been made to a defence budget that had been severely depressed by the prolonged economic calamity of the Cultural Revolution. 2) The modernisation was to replace an arsenal that was antiquated. Just how far behind the Chinese were became fully and shockingly evident to them through America's swift and militarily crushing victory in the Gulf War. 3) The build-up also reflects the unusual conjunction of the availability of greatly increased funds on the Chinese side and the ready availability of modern weapons for sale on the Russian side. 4) However "massive" the Chinese program is, the US defence budget is still as large as the next five or six largest defence budgets in the world combined. 5) Given the backwardness of Chinese technology and the limitation of what can be purchased abroad, it will take a long time for China to acquire a defence force that is fully modernised, even in today's sense of the word. *The New Republic* editorialises that "It is only a matter of decades before China becomes the other military superpower on earth." But as Harold Wilson so nearly said, a "matter of decades" is a long time in politics. By the time those decades have passed, the United States will have made further vast technological advances.

4. China as Human Rights Violator. One justification for hostility towards China, and perhaps the one with the greatest popular appeal, is that its regime is oppressive and shows little respect for human rights.

How concern for human rights translates into foreign policy is a complicated matter. While individuals or single-issue organisations are free to take an absolute position on the question, governments are not. Governments have to balance the claims of human rights against other concerns which also have a moral content (peace, security, order, prosperity). Their place in the hierarchy of interests will vary – sometimes it will be high, sometimes it will have to give way to other compelling interests. To the moral absolutist the result will seem cynical, and governments regularly invite such a response because they persist in speaking of human rights in absolutist terms that they cannot, in the nature of things, honour.

True, there will be some terrible occasions when the violation of human rights will be so horrendous that the absolutist moral approach becomes – or should become – compelling. Such was the case with the murderous regimes of Hitler and Stalin. But mercifully they are the exceptions, not the rule. China today does not constitute such an exception. According to Bernstein and Munro, the best estimate of the number of political prisoners in China currently is 3,000. In a population of 1.3 billion, this amounts to 0.00023%, which is hardly the equivalent of the Gulag or the

Nazi concentration camps. Ironically, back in the early 1970s, when most Americans, liberals and realists alike, were enthusiastically applauding the US opening to China, the Maoist regime *was* in the same league as the Hitlerite and Stalinist regimes.

China today can more reasonably be compared to Indonesia or Saudi Arabia – or India. Of the latter, a recent Council on Foreign Relations report states: "Thousands of Kashmiris have been killed by the security forces. On occasion Indian units have used lethal force against peaceful demonstrators and burned down entire neighbourhoods." It is perhaps worth nothing that, far from suggesting that the United States should penalise India, the report recommends that we develop a "closer strategic relationship" with that country. While one would not want to make a similar proposal in the case of China, it would seem sensible to stop short of ostracism.

One last point: while China's human-rights performance continues to be poor, in important respects the trend is positive. There have been significant improvements in terms of the rule of law, grass-roots democracy and media freedom. Already it is absurd to apply the term "totalitarian" to the regime, as *The New Republic* does. While nothing is certain, and there is no established direct causal relationship between economic advance and political liberalisation, there is certainly a strong correlation between the two. There are therefore real grounds for being optimistic about the likelihood that freedom and respect for human rights in China will increase steadily – perhaps dramatically – over the next decade.

5. The Hostility of China's Political Elite. Bernstein and Munro place a great deal of emphasis on the character of the Chinese ruling elite in explaining the hostility that exists between China and the United States. That elite has become strongly anti-American. It shows a pattern of "irritability, defensiveness, harshness and defiance of American opinion." It uses words such as "hegemonism", "subversion" and "interference" with regard to the United States. This elderly elite is characterised as secretive, intolerant, reflexively defensive, and chauvinistic.

During the second half of the Cold War, these characteristics and the anti-Americanism that flowed from them were held in check by the need for American support against a threatening Russia. But now, with that threat removed and with China's power rapidly increasing, the elite feels no need to keep its true feelings secret. Indeed, they can be turned to advantage. For with communism dead, there is need for a substitute ideology to mobilise support and legitimise the power of the elite. What better substitute than the true and tried formula of emotional, chauvinistic nationalism, directed against an alien superpower?

This analysis deserves at least three comments. First, it may well contain significant elements of truth. But, second, with a closed and secretive elite it is difficult to be certain what those elements are. We knew, or thought we knew, much more about the Soviet elite (all those years of dedicated Kremlinology!) than we know about the Chinese elite – and yet almost all of us were utterly surprised by its supine behaviour in the final crisis of the Soviet system. That experience alone should counsel caution in basing policy on one's supposed understanding of the psychology and motivation of a closed and secretive elite.

A third point also suggests caution. The charges that the Chinese elite directs against the United States are in many respects similar to the charges that Bernstein and Munro (and other Americans) make against the Chinese. Each accuses the other of hegemonistic designs, interference, threatening behaviour, military build-up, and the like. This raises the question of what, in each case, is cause and what is effect. Americans quote Chinese statements to establish that the US must reconcile itself to the enmity of Peking; but it is very likely that analysts in China are simultaneously quoting Bernstein and Munro to establish that American enmity must be taken as a given. Is there not the real danger of a vicious circle here?

6. China's Interference in American Domestic Politics. The inclination to treat China as an enemy has been significantly strengthened by the current charges of Chinese government interference in America's domestic political process. There is no reason to doubt that these charges are true. That said, however, outrage should be tempered by the recognition that if such interference justifies condemnation, then many, many countries have grounds for condemning the United States. For over 50 years the United States has itself interfered in the domestic affairs of other countries on a more or less regular basis – not only Third World countries and not only dictatorships, but developed Western countries, including democracies. The Christian Democratic party of Italy, for example, was massively supported by the CIA in its early days, and there has been much intervention in the domestic affairs of countries as varied as Greece, Chile and the Philippines.

I am aware that pointing this out is likely to draw the charge that one is assuming a "moral equivalence". But if this is not to become an intimidatory device inhibiting free discussion, this is a charge that has to be resorted to with great care. If the United States is always treated as a special case, if what is condemned in others is condoned in America's case because its superior ends justify means that would otherwise be unacceptable, it becomes difficult to discuss issues sensibly. What may have been appropriate in the exceptional circumstances of coping with the "evil empire" of yesterday is not appropriate in the more mundane world of today.

♾♾♾

In their article "Toward a Neo-Reaganite Foreign Policy" (*Foreign Affairs*, July-August 1996), William Kristol and Robert Kagan maintained that "it is hard to imagine conservatives achieving a lasting political realignment in this country without ... a coherent set of foreign policy principles that at least bear some resemblance to those proposed by Reagan. The remoralization of America at home ultimately requires the remoralization of American foreign policy." Again, they argue that "Deprived of the support of an elevated patriotism, bereft of the ability to appeal to national honor, conservatives will ultimately fail in their effort to govern America."

This represents an interesting approach to foreign policy, one that seems to start with the political needs of conservatives rather than the national interest of the United States. Given the title of the Kristol-Kagan article, it should be pointed out that this was not Ronald Reagan's approach to foreign policy. His priority was defeating the evil empire, an enemy in being, not finding a foreign policy that would serve conservative interests.

More to the point, the kind of priority represented by Kristol and Kagan – the need to find a stirring cause that will "remoralize" America – is almost certain to produce an enemy and identify an inspiring conflict between good and evil. As Walter Lippmann once observed, "For the most part we do not first see and then define, we define first and then we see." It is difficult to escape the conclusion that something of this sort typifies much current American thinking about China. It is a dangerous approach to foreign policy.

HENRY A. KISSINGER

April 30, 1997

Dear Owen:

I have read your article in the National Review and can't remember when I have read an article in which I have agreed with every word. I am only sorry I didn't write it myself, but I will plaigerize it liberally.

Warm regards,

Henry A. Kissinger

Mr. Owen Harries
Editor
The National Interest
1112 Sixteenth Street, NW
Washington, DC   20036

The Dangers of Expansive Realism

The National Interest, Winter 1997-98

This article prompted George Kennan, the intellectual architect of the Cold War doctrine of containment, to submit a handwritten letter – at age 93 – endorsing Harries' analysis. Published in the Spring 1998 issue, the letter and article were also reprinted in the *Congressional Record* (3 March 1998), at the request of US Senator Daniel Patrick Moynihan, during the debate over the Senate's ratification of NATO's first round of expansion.

> ... *[I]t is sometimes necessary to repeat what all know.*
> *All mapmakers should place the Mississippi in the same location and*
> *avoid originality. It may be boring, but one has to know where it is.*
> *We cannot have the Mississippi flowing toward the Rockies, just for a change.*
>
> Saul Bellow, *Mr Sammler's Planet*

In many ways, NATO is a boring organisation. It is a thing of acronyms, jargon, organisational charts, arcane strategic doctrines, and tired rhetoric. But there is no gainsaying that it has a Mississippi-like centrality and importance in American foreign policy. When, then, proposals are made to change it radically – to give it new (and very different) members, new purposes, new ways of conducting business, new non-totalitarian enemies (or conversely, to dispense altogether with the concept of enemies as a rationale) – it is sensible to pay close attention, to scrutinise carefully and repeatedly the arguments that bolster those proposals. Even at the risk of making NATO boring in new ways, it is important to get things right.

Before getting down to particular arguments, the proposed expansion of NATO into Central and Eastern Europe should be placed in the wider context that made it an issue. For nearly half a century the United States and its allies fought the Cold War, not, it was always insisted, against Russia and the Russian people, but against the Soviet regime and the ideology it represented. An implicit Western objective in the Cold War was the conversion of Russia from totalitarianism to a more or less normal state, and, if possible, to democracy.

Between 1989 and 1991, a political miracle occurred. The Soviet regime, steeped in blood and obsessed with total control as it had been throughout most of its history, voluntarily gave up its Warsaw Pact empire, collapsed the Soviet system upon itself, and then acquiesced in its own demise – all with virtually no violence. This extraordinary sequence of events was by no means inevitable. Had it so chosen, the regime could have resisted the forces of change as it had on previous occasions, thus either extending its life, perhaps for decades more, or going down in a welter of blood and destruction. That, indeed, would have been more normal behaviour, for as the English scholar Martin Wight once observed, "Great power status is lost, as it is won, by violence. A Great Power does not die in its bed." What occurred in the case of the Soviet Union was very much the exception.

A necessary condition for its being so was an understanding – explicit according to some, but in any case certainly implicit – that the West would not take strategic and political advantage of what the Soviet Union was allowing to happen to its empire and to itself. Whatever is said now, such a bargain was *assumed* by both sides, for it was evident to all involved that in its absence – if, that is, it had become apparent that the West was intent on exploiting any retreat by Moscow – events would not be allowed to proceed along the liberalising course that they actually took. Further, there seemed to be no basis for the United States objecting to such a bargain. For, after all, its avowed objective was not the eastward extension of its own power and influence in Europe, but the restoration of the independence of the countries of the region. In effect, the bargain gave the United States everything it wanted (more, in fact, for the breakup of the Soviet Union had never been a Cold War objective), and in return required it only to refrain from doing what it had never expressed any intention of doing.

Now, and very much at the initiative of the United States, the West is in the process of reneging on that implicit bargain by extending NATO into countries recently vacated by Moscow. It is an ominous step. Whatever is said, however ingenious and vigorous the attempts to obscure the facts or change the subject, NATO is a military alliance, the most powerful in the history of the world, and the United States is the dominant force in that alliance. And whatever is claimed about spreading democracy, making Europe "whole", promoting stability, peacekeeping, and righting past injustices – all formulations that serve, either consciously or inadvertently, to divert attention from the political and strategic reality of what is now occurring – cannot succeed in obscuring the truth that the eastward extension of NATO will represent an unprecedented projection of American power into a sensitive region hitherto beyond its reach. It will constitute a veritable geopolitical revolution. It is not necessary to accept in its entirety the resonant but overwrought dictum of Sir Halford Mackinder ("Who rules East Europe commands the Heartland; Who rules the Heartland commands the World Island; Who rules the World Island commands the World") to recognise the profound strategic implications of what the US Senate is being asked to endorse.[*]

Why is the Clinton administration acting in this way? And – a different question – does it serve American interests that it is doing so, and that its expressed intention is to proceed much further along the same path?

Immediately after the end of the Cold War there was no great enthusiasm either in America or Western Europe for enlarging NATO. In the early days of the Clinton administration, Secretary of State Warren Christopher, Secretary of Defence Les Aspin, and Ambassador-at-Large Strobe Talbott were all opposed to it.

How, then, did it come about that by the beginning of 1994 President Clinton was declaring that "the question is no longer whether NATO will take on new members, but when and how"?

---

[*] When I wrote this, I thought that I was drawing attention to something that was implicit but unacknowledged in the policy of NATO expansion. But in his latest book, Zbigniew Brzezinski directly and honestly links American primacy to "preponderance on the Eurasian continent". In the same chapter he quotes Mackinder's dictum. See *The Grand Chessboard*, New York, Basic Books, 1997, chapter 2.

It was certainly not by a process of ratiocination, vigorous debate, and the creation of an intellectual consensus concerning interests, purposes, and means. To this day there is no such consensus, and no coherent case for NATO expansion on which all of its principal supporters agree.

How Enlargement Happened

The Clinton administration's conversion from indifference, or even scepticism, to insistence on NATO expansion was the result of a combination of disparate events and pressures:

- The strength of the Polish-American vote, as well as that of the other Americans of Central and East European origin.

- The enormous vested interests – careers, contracts, consultancies, accumulated expertise – represented by the NATO establishment, which now needed a new reason and purpose to justify the organisation's continued existence.

- The "moral" pressure exerted by East European leaders, for whom NATO membership is principally important as a symbol that they are fully European, and as a means of back-door entry into the European Union.

- Conversely, the growing eagerness of some West European governments to grant these states membership of NATO as an acceptable price for keeping them out of, or at least delaying their entry into, the European Union.

- The concern and self-distrust felt by some Germans, and not least by Chancellor Helmut Kohl, at the prospect of their country's being left on the eastern frontier of NATO, adjacent to an area of political weakness and potential instability.

- Growing doubts about democracy's prospect of success in Russia, and fear of the re-emergence of an assertive nationalism there.

- The need of some American conservative intellectuals for a bold foreign policy stroke to "remoralise" their own ranks after some dispiriting domestic defeats, the enthusiasm of others for "a democratic crusade" in Central and Eastern Europe, and the difficulty of yet others to break a lifetime's habit of regarding Moscow as the enemy.

Formidable as this combination of pressures was, it is doubtful that it would have been capable of converting the Clinton administration on NATO expansion were it not for the addition of one other crucial factor: Bosnia. The war in Bosnia focused American attention on post-Cold War Central Europe, and it did so in a most emotional way. Bosnia also raised in acute form the question of the future of NATO, as the alliance's feeble response to the crisis cast doubt on its continued viability, and it raised the question specifically in the context of instability in Central and Eastern Europe. The domino theory, forgotten for two decades, was quickly resurrected and applied. "Bosnia" was increasingly understood not as referring to a discrete event but as a metaphor for the chronic, historically-ordained instability of a whole region.

Russia is Russia is Russia

Taken together, these pressures were politically formidable, especially for an administration as sensitive to pressure as was Clinton's. But they had very little to do with America's national interests, and the administration's subsequent attempts to make a case for NATO's eastward expansion in terms of those interests have been perfunctory and shallow.

A much more serious attempt has been made outside the administration, mainly by commentators of a realist persuasion. The case they have made, however, is badly flawed. The realist case is based largely on the conviction that Russia is inherently and incorrigibly expansionist, regardless of how and by whom it is governed. Henry Kissinger has warned of "the fateful rhythm of Russian history". Zbigniew Brezezinski emphasises the centrality in Russia's history of "the imperial impulse" and claims that in post-communist Russia that impulse "remains strong and even appears to be strengthening". Thus, Brezezinski sees an "unfortunate continuity" between the Soviet era and today in defining national interests and formulating foreign policy. Another realist, Peter Rodman, speaks in the same vein, explaining the "lengthening shadow of Russian strength" by asserting that "Russia is a force of nature".

In arguing in this way, these commentators are being very true to their realist position. But they are also drawing attention to what is one of the most serious intellectual weaknesses of that position – namely, that in its stress on the structure of the international system and on how states are placed within that system, realism attaches little or no importance to what is going on *inside* particular states: what kind of regimes are in power, what kind of ideologies prevail, what kind of leadership is provided. For these realists, Russia is Russia is Russia, regardless of whether it is under czarist, communist, or nascent democratic rule.

That approach is enormously counterintuitive, and its weaknesses have been particularly evident in this most ideological of centuries. Has it really made no significant difference to Russian foreign policy whether it is in the hands of a Stolypin, a Stalin, or a Yeltsin? Or to German policy whether Stresemann, Hitler, or Adenauer was in power in that country? In foreign policy terms, was it pointless to have exerted great effort to bring down the Nazi and Soviet regimes?

For most people, merely to ask these questions would seem to answer them. But not so long ago such prominent realists as E.H. Carr and A.J.P. Taylor were prepared to argue an essential foreign policy continuity between the Weimar Republic and Nazi Germany. Indeed, and more seriously, it was the assumption of such a continuity – that Hitler was an ordinary compromising politician in the same mould as the Germans of the 1920s – that led Chamberlain fatally astray with his policy of appeasement.

Already in this century, then, Western statesmen created a terrible crisis and allowed an unnecessary world war to happen because they falsely assumed that the foreign policy of a totalitarian regime would be no different from that of the struggling democracy it replaced. It would be inexcusable – and, almost certainly, again disastrous – if at the end of the century we made the same error in reverse, this time by proceeding on the assumption that the behaviour of another struggling democracy will be no different from that of the totalitarian regime that preceded it.

Spheres of Influence

If in this one respect those who make the case for NATO expansion err in over-emphasising what is weakest in the realist position, in other respects their mistake has been to forget some of the precepts that are its strength. If realism is about anything, it is about a conscientious effort to try to see things as they are. One of the ways things are in international politics is that great powers have spheres of influence. It is one of their basic characteristics, one of the features that qualifies them as "great", that their power radiates out to immediately adjacent regions in the form of significant influence, and that they take a particular interest in those regions. This is as characteristic of democratic great powers as it is of autocratic or totalitarian ones: one of the first important foreign policy acts of the United States, engaged in even before it was an authentic great power, was to claim for itself a huge sphere of influence with the Monroe Doctrine.

To embark on a policy whose deliberate aim is to deny Russian influence in Central and Eastern Europe, to corset Russia within its own boundaries, is therefore a policy fraught with danger. It retains what meagre plausibility it has for two reasons: first, because of revulsion at the fact that in the communist period the Soviet Union ruthlessly and crudely translated the traditional concept of sphere of influence into a totalitarian one of a sphere of dominance, involving puppet regimes, occupying armies, terror, economic exploitation, and ideological regimentation; and second, because for the time being Russia is exceptionally weak. But as Russia recovers, and even if

it becomes a functioning democracy, NATO expansion will become
a risk-laden, destabilising policy – not because extreme Russian
nationalists or neo-communists are bound to come to the fore, but
because, in the nature of things, Russia will again assert its normal
prerogatives as a great power.

Indeed, if some of the arguments now being advanced forcefully
were to prevail, the global picture that would result could be even
worse. For at the same time as the United States appears determined to
commit itself to denying Russia a sphere of influence, many powerful
voices are insisting that it should do the same with respect to China.
That country too should be strictly contained within its borders, and
any attempt by it to extend its influence beyond them should be seen
as illegitimate. Meanwhile, as these two huge countries would be so
constrained, the United States itself, armed in virtue, should feel free to
treat the entire globe as *its* sphere of influence, extending its presence
and imposing its will as it sees fit. Far from promoting stability, such a
policy would create new and dangerous tensions in world affairs.

Ends and Means

Another of the central tenants of realism is that if the end is willed, so
should be the means. The two should be kept in balance, preferably,
as Walter Lippmann urged, "with a comfortable surplus of power in
reserve". In the case of NATO expansion, this tenet is being ignored.
The NATO members are moving to assume very large additional
commitments at a time when they have all made substantial cuts to
their defence budgets, and when more such cuts are virtually certain.
(The French Cabinet, for example, announced in August that the
military draft, which dates back two centuries, is to be phased out
and that defence procurement expenditure is to be cut by 11%.) The
irresponsibility of such a course of action raises the question of the
seriousness of the new commitments being undertaken. After all,
such pledges have been made in the past, only to be broken: Munich,
1938, was the last occasion on which Western powers guaranteed the
security of what is today the Czech Republic.

It is not only in terms of power that realists should be concerned with the balancing of ends and means. They should also consider the suitability of the instruments involved – particularly the human instruments – for the tasks at hand. Not to do so is likely to result in the sort of unpleasant surprise that some realist supporters of NATO expansion got as a result of the March 1997 Helsinki summit. At that meeting, so many concessions were made to Moscow by the Clinton administration that we now have an almost lunatic state of affairs: in order to make acceptable the expanding of NATO to contain a potentially dangerous Russia, we are coming close to making Russia an honorary member of NATO, with something approximating veto power.

Some of the initially most ardent supporters of expansion are now deeply dismayed by these developments. But surely the likelihood of such an outcome was foreseeable. After all, they knew from the start that the policy they were pushing would be negotiated not by a Talleyrand or a Metternich – or an Acheson or a Kissinger – but by Bill Clinton, the man who feels everyone's pain. Kissinger has been clear-eyed enough to label what happened at Helsinki a fiasco.

This image of a Europe "made whole" again after the division of the Cold War is one that the advocates of NATO expansion appeal to frequently. But it is not a convincing appeal. For one thing, coming from some mouths it tends to bring to mind Bismarck's comment: "I have always found the word Europe on the lips of those politicians who wanted something from other Powers which they dared not demand in their own name." For another, it invites the question of when exactly was the last time that Europe was "whole". In the 1930s, when the dictators were on the rampage? In the 1920s, when Germany and Russia were virtual non-actors? In 1910, when Europe was an armed camp and a furious arms race was in progress? In the 1860s, when Prussia was creating an empire with "blood and iron"? When exactly? And then there is the simple and undeniable fact that at every step of the way – and regardless of how many tranches of new members are taken in – the line dividing

Europe will not be eliminated but simply moved to a different place. Only if Russia itself were to be included would Europe be "whole". Anyone who doubts this should consult an atlas.

One final note: During the last few months advocates of expansion have been resorting more and more to an argument of last resort – one of process, not of substance. It is that the United States is now so far committed that it is too late to turn back. That argument is not without some merit, for prestige does count, and undoubtedly prestige would be lost by a reversal at this stage. But that granted, prestige is not everything. When the alternative is to persist in serious error it may be necessary to sacrifice some prestige early, rather than much more later. To proceed resolutely down a wrong road – especially one that has a slippery slope – is not statesmanship. After all, the last time the argument that it is too late to turn back prevailed was exactly 30 years ago, as, without clear purpose, we were advancing deeper and deeper into Vietnam.

Letter to Harries

The National Interest, Spring 1998

I read your article with strong approval. It was in some respects a surprise because certain of your major arguments were ones I myself had made, or had wanted to make, but had not expected to see them so well-expressed by the pen of anyone else. I can perhaps make this clear by commenting specifically on certain of your points.

First, your reference to the implicit understanding that the West would not take advantage of the Russian strategic and political withdrawal from Eastern Europe is not only warranted, but could have been strengthened. It is my understanding that Gorbachev on more than one occasion was given to understand, in informal talks with senior American and other Western personalities, that if the USSR would accept a united Germany remaining in NATO, the jurisdiction of that alliance would not be moved further eastward. We did not, I am sure, intend to trick the Russians; but the actual determinants of our later behaviour – lack of coordination of political with military policy, and the amateurism of later White House diplomacy – would scarcely have been more creditable on our part than a real intention to deceive.

Secondly, I could not associate myself more strongly with what you write about the realist case that sees Russia as an inherently and incorrigibly expansionist country, and suggests that this tendency marks the present Russian regime no less than it did the Russian regimes of the past. We have seen this view reflected time and again, occasionally in even more violent forms, in efforts to justify the recent expansion of NATO's boundaries and further possible expansions of that nature. So numerous and extensive have the distortions and misunderstandings on which this view is based been that it would be hard even to list them in a letter of this sort. It grossly oversimplifies and misconstrues most of the history of Russian diplomacy of the czarist period. It ignores the whole great complexity of Russia's part in World War II. It allows and encourages one to forget that the Soviet military advances into Western Europe during the last war took place with our enthusiastic approval, and the political ones of the ensuing period at least with our initial consent and support. It usually avoids mention of the communist period, and attributes to "the Russians" generally all the excesses of the Soviet domination of Eastern Europe in the Cold War period.

Worst of all, it tends to equate, at least by implication, the Russian-Communist dictatorship of recent memory with the present Russian republic – a republic, the product of an amazingly bloodless revolution, which has, for all its many faults, succeeded in carrying on for several years with an elected government, a largely free press and media, without concentration camps or executions, and with a minimum of police brutality. This curious present Russia, we are asked to believe, is obsessed by the same dreams of conquest and oppression of others as were the worst examples, real or imaginative, of its predecessors.

You, I think, were among the first, if not indeed the first, to bring some of the above to the attention of your readers; and this, in my opinion, was an important and valuable service.

George F. Kennan
Princeton, New Jersey

First Kosovo. Then Russia. Now China.

The New York Times, 16 May 1999

Published when Harries was Editor of *The National Interest*, the *Times* Editor rang him to say that the President would be "responding". Within a week, an op-ed in William Jefferson Clinton's name appeared in the same pages defending the ongoing war.

L ast week, President Clinton attempted a comprehensive defence of his Kosovo policy. Heavy on Balkan history and light on serious analysis, it did little to remove the sense that we are experiencing a foreign policy debacle, one in which bombs are serving as substitutes for thought.

The Kosovo crisis began as one of those small but nasty local disputes that happen regularly all over the world. Usually they are left alone to play themselves out. In this instance, however, we intervened, and an issue that was initially of little geopolitical significance has been elevated into one that threatens to destabilise the whole structure of American foreign policy. Now, three of the most important components of that policy – NATO, United States-Russian relations, and United States-China relations – are all in serious jeopardy.

Madeleine Albright's protestations to the contrary, in all but the most dire of circumstances, some strategic assets are better possessed than used. That applies to armies, and it also applies to alliances. For over 50 years, NATO thrived and became the most successful alliance in history by being inactive. It won the Cold War, acquired authority and an aura of irresistible power without firing a shot in anger. Its whole point was to render its own use unnecessary. True, some knew that it was much less formidable and efficient than was claimed, but they were few.

Then, in March, this alliance called its own bluff and insisted on putting itself to the test against a minor state and on a peripheral issue. It is true that Slobodan Milosevic's ethnic cleansing is a barbaric thing. But contrary to what President Clinton now claims, until things seriously deteriorated after NATO's intervention, it was no worse than what he and other Western leaders had been able to bear with comparative equanimity in Turkey, Kashmir, Sudan, Rwanda – and Croatia. In any case, after seven inconclusive weeks of half-hearted bombing, and of showing much more solicitude for the safety of its own troops than for that of either Kosovar or Serb civilians, NATO has utterly failed to make its will prevail.

Prestige and credibility are important in international politics. Properly cultivated and used, they can be an effective substitute for the actual use of force. But in Kosovo they have been dissipated and squandered, with the result that instead of prestige being an effective substitute for force, increasingly the use of force is being justified by the need to restore credibility.

But in that respect the damage has already been done. The secret of NATO's nervous, tentative and incompetent character is out, and its authority is significantly impaired. So too will be the readiness of NATO members to engage in strategically more valid and urgent ventures in the future. And, most dangerous of all, so will the deterrent power of NATO's leading member, the United States. With its ability to overawe diminished, the United States will have to resort to force even more often. The dangers of miscalculation will multiply.

Over the last decade, we have been assured that old-style power politics is dead and that a new world order, reflecting the realities of both globalisation and American leadership, is emerging. But for any such order to be meaningful, the co-operation of Russia and China will be essential. Unless co-opted, their potential as troublemakers is huge. But as a result of Kosovo, both those countries have been alienated, the fires of virulent nationalism and anti-Americanism have been stoked, and the political moderates there have been undermined. Further, and this is no mean feat, these countries have been driven closer together than they have been for decades.

As far as Russia is concerned, the Kosovo intervention resulted from the same mind-set that – in betrayal of earlier promises and of geopolitical sense – expanded NATO up to the Russian frontier. It is a mind-set that tends to treat Russia with the contempt reserved for a client, dependent and defeated enemy. Thus in the case of Kosovo, no weight was given to the close historical association between Russia and Serbia. Even when the need was felt for Moscow's services as a go-between, it was treated more as a carrier of messages than as a negotiating principal. Given its internal problems, Russia is going to be a difficult and dangerous presence in the world in any case; in almost every way, recent American foreign policy has made the problem worse.

In the case of China, the United States was admittedly the victim of very bad luck with the embassy bombing, though it is the kind of bad luck that tends to accompany gross incompetence. But that apart, military intervention in the internal affairs of a sovereign state, in support of the armed liberation movement of an ethnic minority, had to be deeply disturbing to China (and to any country with a substantial ethnic minority). On the eve of this crisis, American policy toward China had been established on sound lines, even if it was being oversold as a "strategic partnership". Now it has received a severe blow from which it is unlikely to recover any time soon. For those determined to designate China as our next great enemy, this will be good news; for others, it will be deeply disturbing.

⚮⚮⚮

It is not necessary to deny the horror in Kosovo to find it grotesque that a territory, smaller than Connecticut, has been allowed to distort American foreign policy to this extent. Why and how did it happen?

The easy (and, since it is coming to an end, the reassuring) answer is that it is all the fault of the Clinton administration. And there is substance to that answer, for this administration's foreign policy team is surely the weakest in 60 years. Its failure to set and keep priorities, to bear fully in mind the interrelatedness of things, to steer a steady course, to relate rhetoric to substance, has been dismaying.

But blaming the Clinton crowd may be too easy. Many of the faults and weaknesses listed above have a familiar ring. They were the weaknesses that George Kennan and Walter Lippmann castigated Americans for half a century ago. For decades these weaknesses were held in check by the discipline and sense of reality imposed by the Cold War. But in the last few years they have come creeping back, some of them lightly disguised as the new globalism.

There is to begin with the penchant for moralism. Let us be clear: what is wrong is not the impulse to give foreign policy a moral content, but the presumption that doing so is an uncomplicated business, one not requiring calculation and compromise but merely purity of intention. Cheap moralists are as dangerous as cheap hawks – indeed, they are often the same people.

Then there is the lawyerly approach, the inclination to see foreign policy as a series of discrete cases to be settled in isolation one by one, rather than as a continuing process in which everything is connected to everything else, and in which context is all.

Again, and this has been the most blatant weakness of all in Kosovo, there is reluctance to accept that large ambitions – and some American officials now have huge ambitions for the "indispensable nation" – cannot safely coexist with parsimonious means. Talk about the obsolescence of war as an institution and about smart weapons that will do the job without human cost has fed this reluctance. But it has taken a state of only Serbia's weight to prove it wrong. Perhaps the only good thing that will come out of the Kosovo venture is a salutary reminder that it is still true that he who wills the end must also will the means.

Three Rules for a Superpower to Live By

The New York Times, 23 August 1999

Reprinted as "Dangers for the US with its Near Absolute Power" in the *Australian Financial Review*, 26 August 1999.

For the next few decades, perhaps for several generations, the United States is going to be the world's dominant power. Its potential for good and, if it should mess up, for bad is going to be immense. That being so, it is going to be extremely important – not only for America itself but for everyone else – that Americans think clearly about foreign policy. Here are three modest suggestions toward that end.

First, learn to distinguish between the concepts of "victory" and "success", for they are not necessarily the same thing. It is not just that victories can be Pyrrhic, but that even when they come cheap they may not serve your best interests.

To take an obvious example, the British and the French emerged victorious from World War I. But in terms of the terrible loss of human capital, the draining of their treasuries, and the sapping of their will and confidence, that war was not a success. Neither was it in terms of its effect on their ally, Russia, and their adversary, Germany, both of whom became the hosts of brutal totalitarian regimes. On the whole, a compromise peace early on – one that would no doubt have been denounced by the superpatriots of the day – would have served British and French interests much better, as World War II proved.

More recently, and on a much smaller scale, the same distinction is evident in the case of Kosovo. Whether NATO's victory over Serbia amounts to a success is, to put it mildly, extremely dubious. The internal condition of Kosovo in the two months since the end of the bombing has been marked by murder, looting, arson, the absence of civil government, and the mass exodus of one ethnic group. At the same time, relations with China and Russia have deteriorated. In

Western Europe, the prospects of NATO solidarity have weakened rather than strengthened, as the Europeans move toward developing their own collective military capacity. All in all, the episode seems closer to a fiasco than a triumph.

This distinction between victory and success is particularly worth emphasising at a time when the United States possesses the military means to defeat any other country, and when an exceptional readiness to resort to those means is a marked feature of its foreign policy.

A second suggestion: Be on your guard against and reject terms that serve no purpose other than to narrow the range of permissible discussion. It clarifies nothing, for example, to characterise an argument for a restrained and prudent use of American power as "neo-isolationist". There are no serious isolationists in this country today, and the only point of such a term is to denigrate a legitimate position by falsely associating it with a discredited policy from the past.

Other terms to be rejected on similar grounds include "imperialism" and "appeasement". The label "imperialism" only obscures important distinctions between the kind of influence that the United States now exerts and the direct rule engaged in by truly imperialist powers (including the United States itself) in an earlier age.

The same is true of the efforts, witnessed currently in the debate over China, to treat "compromise" and "appeasement" as synonyms. It is an attempt at establishing guilt by association. But, as Hans Morgenthau convincingly argued a long time ago, compromise amounts to appeasement only when it is resorted to in dealing with an insatiable adversary. To condemn all compromise as appeasement is to rule out an indispensable dimension of diplomacy and to condemn foreign policy to a dangerous rigidity.

In each of these cases, what is involved is an attempt to inhibit debate, to intimidate. At a time when open and vigorous discussion is badly needed, that attempt should be resisted.

A third suggestion: If, along the way, you have acquired it, abandon the habit of condemning as "moral equivalence" any attempt to judge the behaviour of the United States by the same moral standards that Americans routinely apply to other nations. During the Cold War – a struggle against what was truly an evil empire – there was some justification in maintaining that similar behaviour by Washington and Moscow should be judged differently, because the intrinsic moral character of the two actors was so different. But that was due less to the unique virtue of the United States than to the special vileness of the Soviet Union, and even then applying double standards was a tricky business, easily abused.

In the more mundane world of today there is no justification for applying one standard to the rest of the world and another to America – over, say, attacks on the territory of sovereign states that have not threatened you, or the extraterritorial application of domestic laws, or the adoption of protectionist measures. The United States should either practise what it preaches or expect other states to emulate its practices.

Not only does insistence on double standards seem hypocritical to others, thereby diminishing American credibility and prestige, but, even more seriously, it makes it impossible to think sensibly and coherently about international affairs. And, as I started by saying, that is a fatal drawback for an indispensable nation.

Understanding America

Occasional Paper No. 80, Centre for Independent Studies (CIS), April 2002 [extract]

Published when Harries was a Senior Fellow at the Centre, this essay was based on a CIS lecture he delivered in Sydney on 3 April 2002 in the wake of the American response to the 9/11 terrorist attacks in 2001. The lecture was extracted in *The Australian* and *The Age* the following day.

As far as American foreign policy is concerned, there have been, and still are, two very different traditions existing alongside each other: realism and American exceptionalism.

From George Washington's warning that "no nation is to be trusted farther than it is bound to its interest" to the Cold War struggle between two great powers, the US has a long and healthy realist tradition. But the doctrine of American exceptionalism – the belief that the US is exceptional, in the double sense that it is superior and that it is different, not only in degree but in kind – has also been a powerful force in the country. From this belief, it followed – psychologically, if not logically – that the US had a mission, a manifest destiny, to change the world in its image.

I would maintain that the foreign policy of the United States can only be understood in terms of a complicated and fluctuating interaction between these two traditions.

A striking example of the clash between them occurred as soon as the United States emerged as a full-fledged great power at the end of World War I. Woodrow Wilson, initially reluctant to intervene in the war, had, once in, come to see it as a crusade to make the world safe for democracy. The League of Nations was to be the instrument for realising the universal ideas of liberty, democracy and peace. To make it work, Wilson was prepared to sign a blank cheque committing the United States to the use of collective force to resist any violation of the borders or sovereignty of any country at any time. His readiness to do so was based largely on the conviction that the actual use of collective force would be unnecessary, because something called "world public opinion" would preserve the peace.

He was opposed by a powerful group of senators led by Henry Cabot Lodge. Liberal historians have been largely successful in representing them as ignorant, backwoods isolationists. In reality they were prudent realists and traditional nationalists who did not share Wilson's faith in world public opinion, were unprepared to sign a blank cheque for collective security, and believed that the United States should not undertake commitments that it might not be prepared to honour when push came to shove. They believed that the United States should promote democracy by its example, not by its power. The position of the senators had been articulated almost a century earlier by John Quincy Adams when he famously proclaimed:

> America does not go abroad in search of monsters to destroy.
> She is the well-wisher of the freedom and independence of
> all. She is the champion and vindicator only of her own.

If, after World War I, American idealism and American realism had been in head-on confrontation, after World War II they complemented and reinforced each other extremely well. In so far as the coming Cold War struggle was a conflict between two great powers – the United States and the Soviet Union – realism came into its own. In office as Secretary of State was that urbane realist, Dean Acheson, and this was the age of influential realists like Hans Morgenthau, George Kennan and Walter Lippmann. But in so far as the Cold War was a struggle between two ideologies, and in so far as it was necessary to re-motivate an America that had rapidly demobilised after victory in World War II, American idealism was an essential counterweight to communism.

When, in March 1947, President Truman outlined what was to become known as the Truman Doctrine, he was responding to a specific crisis in Greece. But he chose to speak in the sweeping, universalist terms of American idealism:

At the present moment in world history nearly every nation must choose between alternative ways of life ... I believe it must be the policy of the United States to support free peoples who are resisting attempted subjugation by armed minorities or by outside pressures ... The free peoples of the world look to us for support in maintaining their freedoms. If we falter in our leadership, we may endanger the peace of the world.

This was Wilsonian language. But while Wilson had called for American commitment at a time when there was no enemy in sight, and had thus alienated realists, Truman did so when there was a very real and powerful adversary. So while realists had opposed Wilson they supported Truman, even if some of them complained that his rhetoric was too extravagant.

Throughout the Cold War, realism and idealism essentially continued to complement each other, with the weight shifting from one leg to the other as circumstances varied. American leaders might have used the rhetoric of "liberation" and "roll-back", but the reality of Soviet power kept their feet firmly on the ground. When a crisis like the Hungarian Uprising of 1956 occurred, prudence prevailed and America refrained from intervening.

So the relationship between American idealism and realism after World War I and World War II differed greatly. What, then, about the aftermath of the third great struggle of the 20th century, the Cold War? The sudden and unexpected collapse of its rival, the Soviet Union, left the United States as the sole remaining superpower in a unipolar world. What, in this entirely changed circumstance, should the United States do?

One answer to that question was given by Jeane Kirkpatrick as early as 1990. A tough-minded realist, a heroine of conservatives and anything but an isolationist, Kirkpatrick wrote in the magazine I edited:

The time when Americans should bear such unusual burdens is past. With a return to "normal" times, we can again become a normal nation – and take care of pressing problems of education, family, industry, and technology. We can be an independent nation in a world of independent nations.

As we now know, that view did not prevail. Indeed, it was soon being denounced as neo-isolationist. It did not prevail, for one thing, because during the long decades of the Cold War the United States had developed deep-set habits of activism on a global scale. Habits are powerful things in politics, and while Americans liked to complain about the burdens of leadership, they grew to expect and enjoy leadership more than they realised or acknowledged.

A second powerful reason why being a "normal" nation did not appeal was that in the preceding four-and-a-half decades a huge foreign policy and security establishment had come into being, which had a vested interest in an activist policy and whose continuing existence could only be justified by it. That establishment was not to shrink but to grow in the post-Cold War period.

And third, having, in the highly-charged ideological atmosphere of the Cold War, put so much stress on the defence and promotion of liberty and democracy, it seemed to many to be only proper and consistent to advance these causes to the utmost – to conduct what some referred to as a "democratic crusade", now that the anti-democratic forces had been defeated.

ॐ ॐ ॐ

After World War I, American idealism and realism clashed head on; after World War II, they were in balance; after the third conflict, the Cold War, they have to a very considerable extent merged to produce a kind of oxymoron: a crusading realism, Wilsonianism with muscle.

It began with George Bush senior who, even before the Cold War was properly finished, was proclaiming a "New World Order". Described in utopian terms as one in which "the rule of law supplants the rule of the jungle ... in which nations recognise the shared responsibility of freedom and justice ... where the strong respect the rights of the weak." In other words, the end of power politics. This vision, remember, was advanced not by a liberal but by a conservative president, and was ardently supported by American conservatives. American power – hard and soft – was to make it a reality.

During the eight years of Clinton's presidency, this vision largely receded. As far as foreign policy was concerned, these were years of ineptitude and opportunism and what Michael Mandelbaum derisively dismissed as "global social work". Clinton's foreign policy team was, in my opinion, the weakest since the 1930s. During the Clinton years, the emphasis was not on changing the world by the exertion of political will, but on the alleged capacity of the forces of globalisation to do the job more or less automatically.

Then came George Bush junior, and quickly afterwards the events of September 11. In terms of the conceptual framework I am offering, how do these events fit in?

First, they have re-energised America's sense of mission very, very powerfully. Those who advocate assertiveness and dominance and a reshaping of the world have been greatly strengthened.

"American imperialism", hitherto a term of abuse used by the left, is now embraced with approval by some influential figures. The sense of mission is expressed in universal, unlimited terms, not just as destroying the perpetrators of the acts of September 11, but as destroying all terrorist groups, everywhere: "It will not end until every terrorist group of global reach has been found, stopped and defeated." The world is conceptualised in simple Manichean terms as a global conflict between good and evil, in which there is no room for neutrality or prevarication: "Every nation, in every region, now has a decision to make. Either you are with us, or you are with the terrorists."

Second, the events of September 11 have changed the emphasis of that mission from a positive one to a negative one: from promoting good to crushing evil. Pace John Quincy Adams, America is now precisely and avowedly going abroad "in search of monsters to destroy."

Third, and following from this, the emphasis has shifted from changing the world by example and influence to changing it by force. The key governmental institution in America's dealings with the rest of the world is now not the State Department but the Department of Defence. There have been statements at the presidential level indirectly hinting at the possibility of intervention in countries considered "timid in the face of terror" and the possibility of first use of nuclear weapons, even against countries that do not possess those weapons.

Fourth, for a nation that considers itself "a city on a hill", the sense of violation and outrage now prevailing in Washington should not be underestimated. Many other countries – Britain, France, Germany, Russia, Japan, Italy – have suffered much, much greater damage by violence in living memory, but the sense of violation, of an upsetting of the natural order of things, in the US is almost certainly greater than it was in any of those.

Fifth, one should also bear in mind the American capacity for ruthless action against those it regards as its violators. (In the last five months of World War II alone, US bombing raids killed more than 900,000 Japanese civilians – and that was before the dropping of the two atomic bombs.)

Sixth, the monsters that the US is committed to destroy, the monsters of terrorism, are particularly elusive and amorphous ones who hide behind facades either manufactured by themselves or provided by others. This makes things more complicated and increases greatly the likelihood that the US will make mistakes, probably serious mistakes, in its war against terrorism, particularly if it becomes frustrated by lack of success.

Finally, the tendency for the US to set aside the restraints of multilateralism and to act unilaterally – a tendency always latent in American exceptionalism – has been increased significantly. Asked by CNN television interviewer Larry King, "Is it important that the coalition hold?" (that is, the coalition to fight al-Qaeda), Secretary of Defence Donald Rumsfeld serenely replied "No", going on to say "the worst thing you can do is allow a coalition to determine what your mission is."

↔ ↔ ↔

During the 1990s, I spent a lot of time arguing with a lot of conservative friends in Washington that the US should use its position of dominance, its vast power, with restraint, discrimination and prudence. I argued that anything resembling a "democratic crusade" or the imposition of a "New World Order" was a bad idea. After all, democracy is not an export commodity but a do-it-yourself enterprise that requires special conditions. Besides, an assertive, interventionist policy was bound to generate widespread hostility, suspicion, and if historical precedence meant anything, concerted political opposition to the US. On one occasion I was even moved to suggest that Clintonian ineptitude might, inadvertently, be a good thing because it served to dampen American enthusiasm for activism and to encourage a sense of limits.[*]

And I regularly quoted the warning that Edmund Burke had once given his fellow countrymen when Britain had been the world's dominant power:

> Among precautions against ambition, it may not be amiss to take precaution against our own. I must fairly say, I dread our own power and our own ambition: I dread our being too much dreaded ... We may say that we shall not abuse this astonishing and hitherto unheard of power. But every other nation will think we shall abuse it. It is impossible but that, sooner or later, this state of things must produce a combination against us which may end in our ruin.

---

[*] *Editors' note*: See the extract earlier in this section from "My So-Called Foreign Policy: The Case for Clinton's Diplomacy".

I, and others who argued along these lines, did not have much success. We were met with assertions, either conscious or unconscious, of American exceptionalism. If other dominant powers that had thrown their weight around – the Spain of Philip II; the France of Louis XIV and Napoleon; the Germany of Kaiser Wilhelm II and Hitler – had been met by hostile coalitions, the US would not, because its nature and motives were different (because the American people were different) and others would realise that they were.

If my warnings had any validity five or ten years ago, they might have more today. The great sympathy felt for the US after September 11 has evaporated and is quickly being replaced by suspicion and hostility. Rosemary Righter, chief editorial writer of *The Times*, has observed: "America-bashing is in fashion as it has not been since Vietnam", and she is talking not of Asia and the Middle East, but of London and Paris and Berlin. And she observes that it is not just a case of the usual suspects on the left, but that a "resurgent anti-Americanism" exists across the political spectrum.

The danger in this is not of a hostile military response. The US is too strong for that. It is rather of a gathering political hostility which leaves America both dominant and increasingly disliked and isolated. This would be an extremely unhealthy state of affairs, not just for the US but for the world.

Let me be clear: After the outrage of September 11, I do not believe that the US could have reacted in any way other than as it did. But doing so will carry a cost. The long-term significance of what happened some months ago may be that it has driven America decisively along a road that – by emphasising its military dominance, by requiring it to use its vast power conspicuously and intrusively, by making restraint and moderation virtually impossible, and by making unilateralism an increasing feature of American behaviour – is bound to generate widespread and increased criticism and hostility. That may turn out to be the greatest tragedy of September 11.

Why Power is America's Weakness

Financial Times, 27 July 2004

Reprinted as "Lesson in the Limits of Power" in *The Australian*, 2 August 2004.

Comparisons may be odious and analogies tricky, but they can be indispensable. Which ones are chosen, however, is a matter of some importance. In the current debate over Iraq, the analogy of choice has been Vietnam. A much better one is the Suez crisis of 1956.

The dictator of a Middle Eastern country incurs the wrath of two leading Western states. The threat he poses is grossly exaggerated and he is regularly compared to Hitler. The two states decide to remove him. They do so without consulting their main Western allies, causing an angry rift between hitherto close friends. The question of United Nations approval or disapproval assumes importance. So does the question of the pre-emptive use of force.

The plan of attack involves the use of phoney evidence. The implementation of the plan is strikingly inept. Popular support for the venture, initially strong, drains away. The whole episode ends with the two principal Western actors embarrassed and with their international prestige seriously damaged.

Analogies are never exact, of course. Britain and France did not succeed in removing Gamal Abdel Nasser, while the US did end Saddam Hussein's rule, and that is a big plus. On the other hand, the Suez crisis did not involve much bloodshed, while the Iraq operation has cost thousands of lives.

What the final balance of similarities and differences will be is uncertain. The Suez crisis caused the downfall of a British prime minister; whether the Iraq crisis will ultimately destroy George W. Bush and Tony Blair remains to be seen.

In the more innocent days of the 1950s, the Westminster convention – that if a minister strongly disagreed with government policy he would resign – was still honoured. One of those who did resign over Suez was Anthony Nutting, the foreign minister responsible for Middle East affairs. He subsequently wrote a book about the crisis, *No End of a Lesson*. It was a good title, for the British did indeed learn some hard truths from the episode.

It was brought home decisively to the British that despite spending no less than 8% of their gross domestic product on defence and having conscripted military forces of 700,000, their claim to "Big Three" superpower status after World War II was no longer sustainable. Conscription was abolished in the UK soon afterwards and, in little over a decade, Britain was to give up every pretence of a strategic presence "east of Suez".

The second part of the lesson was spelt out by General Sir Charles Keightley, who had commanded the Anglo-French force in the venture, in his post-mortem on Suez: "It was the action of the US which really defeated us in attaining our object. This situation with the US must at all costs be prevented from arising again."

All subsequent British leaders have accepted that conclusion, even to the point of abandoning the traditional British policy of always trying to create and maintain a balance against any prospective hegemon. (The French, of course, drew a different conclusion from Suez: never again to rely on America.)

As well as the similarities, there is one basic difference between the British experience of 1956 and the American experience of 2003-04. The former was the result of insufficient power, the latter of excessive power, resulting in hubris.

Errors resulting from weakness are easier to identify and correct than those resulting from strength. Weakness, once recognised, deprives one of choices and compels one to adjust one's ambitions quickly if disaster is to be avoided. When things go wrong for the very powerful, on the other hand, there is always the inclination to blame not the folly and impracticality of one's goals but the implementation of policy, or lack of resolution and support on the part of others, or simply bad luck. Hegemons do not easily learn the lesson of modifying their ambitions. What they are most likely to conclude from failure is that they must pursue those ambitions more ardently and efficiently next time.

Conspicuous among those who will suffer politically from the Iraq episode will be the second-generation neo-conservatives, both inside and outside the Bush administration. It was mainly their influence that, in the space of a few months, caused the "war on terror" to metastasise into a commitment to remake the world in America's image. Polemically brilliant and tactically resourceful, they did not have a prudential bone in their bodies and were strategically reckless – youngish men in a hurry, trying to get done in a year and by the exercise of military power what should have required at least a generation of patient, multi-faceted effort to achieve.

These neo-conservatives will come out of this episode politically diminished. But the impulse they represented – to spread American democratic and liberal values to the rest of the world – will not die. They were merely its latest vehicle, not its creators. The conviction that the US is destined to be the model and inspiration for the world goes deep and is as old as the country itself. For better or worse, it is unlikely to diminish while American power is at its zenith.

Suez forced the British to give up the pretence that they were still an authentic global power. The lesson that Iraq should teach the US is that even the will of an authentic global hegemon will not prevail unless it is exerted with restraint, patience, willingness to compromise, and a respect for the views of other significant operators. Unless, that is, the hegemon behaves as a member of a concert of states. The real success of the terrorists is that they have made it much harder for Americans to accept this.

Costs of a Needless War

The Australian, 18 July 2005

Reprinted as "Two Women and a War" in *The American Conservative*, 29 August 2005.

At the risk of being labelled a male chauvinist, I wish to point out that two of the most unfortunate – and dangerous – political comments made over recent decades have been made by women: Madeleine Albright and Margaret Thatcher.

Start with the former. In 1994, Albright – the then US Ambassador to the UN, past Professor of International Affairs, future US Secretary of State – asked an astonished General Colin Powell ("I thought I would have an aneurysm") a question: "What is the point of having this superb military that you're always talking about if we can't use it?".

Whether the question was genuine or rhetorical, Powell had every right to be startled, for it was an amazing one for a person of Albright's background to have posed. Because for the previous half-century her country had followed a policy that demonstrated powerfully the wisdom of having immense military power and not using it.

That policy was called "deterrence", and its very point was to make recourse to the actual use of force unnecessary. It was brilliantly successful. It saw the US, and the world, through several tense decades without disaster and led finally to the collapse of America's adversary. (The most serious US setback during these years occurred when it did resort to committing its military force actively in Vietnam.)

In response to all this, and in support of Albright and the legion of others who have more recently advocated the energetic use of the US's military might, it could be argued (and has been in the official US document, *The National Security Strategy of the United States*) that that was then and this is now. There is no longer a threatening (but rational) adversary that should be (and could be) deterred;

there are only fanatical terrorist organisations, which cannot be deterred but which should be (and can be) destroyed.

There is some truth in this, but it is very important to establish its limits. Yes, after 9/11 al-Qaeda had to be hunted down and destroyed, and that hunt should continue until Osama bin Laden is either captured or killed. But there is no reason to believe that Iraq could not have been dissuaded from using its (as it happens, non-existent) weapons of mass destruction by a policy of deterrence. Saddam Hussein was a vile and cruel tyrant, but he was not a suicidal fanatic and he did possess vulnerable fixed assets.

It is still a fundamental strategic axiom that the availability of means should not determine ends, and there are very powerful reasons why the US, even as the "sole remaining superpower", should be very parsimonious in using its military force actively.

One is that it is only thus that it can preserve the invaluable mystique of its military power. Consider the prestige that the US military had in the year 2000 and compare it with its standing now. Then, US military power was universally considered to be awesome in its scope and irresistible in its application. Today, after its deployment in Iraq, the world is much more aware of its limitations and less impressed: aware that while it has an enormous capacity to crush and destroy, its ability to control, to impose and maintain order is far less; that while its technology is superb, the human resources at its disposal for protracted occupation or multiple engagements are seriously limited, and the quality of its civilian and military leadership questionable.

The US's military prestige – and therefore its ability to impose its will without recourse to force – has been seriously diminished by Iraq. This will encourage rather than deter its potential enemies.

A second reason why the US should be extremely reluctant to share Albright's enthusiasm for the ready use of force is that its internal consequences are almost certain to be adverse. American wars that result from anything less than a direct attack on the US, and which continue for any length of time, are more than likely to divide the country bitterly.

This happened in the case of Vietnam and it is happening now. The army and even the marines are finding it difficult to attract recruits, and have found it necessary to compel soldiers to stay in the service beyond the terms of their contracts. Barry McCaffrey, a well-informed and, up to now, dedicated supporter of the war, has recently maintained: "The US Army and the marines are too under-manned and under-resourced to sustain this security policy beyond next [Autumn]. They are starting to unravel."

But these are not the only adverse consequences of a ready resort to the use of military force, not at least in the eyes of those who are hostile to big government. For one of the consequences of war is that it inevitably increases the scope and power of the central government responsible for waging it. It is one of the internal contradictions of American neo-conservatism that it simultaneously pursues a domestic policy that seeks to reduce the scope of government and a foreign policy that is bound to increase it.

Today we are witnessing in the US not only substantial increases in government expenditure, but a serious diminution of the rule of law in the form of a partial suspension of *habeas corpus*, a circumventing of the Geneva Convention, a justification of the use of torture, and greater secrecy. (As I write, it is reported that the Bush administration is classifying documents at the rate of 125 a minute or, if my arithmetic is accurate, 180,000 a day!)

One last, but vital, adverse consequence of a ready resort to force by the US: It will provide an extremely unfortunate standard of acceptable behaviour for emerging great powers – the Chinas and Indias and Pakistans and Brazils – that will be leading players in a decade or two. Much has been written about the US's leading role as the setter of "new norms". But what norms are being set by ventures such as Iraq and by claims to greatly expanded rights to initiate preventative or pre-emptive war? And how much will they come home to haunt future generations who have to live with them?

⚮⚮⚮

Which brings me to the second unfortunate and potentially dangerous remark to which I referred in the introduction.

In 1980, early in her prime-ministership, Thatcher made a speech at the Conservative Party conference in which she famously said: "The lady's not for turning." It was said in a particular context and in that context was unexceptional. But the phrase was, with her encouragement, to become emblematic of Thatcher's whole political style, to her admirers evidence of conviction, courage and authenticity, of rising above compromise and calculation and mere "politics". It represents the qualities that make Thatcher such an idolised figure among American neo-conservatives today.

The point I wish to make is a simple one: while it may be appropriate and even admirable in a particular situation (for example, in 1940, when the stark choice was either defiance or disaster in the form of surrender to Nazi Germany), as a general approach to political action a commitment to hold undeviatingly to a line of action, regardless of circumstances or consequences, is foolish and dangerous.

Napoleon showed iron determination and undeviating dedication when he marched on Moscow. The British generals of World War I showed the utmost steadfastness in sending men across the open fields of the Somme and into the bottomless mud of Passchendaele. Hitler was not for turning at Stalingrad.

At another level, Thatcher's own insistence on doing it her way, and her contempt for the collegiate responsibility and compromises of cabinet government, were ultimately to cause her downfall a decade after she made that remark.

Today, as President Bush insists over and over again that we must "stay the course" and "complete the mission", it is worth emphasising that the issue is not some test of character but a matter of cold political calculation. In themselves, firm resolution and unbending determination are not political or military virtues.

Before deciding to complete what one has started, it is necessary to give serious consideration to a number of vital questions: Is the "mission" a realistic one? Is it vital for the US's (or Australia's) national interest? Do circumstances favour its completion within an acceptable time frame? How great a cost – in terms of blood, treasure, moral standing, political reputation, alternative use of resources, domestic harmony – does it justify? And, in the specific case of Iraq, is the mission reducing the threat of terrorism or creating its most fertile breeding ground yet?

As always in politics, circumstances are crucial. To ignore them and to insist that the mission must proceed regardless is to invite recourse to that old play on Kipling's lines: "If you can keep your head when all about you are losing theirs, you have probably misunderstood the situation."

Indeed, prominent US Republican senator Chuck Hagel virtually said as much last month: "The White House is completely disconnected from reality. It is like they are making it up as they go along. The reality is that we are losing in Iraq."

After Iraq

Lowy Institute Perspective, 30 November 2006 [extract]

Adapted from an address Harries gave at the Lowy Institute in Sydney on 29 November 2006, at the time he was a Visiting Fellow at the Institute and Senior Fellow at the Centre for Independent Studies. Edited extracts ran in *The Australian* on 1 December ("The End of Simplicity") and 19 December ("Don't Think It's Over").

We are now close to the end-game in Iraq. By almost common consent, and even in the opinion of British Prime Minister Tony Blair, America's Iraq venture is a disaster. Only a few – those whose spiritual home is the last ditch, or who cannot for political reasons acknowledge what they know is true – still dispute the matter.

The disaster has a significance that reaches beyond Iraq itself, devastating as it has been for that country. It is hugely significant in terms of US policy. Three years ago, in November 2003, I tried to explain why in the second of my Boyer Lectures:

> [T]he Iraq commitment has an importance that goes way beyond the fate of Iraq itself. If, in the end, it turns out successfully, it is likely that the setbacks that have occurred since the end of the heavy fighting will be seen as part of a learning experience, a breaking-in period for a new, revolutionary, strategic doctrine. If, on the other hand, it fails at the first hurdle – if, that is, the United States finds that bringing about security, stability, a decent political order, and an improvement in the living standards of the Iraqi people, is beyond its capacity; if the whole thing becomes a "quagmire" ... then not only will there have to be a reconsideration of the whole global strategy, but the limits of the United States' capacity will have been made evident, and the inclination to resist it greatly strengthened.

I spoke as a sceptical critic of the Iraq project. But *The Weekly Standard*, the influential house journal of American neo-conservatives and an ardent supporter of that project, concurred.

Around the same time as I wrote those words it editorialised that: "The future course of American foreign policy, American world leadership, and American security is at stake. Failure in Iraq would be a devastating blow to everything the United States hopes to accomplish, and must accomplish, in the decades ahead."

What gave the Iraq venture this significance was that it was not meant to be a singular and discrete event. Rather it represented the first application by the United States of an incredibly ambitious foreign policy doctrine. This was the Bush Doctrine, formally proclaimed in the presidential *National Security Strategy* of September 2002. It committed the United States, not only to combating terror, but to actively promoting democracy and a market economy in "every corner of the world" – that is, to transform the whole international system to conform to American values. To that end it would, where necessary, use its vast military force, not only defensively to contain and deter its adversaries, but actively, assertively and pre-emptively. And the document, prepared without any consultation with allies, made it clear that the United States would not hesitate to act alone if necessary.

This represented, and still does, an enormously ambitious and seriously intended project. Only someone ignorant of American history and political culture would have dismissed it as rhetoric. Americans take their doctrines seriously.

So what of the future of the Bush Doctrine now, after the fiasco and tragedy of Iraq? Does failure on its first outing spell an early grave for it? Does it mean that it will have been but a brief passing episode in the history of American foreign policy? I am not as sure about this as I seem to have been three years ago. In any case, in considering these questions it is worth reflecting briefly on the circumstances and forces that gave rise to the Doctrine in the first place.

First, there was, of course, the shock of the terrorist attacks of 9/11, and the tremendous sense of outrage and violation they created in a country whose mainland had not been subject to foreign attack for over a century and a half. And with the outrage came an urgent, angry demand for a decisive response.

Second, there was the fact of a new and inexperienced president having to cope with the crisis – a man who had virtually no experience in international affairs, but one who had strong convictions, including religious ones, and who tended to see things in terms of a single, sharp dichotomy, a Manichean world divided starkly into good and evil, with no middle ground. As a new man facing a major crisis he had much to prove, not least because he was the son of a president whose speciality had been foreign policy.

Third, there was the presence in and around the Bush administration of some well-placed, very articulate and intellectually persuasive neo-conservatives, with an ideological, moralistic and very assertive view of America's role in the world, and an agenda that had on it an attack on Saddam Hussein's Iraq as a priority item.

These three factors in the shaping of the Bush Doctrine were undoubtedly important. But they were also transient factors, and to the extent that one focused on them one might well conclude that the impulse that created the Bush Doctrine is now due to fade. It is, after all, over five years since 9/11 and five years is a long time in politics. Anger and passion fade. Bush is now a lame-duck president, with no control over Congress and low poll ratings. And the neo-conservatives are discredited, divided and with a much-reduced influence.

So does this mean the end of what the Bush Doctrine stood for? Not necessarily. For as well as these three transient factors, the Doctrine also represented two more enduring and fundamental features of the situation – one structural, one cultural – that will not disappear when the Iraq venture ends: America's global hegemony and American exceptionalism.

The United States went into Iraq a confident hegemon, the "indispensable nation" without which nothing important could be done, as Madeleine Albright used to lecture the world. It will come out of it a damaged hegemon but still a hegemon, still far and away the strongest state on earth. It will remain such for at least a couple of decades. When the weak fail, they have no option but to accept the fact and usually there are no second chances. When the very strong fail, they tend to find excuses, regroup and try again, changing their methods and their timetable but maintaining their goals. As hegemon, the United States will still want to impose its will on the world, and that will still represents American values as well as American interests.

Which brings us to the other enduring factor, a cultural one: American exceptionalism, the strange term used to identify the profound belief widely held by Americans since their beginning as a nation that it is their historical – indeed their divinely ordained – destiny to be, in the words of Reinhold Niebuhr, "tutors of mankind in its pilgrimage to perfection", or in the words of President Woodrow Wilson, that Americans are divinely "chosen to show the nations of the world how they shall walk in the paths of liberty." However condescending and presumptuous others may find this conviction, it is deeply-held and as natural to Americans as apple pie. It will certainly survive the Iraq experience.

⚲⚲⚲

So what is likely to happen to American foreign policy post-Iraq?

In my view, there will not be anything like a 180-degree or even a 90-degree change of course, but there will be significant adjustments and alterations as certain lessons of recent experience, and the validity of the realist critique of that experience, are acknowledged. Among the lessons, I suggest, will be these:

- While the US military has tremendous destructive capacity in war, its constructive uses, and its capacity for anything resembling "nation-building", are quite limited.

- Largely because it is a huge, self-absorbed country with a strong commitment to its own values, the American capacity for understanding and interacting with other cultures, particularly non-Western ones, is not impressive. It is a common and profound mistake to think that all other peoples want the same things, have the same priorities, as Americans have. Differences of cultures and circumstances matter. (On this, instead of consulting Bill Kristol, the influential neo-con editor of *The Weekly Standard* and one of the principal supporters of the Bush Doctrine, consult his distinguished father, Irving Kristol, who once expressed the view that "there are many nations where the American ideal of self-government in liberty is simply irrelevant. In those cases we simply have to accept that fact, while using our influence to encourage a little movement in the direction of political decency, as we understand it.") For utopian bliss substitute a little common decency.

- Even the most powerful need the support of others. If you need and want that support, and you do, consult them before you set out on a grand project, not late in the game when you are in difficulties. If you accept former Defence Secretary Donald Rumsfeld's dictum that "the worst thing you can do is allow a coalition to determine what your mission is", be prepared to have a certain sense of loneliness and desertion if and when difficulties arise. To ensure support, a hegemon, however powerful, would be well advised to act as first among equals – *primus inter pares* – rather than throw its weight around and give instructions.

- Pre-emptive or preventative wars, if engaged in at all (and they may sometimes be necessary) need to be short, quick and not very costly in blood and treasure. The American people will not support protracted and expensive conflicts that are not clearly defensive responses to aggression and/or serious provocation. That includes "humanitarian wars".

- The grander and more sweeping the goals of a political enterprise, the greater the likelihood of unintended consequences and consequently a loss of control.

- If you destroy an existing order, you are saddled with the mess and the responsibility for putting something workable in its place. As former Secretary of State Colin Powell succinctly put it to President George W. Bush before Iraq, quoting the warning displayed in china shops: "You break it, you own it." It will be particularly important to keep this in mind in formulating policy toward Iran, a bigger country than Iraq, in the near future.

- It is prudent not to allow too blatant a discrepancy to develop between your ends and means. The moral costs of doing so are likely to come high. Thus if you claim to be promoting freedom, democracy and the rule of law, it will be dangerous to your image and credibility to engage in torture, or "extraordinary rendition", or to violate *habeas corpus*. The more elevated your moral claims, the more blatant the discrepancy.

- The claim that double standards in one's favour are justified – a claim often made by neo-conservatives – fits badly with claims of moral superiority. To say that I am justified in behaving worse than you because I am morally superior to you does not really carry conviction.

- In considering the extent to which other countries should trust America to use its vast power in a non-threatening way, Americans should consider the extent to which they themselves are prepared to trust other states, even those which have much less power than the United States. Trust is a scarce commodity in international politics.

How well these and similar lessons will be recognised and learnt in the near future, I do not know. On the one hand, America has in the past been quick to correct its errors and to be impressive on the rebound. It may turn out that this was the failure that the United States had to have in order to bring its hubris under control – after all, think where we might be now if Iraq had been a walk in the park, a quick and easy success. What might the Bush administration have been determined to take on in that event? On the other hand, there is little reason to place great faith in the Democrats, who are divided and illusion-prone on foreign policy.

And of course, if there is another serious terrorist episode on American soil, something that many experts think is more than likely, all bets are off.

Leading From Behind: Third Time a Charm?

With Tom Switzer, *The American Interest*, May-June 2013 [extract]

Extracted in the *Australian Financial Review* as "US Foreign Policy Staying at Home" (10 May 2013), this was the last essay Harries published and it led the magazine's cover. At the time, he was on the *AI* editorial board, while Switzer was a Research Associate at the United States Studies Centre, University of Sydney, and Editor of *The Spectator Australia*.

A Washington adage holds that someone commits a "gaffe" when he inadvertently tells the truth. This seemed to be what a US policymaker did two decades ago when he mused about the limits to US power in the post-Cold War era. On 25 May 1993, just four months into the Clinton administration, a certain senior government official – the new Undersecretary of State for Political Affairs and a former President of the Council on Foreign Relations – spoke freely to about 50 journalists on condition that they refer to him only as a "senior State Department official". Gaffe or no gaffe, Peter Tarnoff's frank remarks at the Overseas Writers Club luncheon set off serious political turbulence in the foreign policy establishment.

Tarnoff's message was that, with the Cold War over, America should no longer be counted on to take the lead in regional disputes unless a direct threat to its national interest inhered in the circumstances. To avoid over-reaching, he warned, US policymakers should define the country's interests with clarity and without a residue of excessive sentiment, concentrating its resources on matters vital to its own well-being. That meant Washington would, if necessary, act unilaterally where its own strategic and economic interests were directly threatened, but it would otherwise pursue a foreign policy at the same time less interventionist and more multilateral.

At first glance, there was nothing new here. As far back as the Nixon Doctrine, US officials had spoken of more voluble burden-sharing, of asking allies to do more on their own behalf, and of a variable-speed American foreign policy activism that could be fine-tuned to circumstances. And then, within a year of the Soviet Union's collapse, Bill Clinton won a presidential election in part because he promised to "focus like a laser" on domestic issues. Neither during Nixon's tenure nor in 1993 did anyone use the phrase "leading from behind", which an un-named presidential adviser used to explain US policy in Libya in 2011, but this new locution is consonant with the basic thinking of those earlier formulations. In some ways, "leading from behind" is the third coming of a seasoned and generally sensible idea.

Nor was Tarnoff saying anything outside the implicit consensus of presumed foreign policy "wise men" at the time. Many dedicated Cold Warriors and leading foreign affairs experts, Republicans and Democrats alike, had been arguing for the previous three years that, having just won a great victory, it was time for America to embrace a more restricted view of the nation's interests and commitments.

Nathan Glazer proposed that it was "time to withdraw to something closer to the modest role that the Founding Fathers intended." William Hyland, editor of Foreign Affairs at the time, wrote, "What is definitely required is a psychological turn inwards." And according even to Henry Kissinger, the definition of the US national interest in the emerging era of multipolarity would be different from the two-power world of the Cold War – "more discriminating in its purpose, less cataclysmic in its strategy and, above all, more regional in its design."

Notwithstanding all this, and no doubt to his own surprise and chagrin, Tarnoff's remarks started a firestorm of fear and indignation almost the moment reports of his background briefing hit the press. Talking heads denounced not just Tarnoff but the new President for whom he spoke as "isolationist" and "declinist"; some beheld a "creeping Jimmy Carterism" with an Arkansas accent. Foreign embassies went into overdrive as diplomats relayed the news back home. The White House quickly attempted to distance itself from what its press secretary dismissed as "Brand X". The Secretary of State, Warren Christopher, stayed up all night making personal phone calls to journalists and appearing on late-night television to reassure the world that America's global leadership role was undiminished.

The incident could only be described as bizarre. Here was a senior US policymaker saying something that official Washington had deemed outrageous. Yet Tarnoff was not proposing that America pull up the drawbridge from a messy world, nor was he suggesting that Washington withdraw from any international institutions, let alone from any Cold War alliances. He was merely recognising the reality of the emerging post-Cold War world and America's place in it: that, depending on the circumstances and the nature of its interests, the United States could and would pick and choose where to commit its formidable weight.

🚲🚲🚲

This episode from almost 20 years ago is worth recalling as President Obama, at the beginning of his second term, attempts to define a new US role in the world that fits America's changed circumstances and more limited resources. Today, in the wake of the financial crisis and the Iraq and Afghanistan wars, Americans are rediscovering the costs and limits of the use of force. Consequently, the President appears to be in the process of putting into practice the central tenets of what very briefly became known as the Tarnoff Doctrine.

One theme is that it is time for the United States to focus on "nation-building at home", something Obama has stressed several times in recent years. The other theme is the vague, subtle emphasis on caution, prudence, balance, modesty and proportionality in dealing with adversaries and competitors. But just as Tarnoff's nuanced remarks about discriminating leadership ignited a firestorm two decades ago, Obama's efforts to recast the US role in the world have stirred controversy.

Two years ago, an unnamed senior Obama adviser inadvertently coined a foreign policy doctrine in suggesting the United States was "leading from behind" in Libya. According to *The New Yorker*'s Ryan Lizza, the term represented "a different definition of leadership than America is known for", and reflected the reality that the United States now lacks the relative power to impose its will and leadership across a more pluralistic world. Once again, the response was hostile. It's "not leading. It is abdicating", argued syndicated columnist Charles Krauthammer. It "sounds rather pathetic", lamented Maureen Dowd in *The New York Times*. And the phrase, editorialised *The Washington Post*, reflects "extraordinary US passivity" and a "pattern of torpidity" during the Arab Spring.

But however awkward the language, the argument is less foolish than the reaction it provoked. The message is not that passivity is a foreign policy virtue, however passive the second Obama administration may prove to be. Rather, it is that, depending on the circumstances and the national interest, it is sometimes appropriate for Washington to take the lead in mobilising multilateral action and proffering credible threats, but sometimes it is not. Being selective and discerning can be, but is not necessarily, a mask for generic weakness or a disposition to explain away difficult choices.

There are times when the United States is wise and wily, rather than weak and wayward, to be not so visible during a crisis. Sometimes it's better to play a key logistical role from the sidelines rather than take the lead, as with the 2011 Libya campaign. (Never mind, for the time being, whether that was a wise operation on the whole to begin with.) Discrimination and selectivity should take precedence over consistency and comprehensiveness whenever resources are limited, which is virtually always. That was precisely Tarnoff's point, too. *Plus ça change?*

One of the disconcerting things about Obama's more muscular critics, from neoconservatives to liberal hawks, is that they seem to favour American global military interventionism as a binding principle rather than as a course to be pursued only when the effort is commensurate with the stakes, and when other measures have failed. Besides, to insist that the United States must lead globally is to imply that everybody else must follow or else be held in injurious disrepute. That describes a forced subordinate relationship alien to America's basic avowal of freedom and egalitarianism. The United States should be concerned about spreading responsibility and initiative across the world, and building co-operative, not subordinate, relationships.

If such arguments were not persuasive in 1993, they ought to be today. Geopolitical circumstances have changed significantly since then. Public opinion on foreign policy has shifted dramatically. A commander in chief – who has run foreign policy from the White House more than any president since Nixon – recognises the need to balance ends and means. A policy of indiscriminate US global interventionism ("global leadership" in common, high-toned, jingoistic parlance) is not strategically sustainable, even if the economic resources were available to pay for it, which they certainly are not.

☙☙☙

As to changed circumstances, consider that in the 1990s the United States emerged the victor from the Cold War without a shot being fired. It achieved global hegemonic status not by especially assertive or ambitious action on its own part, but by a combination of the self-induced collapse of its rival and the discipline not to gloat about it. The George W. Bush administration had no plan in place to exploit its unexpected dominance, nor did its successor adopt one during the rest of the decade.

Tarnoff was admonished for stressing a more discriminating US world role while advising that "our economic interests are paramount." Yet his boss, Bill Clinton, was generally given a pass for showing little interest in foreign affairs, for having no grand doctrine, and for insisting that the economy should be the country's main preoccupation throughout his two terms in office. Certainly, the US armed forces were maintained at a high level despite post-

Cold War reductions in force strength and the defence budget. But new commitments, over and above the maintenance of America's alliances, were scrutinised mercilessly, and any undertaken were kept limited in time and scope.

Sensibly, the US military often seemed more concerned with effective exit strategies than with implementing ambitious, open-ended, foreign policy projects – whether that concerned the Balkans, Haiti, Somalia or places entirely avoided, like Rwanda. This restraint involved no loss of prestige or influence. Indeed, restraint and discrimination can also win respect. Hegemons are always regarded with great suspicion and resentment by other states. If they throw their weight around, they are likely to bring into being hostile coalitions formed to balance and contain them.

That is partly why Warren Christopher's successor at Foggy Bottom, Madeleine Albright, was able to boast, convincingly if unnecessarily, that the United States was "the indispensable nation" that stood "tall and sees further than other countries into the future." As Thomas Friedman of *The New York Times* summed it up: "Today's era is dominated by American power, American culture, the American dollar and the American navy." Strikingly, the comparative restraint of the new hegemony allowed its dominance to be accepted with comparatively little complaint. Of all people, it was the French Foreign Minister of the day, Hubert Védrine, he who also coined the term "hyperpower", who best reflected the prevailing view: "American globalism ... dominates everything. Not in a harsh, repressive, military form, but in people's heads."

Meanwhile, the United States was experiencing what to all appearances was the longest economic expansion in its peacetime history. Everything that should be up – wages, growth, stock market – was up, while everything that should be down – inflation, joblessness, deficits – was down. Hardly anyone recognised at the time that many of the positive indices reflected bubbles that would later pop, and not until 1999 did the so-called Financial

Services Modernisation Act lay the ground for the debacle to come in 2007–08. America was being widely hailed, abroad as well as at home, as the miracle economy, master for all time of "the great moderation".

That was then. Today, things look very different. The dollar is weak. The debt mountain is of Himalayan proportions. Budget and trade deficits are alarming. Infrastructure is aging. The AAA credit rating is lost. Economic growth is exceptionally sluggish for a nation that is nearly four years out of a recession. And whereas 20 years ago US military power was universally considered awesome in its scope, today, after more than a decade of its active deployment, the world is much more aware of its limitations and costs. It is decidedly less impressed.

In hindsight, it is clear that the terror attacks of 11 September 2001 constituted a major inflection point. As America's alleged "holiday from history" came to an abrupt end, outrage over the attacks, taken together with the mental habits of American hegemony and American exceptionalism, had apparently given US leaders a clear, overriding sense of purpose. A new central organising principle that it had lacked after containment had been retired with laurels arose so crisp and clear as to be too good to be true – because it was. A mature and experienced president might have been able to resist, modify or deflect the temptations of the moment. George W. Bush not only yielded to them; he gave them authoritative voice. Thus, September 11 shifted the balance in favour of those who saw things in sweeping terms – away from prudence and modesty toward an ambitious and assertive use of US power to topple tyrannical regimes and export democracy far and wide. As it happened, in both Iraq and Afghanistan America has been its own worst enemy – inefficient, incompetent and overconfident.

Now, a great power can cope with a bloody nose on the battlefield. The United States coped with Vietnam, after all, in due course. What is more serious is a general loss of credibility and prestige associated not with an episode of bad judgment, but with a generic inability to conduct one's affairs responsibly. It is the latter that truly diminishes a great power's ability to lead and persuade other nations. Washington's demands and requests are increasingly ignored by its longtime foes in Tehran and Pyongyang as well as its largest aid recipients in Cairo and Jerusalem. Its influence is fading at global summits, too: in the G-20, where the Germans reject Washington's loose fiscal policy prescriptions; at climate conferences, where the Chinese, Indians and Brazilians ignore US calls to reduce their carbon footprint; and in security talks, where the Pakistanis refuse to sever ties between their intelligence services and the Taliban.

True, the United States is still the world's largest economy and the issuer of its reserve currency. It is also its lone military hegemon. It is true too that as hegemons go, Washington is not feared. It did not seek to exert absolute control over international events at the height of the Cold War, but that had to do with the Soviet Union's power as well as with the novelty of "an empire by invitation".

Nonetheless, the United States exercises less influence today than it did before the fall of the Berlin Wall, not least for the elemental reason that its allies no longer crave its protection as much as they once did. Although many proponents of an activist and ambitious leadership role acknowledge this point, they do so on the grounds that a reckless president has embraced American weakness. As they see it, decline is less a condition than a choice.

The reality is that the age of American unipolarity, which began with the collapse of Soviet communism, is being replaced by a world populated by new players. To the extent that China, India, Turkey and Brazil become more assertive internationally, it challenges the notion that an activist America can impose its will and leadership across the globe. And a notion thus challenged is a notion weakened, regardless of objective circumstances.

꒦꒦꒦

As to public opinion, in 1993 Tarnoff's proposals, however current among a dominant section of the foreign policy cognoscenti, represented too radical a change for the American people so soon after the end of the Cold War. Today, the environment is different.

Simply put, the American public has tired of the world. It is suffering from foreign policy fatigue. For 70 years – first against fascism, then communism and more recently Islamist fanaticism – it supported and sustained a foreign policy and defence commitment of the most intense and comprehensive kind. Everything else was subordinated to it, and all sorts of domestic concerns were neglected. As America withdraws from Afghanistan – a war that has lasted longer than both world wars of the 20th century combined – there is an overwhelming feeling that it is high time for the nation to concentrate on its own neglected internal problems.

The upshot is that Americans today appear less concerned about foreign policy than at any time since the heyday of isolationism between the world wars. In a polity that is acutely sensitive to public opinion, veritably driven by polls, focus groups and the relentless 24/7 news cycle, this means that foreign policy is severely downgraded in the calculations of politicians. The most obvious exemplar is that more Republicans now care about downsizing government than about a strong defence, and so have learned to love sequestration.

Finally, as to ends and means, we are wise to remind ourselves that one impediment to clear thinking about foreign policy since the collapse of Soviet communism has been the conspicuous divorce of ends and means. In the 1940s, distinguished columnist Walter Lippmann penned the single most important sentence ever written about American foreign policy: "Without the controlling principle that the nation must maintain its objectives and its power in equilibrium, its purposes within its means and its means equal to its purposes, its commitments related to its resources and its resources adequate to its commitments, it is impossible to think at all about foreign affairs."

This idea probably inspired Tarnoff's remarks 20 years ago. But the American political class would have none of it, whether in foreign policy or, as we now see so vividly, in domestic policy. By wilfully ignoring the principle that ends must have some relation to means, a huge gap opened between America's global pretensions and its ability to finance them. And that, exactly, is a gap President Obama seems intent on closing.

In the past four years, the President has jettisoned his predecessor's sweeping doctrine of preventive warfare, aggressive unilateralism and a clear division between those "with us" and "against us". Washington has kept out of hot spots such as the Syrian civil war while playing down, without ever ruling out, the prospect of a pre-emptive strike on Iran's nuclear facilities. This new strategy does not stop Obama from escalating drone strikes against terrorists, nor will it derail his administration's "pivot" of US forces toward East Asia. Nor does it necessarily obviate a strike against Iran if all else fails. But it does allow him to reorder priorities in favour of discrimination and selectivity, to get a good running start on once again matching resources and aspirations.

None of this is about a new isolationism. It's an approach that stresses an unsentimental focus on national interests, pursued with a prudent calculation of commitments and resources, while focusing on rebuilding the US economy. Such realism would require a significantly leaner defence budget, and it would require a far more scrupulous definition of which wars are – and are not – wars of necessity.

Meanwhile Lippmann's axiom is being comprehensively ignored by many conservatives. They simultaneously demand assertive American global leadership, on the one hand, and reduced domestic spending on the other. They make the downsizing of the federal government a high priority while simultaneously demanding an ambitious foreign policy inspired by "vision" and a sense of mission – the kind of foreign policy that has been instrumental in building up the power of the state over the past 70 years, and indeed the power of states throughout history.

For politicians to will the ends but baulk at providing the means is one of the deadly sins of foreign policy. A disjunction between ambition and resources – the attempt to sustain greatness on the cheap – is highly dangerous in terms of American lives and interests.

The imbalance between ends and means isn't just apparent in a reluctance to commit American treasure. It is also apparent in the reluctance to commit American blood. A legacy of the Iraq and Afghanistan wars is an unwillingness on the part of the American public to take casualties on behalf of less than truly vital challenges. American servicemen, for instance, were kept well out of harm's way in the campaign to topple Muammar Gaddafi in 2011. While such concerns may be admirable in humanitarian terms, they are incompatible with a superpower posture and pretensions to global leadership. If a nation is not prepared to take casualties, it should not engage in the kind of policies likely to cause them. If it is not prepared to take casualties, it should resign itself to not having the kind of respect from others that a more resolute nation could expect.

⚜ ⚜ ⚜

The process of implementing a Tarnoff-style doctrine in a second Obama administration would certainly not be without problems. For one thing, deeply-ingrained habits from the Cold War persist despite radically altered circumstances. And if habit – seeing American priorities as they were rather than as they are – has been an impediment to clear thinking about foreign policy, another has been the belief in American exceptionalism: namely, that as a nation born of an idea, embodying a principle, dedicated to a proposition and claiming a manifest destiny, the United States is fundamentally different from other nations in its very nature and hence in its behaviour. This belief underpins the notion that America is a benign hegemon – a provider of "public goods" to the international community, the keeper of order and stability, the promoter of freedom, an unthreatening and disinterested presence to all except those who are evil.

A belief in American uniqueness is not, of course, new. Americans have always maintained that they are more moral and disinterested than other states and that power politics is a game played by the rest of the world but not by them. Nor is it confined to the neoconservative wing of the Republican Party. It was not Paul Wolfowitz but Hillary Clinton who argued in 2010 that "Americans have always risen to the challenges we have faced. It is in our DNA. We do believe there are no limits on what is possible or what can be achieved."

In recent times, however, America has entered a period of upheaval that has shaken the national psyche: persistently high unemployment, a debt larger than gross national product, diminished net wealth, a rising China, a series of what Rudyard Kipling called "the savage wars of peace", and a polarised and dysfunctional political system beholden to special interests. Many Americans are in an increasingly foul mood and are looking for someone to blame.

The danger of American exceptionalism is that it discourages compromise and flexibility, and encourages a sense of omnipotence. And although the United States has shown an impressive ability to bounce back from past setbacks – Civil War, Depression, Pearl Harbour, Vietnam – it will not enjoy the kind of absolute global supremacy that it held in the post-World War II period. Nor is it likely to command the unrivalled power and prestige that accompanied the so-called unipolar moment of the early 1990s.

If political leaders fail to prepare the nation for this reality, they risk leaving the American people open to sad surprise in an era where not every option is available and resources are not unlimited. Despair and frustration could continue to roil the political climate and contribute to what the liberal historian Richard Hofstadter famously identified as "the paranoid style in American politics".

This is the background against which the debate over US foreign policy is now being waged, and the anger and anxieties of the nation perhaps explain why Obama has been so reluctant to give voice to the Tarnoff Doctrine, or something like it, even though he accepts its central tenets. After all, what Tarnoff said 20 years ago – that America no longer has the will, wallet or influence to impose an active and ambitious global leadership across the world – is actually true today, even if it was not at the time. President Obama has an opportunity, and a responsibility, to build support for a foreign policy that stresses realism, restraint, modesty, limits, selectivity and discrimination.

To do that, however, the President will have to stop playing hide-and-seek with his strategic thinking. It is one thing for the administration to embrace prudence and discretion in the deployment of America's still unmatched military power, and to realise the need to be more discreet in using its power and more inclined to act in concert with other nations. It is another thing for the President to state to the American public where Washington should lead and where it should not.

President Obama rightly wants to focus on "nation-building" at home. But only when he articulates an approach that emphasises prudence and modesty in the most forceful and eloquent manner will such a doctrine win public acceptance. His challenge is to match resources with aspirations, to bring commitments and power into balance. He should also explain that the United States has left the realm of necessity and is increasingly entering the realm of choice, where the key word is not "and" but "or", and the key question is not "how?" but "why?".

With Chandran Kukathas (left), William Maley and Francis Fukuyama at the CIS conference Consilium in August 2002

With James Buchanan (centre) and Greg Lindsay at the CIS office in Sydney, March 2002

With Alan Dupont (left), Kishore Mahbubani and Sue Windybank at
the CIS Forum "Asian Power, Asian Values", August 2005

(Left) Presenting the inaugural Owen Harries Prize at the University of New South
Wales in April 2007 and (right) With inaugural Owen Harries Lecturer, Kurt
Campbell, at the Lowy Institute in November 2013

SECTION FOUR

General Foreign Policy

The End of the World as We Know It
The Australian, 10 November 1989

Western intellectuals, at least the most honest and serious of them, are confused and disoriented, in a mental country without maps. For the past 40 years they did have a map, or a model, or to use the fancier term now coming into vogue, a paradigm that explained the world and provided a framework for thinking about it. This was, of course, the Cold War model.

Intellectuals could disagree about details, could take different moral and political positions, could describe the forces involved differently (democracy versus totalitarianism, freedom versus repression, capitalism versus socialism, reactionary forces versus progressive ones, and so on) but the basic model was very widely, if not universally, accepted.

Then, suddenly and unexpectedly, in the late 1980s the model collapsed and lost its validity. In many senses of the term "Cold War" – as it is used by strategists, military people, diplomats, politicians – one can argue about whether it is over. The competition between the United States and the Soviet Union will certainly continue, and some aspects of it will probably be very nasty. But the Cold War as an ideological struggle is over – and since the interest of intellectuals in world politics is essentially ideological, they are not interested in mundane politics.

The Cold War is over as an ideological struggle because the communists have given up, and essentially abandoned their position. Given up the doctrine of democratic centralism, the Brezhnev doctrine, the doctrine of international class war, and the rest of it. And whatever happens to Gorbachev, or after Gorbachev, they cannot go back. Too much has been conceded, too much dirt about the system – its grotesque inefficiency, its pathetic backwardness, its graft and corruption and cynicism – has been exposed for the ideology ever to regain credibility and its ability to inspire and mobilise. For Marxism-Leninism, the dustbin of history beckons.

However, asked recently by the American magazine, *New Republic*, for his views on the present international scene, political commentator Norman Podhoretz's utterly uncharacteristic reply was: "This is one case where it is easier to know what to do than what to think." At about the same time, he undertook to write an article on America's purpose in the world of the 1990s. After a few weeks he rang and said he couldn't do it as, upon reflection, he didn't know what America's purpose should be if, as appeared to be the case, the Cold War was over. For the time being, he would opt for silence.

Not everyone opts for silence. In fact, what we are faced with at present is not silence from intellectuals, but cacophony, not an absence of answers, but a profusion of conflicting ones that demonstrates how decisively consensus has been shattered. This article attempts to sort out the various competing positions – seven by my calculations.

℮℮℮

First, there are the old faithfuls or last ditchers. These respond to the dramatic events of the past few years by claiming that nothing has fundamentally changed. They cling to the old Cold War model and are deeply suspicious of Gorbachev, some maintaining that he is doing no more than conducting an elaborate deception against the West.

Second, the prudentialists. These concede that important changes are underway in the communist world, but that we do not know enough about them, or where they will lead, to make radical changes in our own policy. "Wait and see", or at best a deliberate step-by-step policy, testing the ground at each stage, is their prescription. In particular, the West should be careful not to do anything that relieves the Soviets of the necessity to face hard choices – between more guns and more consumer goods, for example.

Third, the grand designers. If the previous category represents realpolitik at its most nervous, this one includes those realists with a taste for boldness and strategic vision. Former US Secretary of State Henry Kissinger comes to mind. The time is ripe, they argue, for attempting a new European grand settlement, one that will end the division of Europe and the huge military concentration at its centre.

The objective conditions favour such a try. The Soviet Union is losing control of Eastern Europe in any case, and may be glad to cut its losses on the American side. Western Europe is likely to become more independent as the Soviet threat is perceived to be diminishing and as the process of unity proceeds in the European Community. Too much prudence, they maintain, may result in a historical opportunity being missed: Seize the Day.

Next, and more soberly, there are those who may be termed the classicists. They argue that what is happening in the world, now that the totalitarian threat is receding, is a return to the "classical" power politics of the 18th or 19th centuries. Instead of the bipolarity of the Cold War, there is multipolarity; instead of a highly charged ideological rivalry, the cooler politics of limited national interest. What America and the West should be doing is preparing for this new game, one in which they are not very experienced and which is, in some ways, alien to their nature.

My fifth category I call the triumphalists. These are the people who argue that the West has won the Cold War, that liberal democracy has defeated Marxism-Leninism, and that the West should behave like a victor and press home its advantage by promoting a "democratic revolution" throughout the world. It is a view vigorously advocated by a number of younger American conservatives. In the latest issue of *The National Interest*, for example, Elliott Abrams gives this advice to the State Department: "It should take as a central task propagating America's values around the world – not just cheering but leading the democratic revolution." This, I should mention, is a divisive issue among conservatives. Many – and I include myself – think that it is neither in America's competence nor its interest to conduct an intrusive policy of this kind.

Sixth is a group that goes much further than any of the others – let's call them the euphoric welcomers. These maintain that the whole nature of international relations is being transformed fundamentally. Everything is changed, changed utterly – and they like what they see.

For the euphoric welcomers the crucial concept is "interdependence". They maintain that, with the development of technology and communication, the interests and activities of the industrialised states of the world are becoming so intertwined and interlocked – so mutually dependent, so finely meshed – that sheer self-interest demands co-operation and rules out war as an instrument of policy. Not merely economic interests but environmental, ecological, demographic and other concerns point in that direction, and the decline of ideological hostility removes the main barrier to proceeding along these lines. Military and strategic aspects of international politics will decline in importance: international relations will become more benign and co-operative.

Seventh and last, there is the back-to-isolationism school. Its most vocal and influential representative is Pat Buchanan, once chief speech writer for Nixon, then Reagan, and now a syndicated columnist and television talk-show performer in America. His message, which consciously echoes that of the left-liberal George McGovern in the 1970s, is "Come home America" – the anticommunist mission is accomplished, now let the Europeans and the Asians look after their own security. It is not an unimportant voice, and for different reasons it has supporters on both the left and the right.

The range covered by these seven positions indicates the extent of the prevailing confusion and flux. But it is even worse than that. Most intellectuals are not sure which group they belong to. There are bits they agree with and disagree with in most positions, and their views tend to vary with their moods or what's happened lately.

That, I have to say, with regret and some shame, is also the condition in which I find myself. So if you have been feeling intellectually inadequate lately because you haven't been able to make sense of what is happening, cheer up and join the party.

The confusion exists on both left and right. On the right there is talk of a "conservative crack-up" because the glue of anti-communism that has held the various conservative groups together is dissolving. The left is divided into those who think Gorbachev is a good thing – that at last he may produce a viable socialism – and those who think he is a traitor and a disaster to the cause.

Some years ago, former US Secretary of State Dean Acheson wrote a book called *Present at the Creation* about how he and a group of other remarkable men – George Marshall, George Kennan, James Forrestal and others – had shaped a global foreign policy for the US. In the 1940s, these men, tempered by the recently-ended war and thus shorn of frivolity and illusion, provided a conceptual framework that endured for 40 years.

But we are now present at the disintegration of that framework. Whether a new group of thinkers and policymakers – conditioned by opinion polls, the 30-second television sound bite and the 800-word editorial page article, rather than by world war – will be up to providing an equally sound and enduring basis for policy remains to be seen.

The New World Order? Take Your Pick

Sydney Morning Herald, 19 September 1991

This article was based on the John Latham Memorial Lecture that Harries delivered at the University of Sydney on 12 September 1991, the year that saw, as he put it, "the final dramatic collapse of Soviet communism – indeed, of the Soviet state." The full lecture was published as "The Fog of Peace" in *Quadrant*, November 1991.

When the President of the United States, the world's only all-round superpower, talks about a "New World Order", it is necessary to pay attention. George Bush, not hitherto known as a bold conceptualiser, used that phrase during the Gulf crisis. What, if anything, did he mean by it? I think it true to say that in Washington the jury is still out on that. But there are basically four views which are interesting and influential in the current US foreign policy discussion.

First, there is what may be called the interdependence or Global Village Model of the future. The essential thesis here is that, with the technological conquest of time and space, the countries and people of the world are now so closely intermeshed that the old zero-sum game of power politics (whereby your gain must be my loss) is rapidly giving way to a new order characterised by harmony and mutual dependence.

It is worth pointing out that this way of thinking is not new. (You will recall the saying that no truly bad idea ever really dies.) Immediately before World War I, Norman Angell was using similar arguments about the degree of integration in Europe (as unprecedented at that time as it is now) to maintain that war had become a counterproductive, unprofitable and irrational institution. The fact that the Great War followed shortly afterwards did not prevent him subsequently receiving a Nobel Prize and a knighthood.

In the 1970s we had the period of detente and now, with the end of the Cold War, this kind of thinking has really come into its own. What is one to say? That there is a vastly greater volume of interaction is indisputable. That this necessarily involves more harmony and peace, however, is eminently disputable. Many of those who equate the "global village" with amicable relations seem to have little experience of real villages – and the degree of envy, malice, rivalry and vindictiveness that their intimacy can accommodate and even foster.

There is one other, rather dramatic, way of making the general point (though it is not a very palatable one to conservatives): the most interdependent social unit that human beings ever enter is the family – and it is in the family that most murders occur.

The second version of the new world order is the Pax Democratica Model. Stripped to its barest bones, this is based on two propositions. First, liberal democracy has emerged triumphant from the Cold War and it will be the dominant political system of the coming decades. Second, since the historical record shows that democracies do not fight each other, this means that we are heading towards a more benign and peaceful world.

Both these propositions have some substance. The prestige of liberal democracy is undoubtedly higher than it has been for a long time and democratic governments have been established in many more countries in recent years. It is also true that the historical record yields few if any examples of democracies going to war against each other.

That having been said, there is something facile about all this. In the first place, the extent of the "democratic revolution" is surely exaggerated, with many countries (whose adherence to democracy is skin deep, merely formal, and almost certainly fleeting) being counted to swell the numbers and justify the optimism.

As for the second proposition – democracies are not bellicose and do not fight each other – it is worth bearing in mind several things. One, until a couple of generations ago there were only a very few democracies to test this hypothesis. Two, virtually all the democracies that existed until recently were Christian and north

European countries (mostly Protestant, mostly Anglo-Saxon or Nordic) with relatively high living standards, and any characteristics exhibited by them might have had more to do with that shared background than the fact that they were democracies. Three, for the past 60 years democracies have had their hands full dealing with totalitarian enemies who have distracted them from any intramural conflicts among themselves. Four, the fact that democracies have not fought each other does not establish that they are non-belligerent. One of the first inventions of modern democracy, it is worth recalling, was the *levée en masse*, which mobilised the entire male population of revolutionary France and made it available to Napoleon for a two-decade assault on the rest on Europe. And, of course, most democracies have often yielded to the temptation of initiating splendid little wars against non-democracies.

More generally, as we witness the disintegration of the vast Soviet empire, it may turn out that we are also going to see the triumph of democracy. But the difficulties are formidable. What we certainly are going to witness – are witnessing – is the resurgence of nationalism, held in check and suppressed for half a century. There are ominous signs that we are going to experience what someone has described as a proliferation of tribes waving flags.

Note, finally, that those who think that the universal spread of democracy would eliminate war are committing themselves to one explanation of war – that it is the outcome of the way particular states are organised internally. This rejects another explanation that has a long and respectable pedigree – that it is a product of the way states are organised in relation to each other. I tend toward the latter explanation as the crucial one.

ॐ ॐ ॐ

Both the models so far discussed – interdependence and Pax Democratica – assume the declining efficacy of force, a major theme in the first year after the Berlin Wall came down: that economic power is about to displace military power as the principal measure of things. Then came the Gulf War, which caused people to think again. The much-heralded new economic superpowers – Japan and Germany – played a marginal, not to say feeble, role in that affair. Political and military power were the decisive currency. Partly as a result of this, two other versions of a new world order have gained favour.

So we come to the third of the quartet: the Collective Security Model, whereby the international community organises itself to deter, thwart and punish acts of aggression by collective action. This is really a retread of a pre-1939 favourite, and its popularity now derives from the prominence of the UN in the Gulf War, and more specifically from the fact that the Security Council for once functioned according to the manual, with no vetoes obstructing it.

In New York in February, Mr Bush associated himself with this view, saying: "So the New World Order, I think, foresees a revitalised peacekeeping function of the United Nations." This raises the question: how typical was the Gulf crisis and how much can we generalise from it? In one sense, I think it was typical enough. There will always be bully boys like Saddam Hussein, seeking regional hegemony and prepared to strike at weaker neighbours. But in other respects, it was a special, probably unrepeatable, case:

- It involved crude, unambiguous aggression by a perfect villain, one not only lacking any redeeming virtues but who was obligingly stupid.

- The presence of oil gave the crisis great urgency, while Saudi Arabia provided a secure land base for operations.

- The crisis occurred at a time when the Soviet Union desperately needed Western help, and China was concerned to rehabilitate itself after the Tiananmen Square debacle.

Is it likely that such a helpful set of circumstances (including the fact that the transgressor was not a veto-possessing member of the Security Council) will accompany future crises?

There is another way of interpreting the Gulf War – not as the beginning of collective security but as a manifestation of American supremacy, a Pax Americana, in what is now a unipolar world.

Is it this, the fourth possible outcome, that is the lesson to be drawn from the end of the Cold War and the Gulf War? Take the Gulf crisis first. In an enormously impressive political and military performance, the US shipped a huge force to the region and kept it there for months. The irony of this tremendous effort, however, is that it establishes conclusively that the Gulf War cannot serve as a precedent, for such an effort cannot be replicated regularly.

This was the first US military operation in its history that the US felt unable to pay for by itself. Furthermore, many Americans do not share an appetite for an active, outward-looking, global leadership role for America. What motivates many of the people holding such views is a concern about the magnitude of the nation's domestic problems. It seems doubtful whether America will have either the capacity or the will to sustain Pax Americana. And there are two other aspects to bear in mind: first, there are serious grounds for doubting that in the absence of a life-threatening ideological enemy representing evil incarnate, America has the staying power to impose and manage a Pax Americana.

Second, if indeed the US is the only remaining superpower, and if it behaves in an assertive manner, then by all the rules of power politics, what one should expect before long is the emergence of a coalition of states to balance and contain American power.

&ℰ&ℰ&ℰ

Each of these four versions of the new world order has some plausibility. All four also have one other thing in common: they are all essentially optimistic. But the picture is not uniformly bright, and if we are not to be surprised by the world yet again, we need to cultivate and keep in good order that imagination of disaster which is natural to conservatism, but alien to liberalism.

So let me observe that future historians may well decide that the most suitable label for the era that is just beginning will be "The Age of Proliferation". Proliferation, that is, of nuclear weapons, of chemical and biological weapons, and of the ballistic missiles to deliver them.

A lot of people spent the Cold War predicting and being terrified of a nuclear holocaust. In fact, the principal actors of the Cold War were rational calculators of nuclear risks and there was little danger of nuclear war. In addition, the control and discipline exercised over others by the superpowers, as well as their willingness to extend nuclear protection to their allies and clients, limited the horizontal proliferation of nuclear weapons. Those restraints and inhibitions are now weakening.

After 45 years of Cold War, only five countries openly acknowledge that they have nuclear weapons. Another five countries – India, Israel, Pakistan, South Africa, North Korea – have them but are reticent about admitting the fact. In addition, there are at least 10 and possibly 12 "threshold" states – ones that are capable of producing nuclear weapons in a period of a few years or less: Japan, Germany, South Korea, Taiwan, Iraq, Brazil, Argentina, Iran, Libya and Syria. And within a decade, according to the US Defence Secretary, Dick Cheney, 15 countries will acquire ballistic missiles, the means of delivering nuclear, chemical and biological weapons.

Whether the threshold states proceed to make weapons will depend not on technical considerations but on political ones. Unfortunately, it is likely that a significant number of them will decide that in the more uncertain, volatile and uncontrolled post-Cold War world, the case for acquiring them is the stronger.

The lesson to be learnt from the past two years – the two most exhilarating in modern history – is not that we have reached a sunlit plain where there will be no more problems, no more dangers, no more evil. The lesson surely is that even horrendous problems can be dealt with if the will and courage to prevail are strong. A banal enough lesson. But just as Hannah Arendt once examined the horrors of Nazi Germany and declared the banality of evil, so can we perhaps now examine the fall of the other monstrous totalitarian system and declare the blessed banality of courage and fortitude.

Fourteen Points for Realists

The National Interest, Winter 1992-93

How should an aspiring realist approach the post-Cold War world and the problem of formulating a foreign policy suited to it? What sort of attitudes should he cultivate, what assumptions should he make? And, just as important, what should he be careful to reject and avoid? Here are some suggestions:

1) View with extreme scepticism the current outpouring of claims that what has been true about relationships between states from the time of Thucydides until yesterday no longer holds. Interdependence, transnational institutions, the spread of democracy, the obsolescence of war, the new primacy of economics, the dilution of sovereignty – take your pick, all have been nominated as revolutionising international politics and falsifying classic realist premises. Do not allow your scepticism to be modified because some of these claims have been advanced by conservatives.

Similar or identical claims have been advanced in earlier periods and proved spectacularly and dangerously wrong. They invariably underestimate the durability and tenacity of the past. It is going to take a long time to alter the international system in any basic way. And to be prematurely right in international affairs, to anticipate a trend too early and to act on it, can be as fatal as being dead wrong.

2) Resist the notion that we must now find a new, grand, elevating cause to perform the same function as anti-communism did until recently – that of providing coherence, unity, and high moral content to foreign policy. The Cold War was exceptional, not typical. The post-Cold War world is a fragmented and pluralist one, requiring diverse and particular policies, not one big policy based on one big concept – or, even worse, on a "vision". To adapt one of Harold Macmillan's better remarks, if you want a vision, consult a saint not a politician.

3) Also, discard the habit of making foreign policy in terms of sweeping doctrines that purport to lay down general, binding

principles and rules of conduct that must be followed consistently, across the board. Elevate discrimination and selectivity over consistency and comprehensiveness. If anyone accuses you of "double standards" for doing so, relax and live with it. Dean Acheson once explained very clearly why you should:

> The United States, in my judgment, acts in regard to a foreign nation strictly in regard to its interests or those wider interests which affect it. And if it is to American interests or those wider interests which affect it to do one thing in one country and another thing in another country, then that is the consistency upon which I propose to advise the president. And I am not in the slightest bit worried because somebody can say, "Well, you said so and so about Greece, why isn't all this true about China?" I will be polite, I will be patient, and I will try to explain why Greece is not China, but my heart will not be in the battle.

Discrimination is always necessary because circumstances alter cases. In the 1990s it will be particularly important, because the resources available for foreign policy are going to be more limited and choices will be unavoidable.

4) As the essence of the realist disposition is a concern to see things as they are, apply yourself to unlearning and discarding the habits, assumptions, and categories that depended on the conditions of the Cold War for their validity. For example, stop thinking as a matter of course in terms of a unified political entity called "the West", because in the absence of a threatening "East" it increasingly lacks substance and conviction. (Already, the French and Germans and the Japanese clearly do not think or act in terms of a united West.) Similarly, the concept of a "Third World" has lost most of its relevance in the absence of first and second world conflict. Now that the United States is not engaged in a global struggle against a serious enemy, huge tracts of the world that used to be regarded as important may be viewed with geopolitical indifference, and the same applies to millions of "hearts and minds".

5) While the United States should be prepared to promote democracy in a modest, non-insistent way (because democracies are more peaceful towards other democracies and therefore easier for America to live with; and because doing so is consistent with America's sense of itself), it should certainly not make the promotion of democracy a major – let alone the centrepiece – feature of its policy, as some have eloquently urged.

By its very nature, democracy is a do-it-yourself enterprise, not an export commodity. Americans do not have the understanding of other societies and peoples, the attention span or staying power, to engage in an active, interventionist policy of democracy promotion on a large scale. Only trouble – for the United States and for others – will result if they try. Unless you are prepared to support conquest and prolonged US occupation of targeted countries, resist the argument that America's success in fostering democracy in post-World War II Germany and Japan validates a democratic crusade now.

I don't often find occasion to quote Brent Scowcroft – who does? – but I agree with him that as far as promoting democracy is concerned, America should be content merely to "nudge" other countries, rather than attempt to interfere deeply in their internal affairs.

6) In terms of regional involvement, the United States should increasingly (but not abruptly) leave Europe to the Europeans – and that emphatically includes Yugoslavia. That is the way the Europeans seem to want it, and America should respect their wishes. Some Europeans – notably the French – may soon come to feel a new need for a continuing American commitment to Europe, and when they do, the United States should consider dispassionately whether its interests would be served by a positive response. In the meantime, nothing will be lost and something will be gained by making it clear that the United States does not insist on clinging to Europe, does not demand a major role there.

The United States should concentrate its attention on the north Pacific, where the intersecting interests of three great powers and a divided Korea make the danger of a general conflagration real, and where American sea and air power can be effective; and on the Middle East, where the combination of oil, religion, passionate hatred, sophisticated weaponry, an old-fashioned readiness to resort to force, and commitment to Israel requires American involvement.

The regional relationship between Ukraine and Russia is of great importance, but it is difficult to see how the United States could play a major role if the relationship were to deteriorate seriously. Good offices, yes – but beyond that intervention would be both dangerous and probably ineffectual.

In all three cases America's principal concerns should be to maintain regional equilibrium and stability, and to prevent the emergence of an irresponsible nuclear power capable of endangering world peace.

7) As I am not one of those realists who hold that the international system counts for everything and the individual character of countries and regimes for nothing, I believe that we should keep well in mind the peculiar and exceptional character of some of the leading actors on today's international stage. Three of the leading four states – Germany, Japan, and Russia – have been traumatised by humiliating defeat and collapse, well within living memory. It is too early to say with certainty how this experience will affect Russia, though most of the signs are bad. I don't think it unfair to say that Germany and Japan are in some respects neurotic states. They tend to have violent mood swings – from arrogant assertiveness and insensitivity to timidity and self-pity. Both are reluctant to assume responsibility and have little experience in wielding it.

Another major actor, France – also defeated and occupied in living memory – is obsessed with status and bitterly resents dependence on America. And then there is China – inward-turning, unable to reconcile its ideology and its economic practice, substantially increasing its military spending, soon to face a succession crisis. There is enough in all this to temper any bliss-was-it-in-that-dawn optimism.

8) It has now become something of a cliché to say that the post-Cold War world is assuming a triangular shape, with the United States, Europe, and the Asia-Pacific as the three centres of power. Bear in mind that, in political terms, a system of three is inherently unstable. Bismarck once observed that in a game of five, the object should always be to be one of three. Likewise, in a game of three, the aim should always be to be one of two – or at least to avoid being isolated while the other two draw closer together. In this respect the United States starts with an advantage, in that in recent decades it has had a very strong relationship with both the others, while the relationship between Japan and Europe has been weak. It should be a central objective of US policy to ensure that this advantage is not dissipated.

Down the road, it might come to a choice between putting the European or the Asian relationship first. If it does, many Americans would not hesitate to opt for Europe. Indeed, many see a united Europe as an unmitigated good for the United States. For example, *The New York Times* editorialised on 18 September 1992: "The US has a strong stake in European integration; it would dampen historic rivalries, encourage international co-operation and promote global prosperity." Perhaps. But it is worth reflecting that a united Europe is the only entity that could, in the foreseeable future, challenge and surpass the United States as an all-round power. Europe is also currently the pace-setter in undermining international free trade.

9) Be aware that being – or being seen as – the world's only remaining superpower is not altogether a comfortable situation to be in. The historical tendency has been for other states to gang up on and challenge the No. 1 state. Perhaps the United States will be an exception to this, as to some extent Britain was. But it is worth remembering that Britain succeeded in this respect by remaining

relatively detached and unthreatening, content most of the time to act as a balancer of last resort, rather than an assertive leader, active instigator, or bossy "policeman".

10) Do not take American policy in the Gulf crisis as a suitable model or precedent for post-Cold War regional policy. Expeditions involving half-a-million men and half-a-dozen aircraft carriers cannot be repeated on a regular basis. Other countries will not cough up $50 billion to pay for such American commitments, especially if they were not consulted before the commitments were made in the first place. Unilateral initiative on this scale was a luxury the United States could once afford; no more.

11) Be cautious about yielding to the temptation of using the United Nations – and particularly the Security Council – as an instrument of American policy, now that the Soviet veto is effectively removed. While doing so might have short-term advantages, it would create precedents that could well come back to haunt you in the future. It would also strengthen misunderstandings in American minds as to how international politics really works – for example, by encouraging the belief that a range of actions can only acquire legitimacy and moral acceptability if they are based on a UN "mandate"; or by creating the illusion of action when in reality problems are being evaded.

12) Do not listen to those who sneer at the maintenance of stability, order, and equilibrium as unworthy foreign policy objectives. The international state system is inherently unstable, and the forces unleashed by the collapse of the last great empire – the Soviet empire – make it especially so today. Instability can very easily and quickly get out of hand, and the cost of treating it complacently comes high. As a satisfied "have" country, but one whose primacy is diminishing, the United States has a particular stake in stability at this time. It needs a period of equilibrium – one in which excessive demands will not be made on its resources and energy – to buy time, so that it may attend to serious domestic problems and put its house in order.

13) Pin up on your wall, declaim in lectures, essays, debates and casual conversations, print in your Christmas cards, and otherwise propagate in every way you can, Walter Lippmann's great sentence:

> Without the controlling principle that the nation must maintain its objectives and its power in equilibrium, its purposes within its means and its means equal to its purposes, its commitments related to its resources and its resources adequate to its commitments, it is impossible to think at all about foreign affairs.

This is a truth of which Americans – more apt to focus on ends than means when it comes to dealing with the rest of the world – need always to be reminded. But it is going to be particularly necessary during a period of diminishing primacy.

14) Some will tell you that the kind of realist precepts advanced here might be all very well for other countries but are inappropriate for the United States, are fundamentally at odds with the American ethos. Treat this view respectfully – it is held by some individuals with whom you are likely to have much in common – but reject it.

America has a perfectly good realist tradition, extending from its beginnings until now. Washington's farewell address; the Louisiana Purchase; the Monroe Doctrine and its corollary, as well as the actions based on them; the Mexican and Indian and Spanish wars (perhaps the most successful series of wars of acquisition since the days of the Romans); the coalition-building of World War II and the Cold War – it is absurd to say that realism is alien to the American tradition. In opting for realism now, the United States would be following a course that has served it well in the past.

The Collapse of "the West"

Foreign Affairs, September-October 1993 [extract]

Extracted as "'The West' Is Only a Flag of Convenience" in *The New York Times* (28 August 1993), a shorter version also ran as "Survival of 'West' Doubtful Now Cold War Is Over" in *The Straits Times* (Singapore), 2 September 1993.

Old Thinking in a New World

Underlying the recent debates over Bosnia, the Balkans and Eastern Europe more generally, there is a much broader and unanswered question about the condition and future of the West. The proponents of intervention in the Balkans believe that, simply put, the West should go East. William Pfaff was surely speaking for many when he argued eloquently in these pages that the West should act through NATO – "the true Great Power in Europe today" – to guarantee existing frontiers in the Balkans and Eastern Europe, "so as to deprive transnational ethnic rivalry of its political and military explosiveness." The NATO guarantee to these new states should be backed up by force if necessary. Only such a policy, it is claimed, can both recover for the West the moral and political ground it has lost through its mishandling of the Yugoslav crisis and lay a base of stability for the future of Eastern Europe.

There are specific problems with such a course of action. But more important, the various policy proposals and position papers advocating such a course reflect a philosophical inertia, an inability or unwillingness to jettison old concepts and modes of thought in the face of utterly changed circumstances. In particular, such proposals for what amount to a new NATO are based on a most questionable premise: that "the West" continues to exist as a political and military entity. Over the last half century or so, most of us have come to think of "the West" as a given, a natural presence and one that is here to stay. It is a way of thinking that is not only wrong in itself, but is virtually certain to lead to mistaken policies. The sooner we discard it the better. The political "West" is not a natural construct but a highly artificial one. It took the presence of a life-threatening, overtly hostile "East" to bring it into existence and to maintain its unity. It is extremely doubtful whether it can now survive the disappearance of that enemy.

A Child of Danger and Fear

The countries of the West share vast commonalities: a common history, culture, and political values and institutions. It is in all this – the glory that was Greece and the grandeur that was Rome, Christianity, the Renaissance, the Reformation, the Enlightenment, the French and Industrial revolutions, representative democracy, the rule of law, the market economy – that many find the basis of Western unity. In this view, the threat from the East was just one additional factor, and by no means the most important one, in the creation of a political "West".

But those who argue thus overlook the fact that while all these common features had existed long before the Cold War, they had never created or sustained a united West before the appearance of a shared and formidable enemy. A common civilisation is one thing, political unity is another, and they should not be confused. In fact, relationships among the countries of the West have been marked by division and by particularly bloody internecine conflicts throughout their history – to the point that fratricidal warfare might well be offered as one of the distinguishing characteristics of Western civilisation, as opposed to civilisations that have been less marked by political fragmentation, the development of nationalism and sophisticated military technology.

Something approaching a united "West" has been spoken of only three times in modern history: in 1917-18, 1941-45 and the Cold War years. In the first two instances, the term is a complete misnomer, since the enemies – Germany and Austria-Hungary in the first case, Germany and Italy in the second – were full-fledged members of the West. The conflicts could more accurately be described (and, indeed, they sometimes have been) as Western civil wars.

But if one stretches the point and allows all three as examples, it becomes clear that the notion of a political "West" is one that has been attractive to Europeans only when some or all of their countries have been in great and imminent danger. Desperation and fear have been its parents, not natural affinities. They have been the forces that have driven Europeans to unite among themselves and to associate with the United States under the banner of "the West". Further, it is a concept that, in the European experience, is associated with the prospect of subordination and, for proud nations accustomed to being leading actors in their own right, a certain amount of humiliation. For, once in being, "the West" has always and necessarily been dominated by the United States, a country long viewed by many Europeans as unsophisticated in international affairs.

Fair-Weather Foes

In the absence of an overriding threat that one is incapable of handling on one's own – and sometimes even in the presence of such a threat – the inclination on both sides of the Atlantic has been to emphasise not unity, but the difference and incompatibility of Europe and America. Thus, even before final victory was achieved in 1945, the prevailing model of the political world had become that of the "Big Three", with Franklin Roosevelt more suspicious of Britain and its empire than of the Soviet Union; and immediately after victory, Harry Truman ruthlessly and abruptly ended Lend-Lease aid to Europe without any obvious concern for the overall well-being of "the West".

Even later in the 1940s, as the clouds of the Cold War were gathering rapidly, most Europeans who thought about such things – George Orwell for one – conceived the world in terms not of two groupings but of three, with Europe and the United States constituting not one but two of them. In an article written for *Partisan Review* in 1947, Orwell saw the two as divided not only as separate power blocs but ideologically as well. Europe stood for democratic socialism, the

United States for capitalism. He longed for a self-sufficient United States of Europe, able to hold out against both America and Russia – that is, for Europe as the original "Third World".

As it was at the beginning of the Cold War, so it was at the end. Two years ago, as soon as the Soviet Union disintegrated, what we immediately started to hear propounded on both sides of the Atlantic – and what we were still hearing from President Clinton during the July Tokyo summit this year – was a tripartite or tripolar version of the world, with Europe and the United States again constituting not one but two separate sides of the triangle, and with Japan/Asia as the third. Far from stressing the continuing existence of "the West", once free of a Soviet threat many Europeans immediately began anticipating, often with ill-concealed glee, a post-Maastricht United Europe that would supplant the United States as the dominant economic and ultimately political force in the world.

In particular, it was claimed that Europe, led by a reunited Germany, would take the lead in dealing with the countries of Central and Eastern Europe. When fighting broke out in Yugoslavia in the summer of 1991, for example, the immediate reaction of Jacques Delors, President of the European Commission, was: "We do not interfere in American affairs. We hope they will have enough respect not to interfere in ours." The fact that the United States had liberated Monsieur Delors' country from occupation by one totalitarian regime during his lifetime, and had subsequently protected Western Europe against the threat posed by a second such regime for four decades, was neither here nor there. To say again: once deprived of a threat or some other serious trouble it cannot cope with, there is a strong tendency for Europe to treat the United States as a rival (and sometimes as a naïve, heavy-handed and incompetent rival), not as a leader or a partner.

Subsequently, of course, the momentum toward European unity has faltered and Maastricht has become a divisive rather than uniting symbol. The European economy has gone into what looks increasingly like a prolonged structural recession. Almost to a man, European political leaders have become deeply unpopular in their own countries, their authority attenuated and their ability to conduct forceful foreign policies limited. And a nasty, racist form of populism has spread through much of the continent. As all these things have happened, and as Europe has proved embarrassingly incapable of dealing with the Bosnian crisis, European confidence that it can dispense with American leadership and operate as an independent force has drained away, and we have been hearing more, again, of "the West". But if and when things improve significantly for Europe, we should anticipate another reversal.

American Arguments

If European needs and insecurities constitute one condition for the continuation of "the West", there is also an obvious second condition: US willingness to respond to those needs. That, too, has in the past required a deep sense of danger – danger to *American* interests – to overcome America's moralistic distaste for European power politics. In 1917, it took a lot of German provocation before the New World finally did come in to redress the balance of the Old. In 1941, it took Pearl Harbour and Hitler's foolish declaration of war on the United States to produce a decisive, if involuntary, intervention. And in 1946-49 the rapid spread of Soviet power into Central Europe provided the incentive, after the United States had initially responded to the end of World War II with instant and comprehensive demobilisation. Absent a sense of danger, America's aloofness has been as marked as Europe's assumption of independence and superior sophistication.

So, what are the prospects of continuing close American association with Europe in the political enterprise labelled "the West"? At present the odds are somewhat against it. On one side of the scale, and it is not negligible, is the weight of habits of involvement and leadership acquired over the last half-century.

Americans have got used to their country being a superpower and a leader, and they like it more than they care to admit (or possibly know). There are powerful groups in the United States – in the military, most obviously, but elsewhere as well – that now have a major vested interest in "the West". And there are various arguments that they can advance in support of continued commitment to it.

One is the idealist argument that the United States has a new post-Cold War mission to promote democracy throughout the world and that this is best done in co-operation with other established democracies. Another is the realist argument that American participation is necessary in order to keep an eye on Germany and ensure that it does not go off the rails a third time before the end of the century. Beyond Germany is the even greater uncertainty about the future behaviour of Russia and the need some feel for an American commitment to Europe in order to forestall any major misbehaviour on Moscow's part.

These are not negligible considerations and arguments, but neither are they compelling and conclusive. As for spreading democracy, a sense of mission has never on its own been sufficient to lead the United States to commit itself to a policy of heavy involvement or close association with Europe, and this is unlikely to change. In June of this year, the House of Representatives voted to kill the National Endowment for Democracy, the agency created during the Reagan years to promote democracy abroad. Even if the Senate were to reverse this vote, it is a significant sign of the times. There is the further constraint that Europe's zeal for spreading democracy is comparatively limited, and that, at this post-imperial stage of their history, European countries lack the confidence and assertiveness necessary to sustain serious intervention in the affairs of other countries.

As for concern about the future behaviour of Germany and Russia, as of now both cases lack the sense of a clear and present danger that has been necessary in the past to overcome American inhibitions and to cause the United States to commit itself to "the West" – and, for that matter, that has also been required to create a "demand" for such a commitment on the part of Europeans. In the absence of such a sense it is highly questionable whether, should a German or Russian crisis erupt quickly, the United States could mobilise the political support necessary to intervene decisively and expensively (in terms of casualties even more than of money, though the latter constitutes an increasing restraint also).

When that good Atlanticist, Jeane Kirkpatrick, wrote in 1990 that in the post-Cold War era "the United States should not try to manage the balance of power in Europe – we should neither seek to prevent nor assist Germany in re-establishing a dominant position in Europe or Central Europe. We could not control these matters if we tried and there is no reason to try," she was expressing a view that many Americans share. In the cases of both Russia and Germany, if things were to deteriorate seriously, the United States would undoubtedly use its very considerable political and economic clout in an effort to prevent trouble. But there would be legitimate doubt about Washington's willingness to commit American forces on a significant scale in either event. This would limit both the capacity and the acceptability of American leadership.

The "Nogood Boyo" Approach

The most powerful argument for substantial American withdrawal from the kind of serious, sustained and expensive participation necessary to maintain "the West" as something more than a reassuring fiction is the urgent pull of domestic matters, long neglected or relegated to subordinate status during the Cold War. One does not have to be an isolationist or a "declinist" to believe that the time has come to alter the country's priorities in favour of domestic concerns; and it is not only Patrick Buchanan who has been saying "Come home, America." It was William Hyland, at the time sitting at the heart of the American foreign policy establishment as editor of *Foreign Affairs*, who opined that "What is definitely required is a psychological turn inwards." This view has been echoed by many others, one of the most recent being Zbigniew Brzezinski, who has called for "a period of philosophical introspection and of cultural self-critique", necessary, he believes, in order to tackle the moral, social and economic malaise that afflicts the "permissive cornucopia" that the United States has now become.

To the extent that such attitudes prevail and such advice is taken, they are inimical to a united and purposeful "West", which requires an active, outgoing and engaged America. There is good reason to believe that in the Clinton era such attitudes will prevail. President Clinton has an ambitious domestic agenda and little interest in or feel for foreign policy. He has equipped himself with a team that, to put it mildly and politely, is unlikely to press him hard to adopt ambitious, activist policies abroad, except in the area of trade. If the Bosnian crisis is any indication, one can expect that in Clinton's Washington "the West", together with the United Nations, will be used as devices not to facilitate action but to justify inaction. The United States wants to take decisive action, it will be claimed in a variety of situations, but it must be *multilateral* action and a proper international *mandate* must be given. If these conditions cannot be fulfilled, then the United States will, regrettably but justifiably, do nothing. In practice, whenever it has looked remotely as if the Europeans might agree to an American proposal regarding Bosnia, there has been a rapid backing off on Washington's part. After the character in Dylan Thomas's *Under Milk Wood*, this rationalisation of passivity might be labelled the "Nogood Boyo" approach to foreign policy: "I want to be good, but nobody'll let me."

In fairness, it should be added that these would be difficult times for any administration as far as foreign policy is concerned, for today's conditions are novel and puzzling for Americans. Framing choices in terms of all or nothing makes little sense. Earlier experiences of confronting clearly identified enemies in extreme situations, and of leading great alliances in bipolar situations, are not very helpful and may be misleading (particularly if they lead to an incessant and indiscriminate stress on leadership). Washington will have to learn to play new and different games.

While it is doing so, the concept of "the West" is likely to revert to what it has been for most of the past: a concept of last resort, held in reserve for when things go seriously bad and individual countries or restricted alliances are unable to cope on their own. One must assume – unless one has come to accept the fatuous nonsense that war as an institution is dead – that such circumstances will again return to haunt us one day, perhaps sooner rather than later. Indeed, if those who speak of "the Clash of Civilisations" (Samuel Huntington) and of "the West and the Rest" (Kishore Mahbubani) are right, the idea of a political "West" may achieve greater authenticity in the struggles of the future than it did even in the days of the Cold War. But meanwhile the notion has lost much of its definition and *raison d'etre*.

W. H. Auden once wrote of Brussels, the city that subsequently became the headquarters of the European Community and NATO, and thus of the West:

> Its formula escapes you; it has lost
> The certainty that constitutes a thing.

For the time being, at least, these words can properly be applied to the West itself.

The Next Cold War? Asia v. the West

National Review, 1 August 1994 [extract]

Reprinted in *Quadrant* as "Asia v. the West", October 1994.

"Sam Huntington's ghost lurked in every shadowy corner." Thus the American ambassador to Indonesia reported on the Asia-Pacific regional conference in Jakarta in August 1993. He was referring to the initial impact of Professor Huntington's thesis that we are entering an era that will be dominated by the "clash of civilisations" – conflicts caused by and reflecting cultural differences. Ten months later, I return from another such conference in Kuala Lumpur to report that the impact has not diminished. As we talked, difficult dealings with North Korea over nuclear weapons served as a grim warning of the potential costs of cultural incomprehension and antagonism.

It is the spectacular rise of Asia – first Japan, then a cluster of small Confucian "tigers", now China itself, and tomorrow probably India – that gives Huntington's thesis most of its plausibility and relevance. For the first time in several centuries, the primacy of Western civilisation is under serious challenge.

Several recent episodes in Western-Asian relations have given dramatic evidence of how cultural differences can lead to conflict. Although most Asian countries welcome an American strategic presence in the region, and although a vast and mutually beneficial economic relationship now exists, questions of "values" and behaviour have soured relationships significantly. In the MFN [Most Favoured Nation] dispute with China, different views of human rights and their relationship to public order and economic progress precipitated a serious controversy. In the case of the Singapore caning, different views as to how heinous certain forms of misbehaviour are, and how acceptable or repugnant certain kinds of punishment are, led to bitter exchanges.

These disputes have occurred because the government of the United States, and sections of its media and public, have taken strong exception to certain aspects of the behaviour of an Asian government and demanded change. In doing so, they have behaved as the West has regularly behaved toward non-Western governments for the last two or three centuries – i.e., they have laid down the law from a presumed position of superior enlightenment, making their demands not in terms of merely Western values but of universal ones; or, more accurately, acknowledging no differences between the two: Western values *are* universal.

Bearing in mind the civilisational solidarity postulated by Huntington, it is worth noting that the initiator in these instances has not in fact been "the West" but the United States. To the best of my knowledge, the European countries have mostly kept their distance. (Indeed, in Britain the main interest in caning recently has taken the form of largely sentimental recollections in the correspondence columns of *The Times* concerning the prowess of an ex-headmaster of Eton.)

On the other side, however, there has been an impressive closing of ranks. Instead of submitting to Western pressure, or resisting passively and silently, or merely blustering – all common responses in the past – Asian spokesmen have taken the offensive and launched a sustained intellectual campaign.

If Huntington is right, these episodes are worth looking at closely, both as a foretaste of what is to come and as lessons in how best to respond when it does come.

American Behaviour

What can be said about American behaviour in these episodes? Well, let's begin with some things that should not be said.

First, I believe that it is a mistake to interpret American behaviour as representing a patronising and contemptuous sense of superiority toward China, or toward Confucian countries in general. Western attitudes have historically been, and are, much more complicated than that, inclined as often as not to see Confucian societies as paragons rather than inferiors.

It was the Indian historian K. M. Panniker, not a Westerner, who commented sardonically on the tendency of 18th-century intellectuals – starting with Voltaire – to become infatuated with China: "China became the example of enlightened government. As it was distant and but imperfectly known, the realities of China's despotism did not interfere with the theory of paternal government." For some it still does not, though distances have shrunk and more is known. Henry Kissinger and Richard Nixon, to take two prominent examples, showed a tremendous admiration for Chinese diplomatic skill and insight even though China's foreign policy had zigged and zagged since the communists took over, on occasion leaving it completely isolated. In recent years, admiration may have shifted largely from the political to the economic performance of Confucian countries, but it is still there.

Second, I think it is an error to interpret American policy toward Asia as essentially driven by economic fear, as the Malaysian Prime Minister, Dr Mahathir, did in the interesting speech he delivered in Peking this May. "This proselytising for democracy," he declared, "veiled only slightly the objective of eliminating competition before it begins." He continued: "They would like the East Asian democracies to be weak and unstable like theirs, or worse. Maybe there is no grand conspiracy by the West to undermine all the East Asian economies. But conspiracy is not necessary. It is sufficient for everyone to see the danger threatening them for them to act in concert."

Again, this is demonstrably wrong. Western countries do not act in concert; they disagree and compete. If one country takes a tough attitude toward Asian governments, others are likely to try to cash in by being accommodating and uncritical. Even where there are no prospects of cashing in, France often stays out-of-step on principle.

In the United States itself, it is certainly true that there are some economic interests, usually those representing old and inefficient industries, which would like government action that would have the effect of curbing Asian competition. But there are more economic interests which are flatly opposed to any action that would in any way threaten the huge and growing economic relationship between the United States and China. Claiming that withdrawing MFN status would abolish 170,000 American jobs and in effect impose a $10 billion tax on American consumers, the latter comfortably prevailed in the recent dispute.

Third, it is a serious error to characterise the American position on these issues as either cynical or frivolous. If it could properly be so characterised it would not be half as worrisome as it is. A concern for promoting democracy and liberty and what we have come to call "human rights" is bred in the American bone. From Thomas Jefferson's proclamation of the newly-formed country as the "Empire of Liberty" onward, it has been an article of faith that the country exists, not only to promote the freedom of its own citizens, but to serve the cause of freedom throughout the world. Disagreement has centred mostly on how best to do that – whether by example alone, or by active crusading. There is nothing unusual or particularly anti-Asian or anti-Confucian about American behaviour in these instances, therefore, and one does not have to look for special circumstances to explain it; for better or worse, America is just being itself.

The Three Cs

If the United States is not guilty of these particular charges, what, if anything, is wrong with American policy in these instances? In my opinion, plenty. Nearly all of it can be presented in terms of three Cs: Consequences, Circumstances, and Capacity.

Politics is about *consequences*, not about purity of intention, self-therapy, or feeling good. In a celebrated essay, Max Weber distinguished between "the ethic of ultimate ends" and "the ethic of responsibility". The former represents the absolutist religious view that one must always do what is right regardless of consequences; the latter holds that there is an obligation to take into account foreseeable consequences in deciding on one's actions. An individual is free to follow the first ethic – to, for example, treat human rights as absolute, to be respected whatever the consequences and cost. But once it enters the realm of politics, the promotion of human rights has to take its place in a hierarchy of interests and values, including such basic concerns as the promotion of security, peace, order and prosperity. The place of human rights – or for that matter any other single interest – in that hierarchy will vary from occasion to occasion, and no responsible government will be able to put them always at the top. Political wisdom – statesmanship – involves not mechanical consistency and uniformity in applying principle, but discrimination and judgement.

This way of thinking is uncongenial to Americans. They are inclined to approach politics in terms of an ethic of absolute ends, one that scorns discrimination and compromise and demands consistent rectitude. But in so far as the country's rhetoric and posture are absolutist and moralistic, it inevitably leaves itself open to the charge of hypocrisy and double standards. Because in the end a country has to discriminate and calculate. (What weight to give to the China trade? What to promoting Chinese co-operation in dealing with North Korea?) Thus, because of an absolutist rhetoric, the difference between the American approach to human rights in China and in, say, Saudi Arabia (or even Libya, which enjoys MFN status) has provided Asian critics with an easy target. So has the difference between the American attitude towards China and human rights today and tolerance of much worse practices 20 years ago, when China was valued as a "card" in the struggle against the Soviet Union.

A second set of weaknesses in the American position can be summed up by the word *circumstances*. Just as no proper concern with consequences is shown, so also are differences in circumstances played down or ignored. In the case of China, there are the obvious facts that it contains about five times as many people as the United States; that in the last 60 years it has experienced invasion, civil war, mass famine, political purges, and chaotic upheaval; that it has no tradition whatsoever of liberal democracy. In the case of Singapore, there are the equally obvious facts that it is only three decades old; that it inherited many authoritarian practices (including caning) from its colonial experience; that it is very small and works on slim margins of safety (in the same way as, for example, Israel does in some respects).

There is no taking into account that Asian countries started on the road to modernisation much later than Western countries, and that in the comparable, earlier stages of their development many Western countries showed much less than perfect respect for human rights. Well into the 19th century, for example, the British hanged (rather than caned) people for stealing or destroying property. Sweated labour was a common feature of the American scene until quite recently. And it was not until very late in the piece that the United States extended human rights in any serious sense to blacks and Native Americans.

Let it be clear that the point is not whether there are or are not universal standards, but how those standards ought to be applied in different circumstances. Americans – and perhaps Western liberals in general – tend to work on the maxim that "one size fits all". Conservatives, on the other hand, tend to agree with Edmund Burke that "government [is] a practical thing made for the happiness of mankind, and not to furnish out a spectacle of uniformity to gratify the schemes of visionary politicians."

A third respect in which American policy can be properly criticised is summed up by the word *capacity*. Except in very special circumstances, usually involving conquest and occupation – as in Germany and Japan after 1945 – no country has the capacity to impose democracy on another. Before intervening in the affairs of another country in the name of human rights and democracy, therefore, a government should consider carefully its capacity to achieve intended consequences, rather than to create unintended ones. For unless one believes in inevitable and irreversible progress, it is always possible to make things worse as well as better. The United States, let it be remembered, intervened in the most forceful way in the internal affairs of Haiti for 19 years, and left it in an utter and disgraceful shambles.

America's understanding of other societies and cultures is not profound; its experience of dealing with them is not extensive. Except when it is engaged in what is perceived as a life-or-death struggle like the Cold War, its attention span tends to be short. And once engaged in an enterprise it is impatient for results and eager to move on to something else.

These are not characteristics that equip one for intervening deeply in the internal affairs of other countries. One remembers the decisive American intervention in the Philippines a few years ago and the intense excitement and optimism in the United States about Mrs Aquino and "People Power". Hardly anyone in America now gives the Philippines a passing thought – it is yesterday's issue. Meanwhile nothing very much has changed for the better in its political life; it is still the same old game. American "can do" optimism is not very well suited for dealing with the intractable, dense material that makes up alien cultures. It is very difficult to carry things through to successful conclusion. It is very easy to create, and to leave, an unstable mess which others have to live with.

Confucian Confusion

That's one side of the coin. Now let's look at the other – at how Asian countries have comported themselves in these recent disputes. If Americans have proceeded by appealing to, and making their claims in terms of, universal values, Asians have responded by evoking particular civilisational values and circumstances, according to Huntington's script.

In considering their response, we quickly come up against a serious problem with the concept of "civilisation". Any notion of a civilisation is such an abstraction, such a simplification of an indefinitely complex reality, that it must to some extent be arbitrary. Depending on one's standpoint and interest, it is possible to reach quite different, though equally plausible, conclusions regarding the defining characteristics of a civilisation.

This applies to all civilisations. Which best captures the essence of the West: its humanism or its exceptional predilection for warfare? A case can be made either way. As for Confucian society, it is only a few decades ago that it was aggressively argued – not least from the left – that the ethos of Confucianism was uncongenial to the requirements of capitalism, and therefore it was wrong to try to "foist" a market economy on this region. Well, so much for that argument.

In recent disputes, great stress has been laid on the importance that Confucian civilisation places on order as opposed to freedom. But the question arises: What sort of commitment to order does a civilisation have if it inflicts upon itself the terrible convulsions of a Great Leap Forward and a Cultural Revolution within a decade? These are estimated to have killed over 20 million Chinese. They deliberately sought to destroy continuity and bring about instability. So how plausible is the claim that this civilisation puts a high premium on order and cannot therefore extend human rights at a pace that will endanger it? (Attempting to answer this question by saying that the chaos of the 1960s was brought about by communism, not Confucianism, only pushes the problem back a step. How come an order-loving Confucian civilisation gave rise to a revolutionary regime dedicated to making and remaking society at will?)

Again, while it is quite right to regard order as an essential condition for political and economic progress, it is also true that the argument from order is easily and often abused. If patriotism is the last refuge of the scoundrel, order is often the first refuge of an authoritarian. Those who impose order are also its main beneficiaries, and "*Cui bono?*" is an old and sensible question in politics.

The East Strikes Back

Besides defending their own behaviour, the Asians have also launched a vigorous counter-attack against the United States. This counter-attack contains two elements, the socio-cultural and the geopolitical.

On the socio-cultural front, the argument may be summed up in the short biblical admonition: "Physician, heal thyself." American society is so sick, it is said, that far from preaching to others, Americans should be attending to their own ills. Crime, the breakdown of the family, the poor work ethic, the low rate of saving, the indulgence of the individual in the form of excessive solicitude for rights – all this, as Kishore Mahbubani puts it, represents "massive social decay … But instead of travelling overseas with humility, Americans confidently preach the virtues of unfettered individual freedom, blithely ignoring the visible social consequences."

Of this line of argument, I would say the following: First, and just as was the case with left-wing critics of the US in earlier days, everything that the Asian critics know about American civilisation they know because Americans told them. America washes its dirty linen in public; authoritarian governments do not. Who, except the people who live in them and who are not free to speak, knows what are the faults and weaknesses of tightly-controlled authoritarian states? Who has the crime statistics for China? Who would believe any offered by the government in Peking?

Second, serious as the United States' problems are, statistics give a misleading picture of the overall condition of the society. The pathologies they describe are largely concentrated in the inner cities and in the black minority. For example, the murder rate among American whites is actually lower than that of Britain and Italy. The ordinary lives of the majority of Americans are largely unaffected; even in Washington DC, which suffers from most of the pathologies described above, it is possible to live a more or less normal working and social life.

Third, it would be a serious mistake to write off the United States on the basis of its current troubles. Remember Adam Smith's observation that "There is a lot of ruin in a nation." Bear in mind, too, that as well as having the capacity to make big mistakes, the United States also has great energy and capacity for recovery. After a devastating Civil War, the United States quickly recovered and began a long period of spectacular economic growth, overtaking Britain and Germany. During the Great Depression of the 1930s, some of the cleverest people around wrote the United States off as a failure, doomed to irreversible decline. Then it came roaring back and in a few years it was a superpower, producing nearly half the world's wealth.

Fourth, brilliant as are the economies of Asia, in a real sense they are still parasitic on the basic science of the West, which continues to make most of the fundamental breakthroughs on which the technological and communications revolutions depend. Until that ceases to be the case – until, say, Confucian societies have produced their first dozen and a half Nobel Prize-winning scientists – it would be wise to moderate any contempt for the West. (Just to provide a standard of measurement, the Cosmos Club in Washington DC numbers 29 Nobel Prize-winners among its past and present members.)

The same general point applies in the geopolitical area. I would be the first to agree that over the last year the conduct of American foreign policy has been quite feeble. Many Americans share that view and express it openly – spontaneous, unforced, and genuine self-criticism (as opposed to the cruel and compulsory version practised in China) being a Western civilisational characteristic. But it would be a very serious and dangerous error to equate the performance of the Clinton administration with the likely longer-term performance of the United States. It could also be a disastrous error – the kind of error that Saddam Hussein made – to act on the assumption that, in dealing with the United States, "it takes only one soldier to be killed before the whole force will be withdrawn" (Dr Mahathir again).

Little tigers should proceed with caution when they are tempted to characterise big tigers as made of paper. They should be particularly careful if they are likely to need the presence of the alleged paper tiger to provide a stabilising presence in their region. If they assume that China will be a comfortable neighbour, benign and easily managed; or if they are prepared to accept a resumption of the old Middle Kingdom, with themselves as tributary states; or if they are unworried at the prospect of an unpredictable Kim Jong II in possession of nuclear weapons – then, of course, there is no problem.

But, if these conditions do not apply, if they are not prepared to put their trust in a belief that Confucian civilisational harmony and solidarity will override the old truths of power politics (and North Korea, apart from anything else, puts great strain on the notion of civilisational solidarity), then they are going to need the United States, and they should adjust their behaviour and rhetoric accordingly.

For no one else can play the role of balancer to China, should the US vacate the field. Japan would seem the likeliest candidate, but I do not think that Japan can adequately play this role. For one thing, the Japanese homeland is too vulnerable to allow it to do so with any conviction. For another, the psychology is wrong. While Japan is too inhibited and passive to play the balancing role today, once activated and set in motion it could well become too assertive and insensitive to do so. Lee Kuan Yew's gibe that encouraging Japan to send its soldiers abroad, even as part of a peacekeeping force, is like giving chocolate liqueurs to an abstaining alcoholic has its point.

Be Warned

To the extent that Huntington's hypothesis is responded to as a prediction, it may become self-fulfilling. To the extent that it is responded to as a timely warning, it may serve to avoid or mitigate conflict.

I believe that the consequences of the recent fiasco with regard to human rights and MFN may be salutary on the American side. It should serve as a warning that allowing Americans to feel virtuous should not be the object of foreign policy, and that making threats that the country is then not prepared to implement (for very good reasons) is an efficient way of squandering prestige and credibility. To the extent that the United States is serious about promoting human rights, the episode should encourage serious thinking about more effective ways of doing so, whether by promoting economic development and betting on the liberalising effects of modernisation, or by finding other less self-lacerating ways of bringing pressure to bear on the Chinese.

Whether the recent episodes will affect attitudes and behaviour on the Asian side, I don't know. On the face of it, they are less likely to act as an effective warning, because it was the United States which both initiated the incidents and then ignominiously backed down. Indeed, these incidents may be seen in Asia as a sign of things to come – a confirmation of Huntington as predictor – and thus foster not only resentment and hostility toward the United States but also contempt.

Whether the hypothesis of "civilisational conflict" is accepted or rejected, it will be as well to keep in mind the element of truth contained in the maxim: "Everybody's strategy depends on everybody else's." It is a maxim applied to the Western game of poker, but it probably applies just as well to *go* and other Asian games – and to international politics, whether of the traditional power-political kind or of the new culturally-determined variety that may be on the way.

Realism in a New Era

Quadrant, April 1995 [extract]

This essay was originally delivered as the inaugural Richard Krygier Memorial Lecture at La Trobe University, Melbourne, in February 1995. Krygier was the founder of *Quadrant* during the Cold War and was, according to Harries, "a man of imagination, tenacity, modesty and courage. And he had the not inconsiderable virtue of being right on the big issues of his time." A revised version was published in 1996 as "Does Realism Have a Future?" in *Conservative Realism: New Essays in Conservatism*, editor Kenneth Minogue.

There is a sort of circularity about this century. When it began, capitalism was thriving, democracy was spreading, and there was an unprecedented interdependence both within Europe and between European states and their colonial possessions. Liberal internationalists were declaring that war was incompatible with the needs of modern industrial society and was therefore becoming obsolete.

As the end of the century approaches, capitalism is again spreading unprecedented prosperity to new parts of the world, democracy has experienced another wave of expansion, and *interdependence* is once more one of the vogue words of the day. Led by Francis Fukuyama, intellectuals have again been declaring the final triumph of liberal democracy and the end of power politics. And US President Bill Clinton has been enthusiastically echoing them: "In a world where freedom, not tyranny, is on the march, the cynical calculus of pure power politics simply does not compute. It is ill-suited to the new era."

But in the years between 1914 and 1991 – throughout what Eric Hobsbawm has called the short 20th century – power politics, realism, war, and the Cold War in fact prevailed and shaped the age. This was certainly so during the worldwide conflict between two superpowers, with its intense suspicion and sense of insecurity; two global systems of alliances and clients; huge military budgets; and an obsessive concern with the balance of power. What could conform more closely to the realist paradigm of international politics as an affair of interests, power and conflict than all this?

On the communist side, of course, the subordination of socialist ideals and ends to the dictates of realism had been mandatory from the beginning of the regime. Once the Cold War began to take shape, so too did the United States cast aside for the duration of the struggle its traditionally declared repugnance of European-style power politics, and embraced realism. The leading practitioners of US foreign policy in the Cold War – Dean Acheson, George Kennan, John Foster Dulles, Richard Nixon and Henry Kissinger – were avowed realists.

And yet, no sooner did the United States have its resounding triumph in the Cold War than influential voices were immediately raised insisting that the days of realism were now over. Why has this claim been made so insistently in the last three or four years? How valid is it?

⚙⚙⚙

One reason why realism has been discredited and discounted has to do precisely with how the Cold War came to an end – which, on the surface at least, seemed to contradict the logic of realism.

Consider: one day there are two superpowers armed to the teeth and in deadly rivalry. Then, quite suddenly and with virtually no warning, with no-one predicting it, the conflict ends abruptly, without a fight and with virtually no bloodshed. One party, hitherto intransigent, in effect gives up and disintegrates.

Now, according to realists, this sort of thing is not supposed to happen. For sovereign states, and particularly great powers, it is asserted, survival is the most basic interest. They will fight savagely to preserve it. As the English realist Martin Wight once put it, "Great Power status is lost, as it is won, by violence. A Great Power does not die in its bed."

But according to most Western liberals – which is to say, most Western opinion-makers – the Cold War ended when the Soviet

Union did just that. It collapsed, either as the result of internal problems, or because of the enlightened policies of a great statesman, Mikhail Gorbachev; or through some combination of the two. It had little or nothing to do, they insist, with what was happening in the Cold War with power politics.

In 1991, Strobe Talbott, then a senior editor of *Time* magazine and now US Deputy Secretary of State, spoke for most of these liberals when he dismissed as a "conceit" the claims that "anything the outside world had done or not done or threatened to do" (and he particularly meant the policies of the Reagan administration) had played any part in the demise of the Soviet Union. It was Gorbachev alone who deserved the credit. He, not Ronald Reagan, was crowned "Man of the Decade" by *Time* magazine.

Now, if true, that account of things clearly undermines the realist case. But *is* it true? Before deciding that, I suggest that you watch a remarkable four-part television program, *Messengers from Moscow*, produced in Britain and recently shown by the BBC and by PBS in America. In the fourth and last instalment, a series of Russians who held some of the most senior positions in the party, the military, the Ministry of Defence, the KGB, and the Foreign Ministry, testify in frank and unqualified terms about the last years of the Soviet regime. To a man, what they say is that the Reagan administration's policies were crucial factors in the collapse of the Soviet Union – the administration's greatly increased defence budget, its blunt condemnation of the "evil empire" (which repudiated a decade of polite detente), its putting Pershing II missiles into Europe, its giving Stinger missiles and other aid to Afghanistan, and, most of all, its initiating of SDI, the much derided "Star Wars" program.

It was these American policies, the senior Soviet officers testify, that converted the existing chronic problems of the Soviet Union into a terminal crisis. Faced with them, the regime realised that it could no longer compete with the United States, certainly not without transforming itself into something more modern and efficient; it tried desperately to effect such a radical and rapid transformation; there were spectacular unintended consequences; things got completely out of hand; the regime collapsed and the state disintegrated.

These senior ex-Soviet officials may be wrong, of course. But if they are not, the realist position remains essentially undamaged. Many things combined to bring down the Soviet Union, but of enormous importance among them were the policies of the Reagan administration.

ക്കക്ക

However the Cold War ended, its ending generated tremendous euphoria and optimism, and this is a second reason why realism fell into disfavour. It was at odds with the new spirit of the times. Realism is a dour and pessimistic doctrine, one that stresses the inevitability of conflict, the intractability of interests, the dangers of life in a world of sovereign states. The virtues it most strongly recommends are the unexciting ones of prudence and vigilance. It carries most conviction when there are evident threats, a gathering storm; least conviction when the skies are blue and clear – and they seemed very blue and clear between the fall of the Berlin Wall in 1989 and the collapse of the Soviet Union in 1991. In such good times, realists are especially likely to be dismissed – as threat-mongers, cynics, and, most of all, as irrelevant and outdated.

Liberals in particular were in the mood so to dismiss realism. They had spent most of the Cold War in either futile opposition to, or very reluctant support for, a realist policy that was temperamentally uncongenial to them. Now, with the Cold War ended, it could be enthusiastically rejected as the *bête noir* it really is for them.

Realism is an affront to liberalism in many ways:

- It stresses conflict as a central and enduring fact of life, while liberalism asserts a true and peaceful harmony of interests, obscured only by temporary and removable ignorance and misunderstanding.

- Classical realists like Reinhold Niebuhr and Hans Morganthau postulate a universal and unchanging human nature, one that has an incorrigibly selfish and power-seeking component in it; liberals believe either in the innate goodness of man, or in a malleable human nature that can be made good by wise policy and a suitable environment.

- Again, liberals believe profoundly in the redeeming power of institutions – such as the League of Nations, the UN, the European Union, APEC, or whatever – to change, to transform reality. They have a sort of "Build it and they will come" approach to the relationships between structures and behaviour. Realists, on the other hand, believe that institutions essentially reflect reality and have a very limited capacity to change it. (As that old Australian realist, Robert Menzies, once said of faith in the United Nations: believing that it can transform international politics is like believing it is possible to erect a house which will then proceed to dig its own foundations.)

The liberal rejection of realism since the end of the Cold War has come in various forms, most of them representing very durable ideas and powerful longings. As the English journalist Frank Johnson has observed, "In politics, Utopia is always an important country, always one of the Great Powers." And as the Polish satirist Stanislaw Lec sardonically advises, "When smashing the monuments, save the pedestals. They always come in handy."

The most superficial utopian, anti-realist line has been salvation through the United Nations, now free – with the Cold War over and its vetoes ended – to function as it was supposed to, thus transforming the nature of world politics. A short but adequate response to this is that if the UN is the answer, the question is wrongly framed. The UN does not replace power politics, it merely disguises it.

A much more interesting version of post-Cold War optimism, and one that challenges realism more effectively, is the salvation-through-democracy thesis: democracy is spreading rapidly; the historical record shows that democracies do not go to war with each other; therefore we are moving to a state of affairs in which war will become obsolete. Now, we can quibble about the details, but the historical claim is in fact pretty sound.

This leaves us with a crucial question: whether what has been substantially true up to now of a limited number of democracies, overwhelmingly Western in culture, will remain true of a much larger and culturally diverse number of democracies in the future. That is, is it the political system or the culture that has been the crucial factor in the case of Western democracies? This is one of the many forms in which the question of culture is increasingly intruding itself into international politics.

The democratic argument does draw attention to one of the serious shortcomings of realism. In its stress on the structure of the international system, that is, the state of anarchy among sovereign states, realism attaches little or no importance to what is going on *inside* states – what kind of regimes are in power, what kind of ideologies prevail, what kind of leadership is provided. According to realists, the foreign policies of all states are basically driven by the same systemic factors – they are like so many billiard balls, obeying the same laws of political geometry and physics.

This is enormously counterintuitive and a real weakness, especially in an age of ideology. Did it really make no difference to German foreign policy whether the regime in power was the Weimar Republic or the Nazis? Was it not precisely the failure to recognise the difference that led Neville Chamberlain and other hard-headed conservatives to think that they could cut a deal with Hitler in the traditional way? I shall be returning to this question later in a different context, for it is pertinent today when thinking of Russia.

A third challenge to realism in the post-Cold War era is even more fundamental and strikes at the basic premise of the realist approach. The political world is, according to realists, chopped up vertically into sovereign states. These states have boundaries that they control and defend and regard as inviolable. International politics is about relations between these vertically-divided states.

Until now that has been a basically true picture of the political world. No longer, say an increasing number of influential voices, who claim that this vertical version of the world is rapidly being replaced by a horizontally-ordered one. The decisive forces in today's world – even more so in tomorrow's world – it is asserted, are capital, technology and, especially, information. Increasingly, and with ever greater velocity, these spread horizontally across the surface of the earth, recognising no impediments, no national limits. We are moving rapidly towards a borderless world in which sovereignty is a myth, the state a fiction, and interdependence and integration the overriding realities. In such a world, state rivalries and military force make little sense – the realist's world is an anachronism.

This is a sermon preached by many leaders of industry and by academics and intellectuals. You could hear it, for example, in Rupert Murdoch's recent Bonython lecture[*] – and he himself embodies much of what this worldview is about.

What can one say about it? A lot, but I'll just make two points. First, while it presents itself as a cutting-edge view, it has a very familiar ring to it. A century and a half ago, Marx and Engels were declaring that "in place of the old local and national seclusion and self-sufficiency, we have interaction in every direction, universal interdependence of nations," and they went on to announce the withering away of states. Well, they have been a long time withering and have shown themselves to be extremely tough, durable and adaptable institutions.

Second, this picture of the world is very Western-centred. If the United States and European countries have allowed their borders to become very porous in many respects, this is certainly *not* true of much of the rest of the world – not of Japan or China or Iran or Korea, for instance. Henry Kissinger recently observed that there is little Wilsonian idealism in Asia; and, he could have added, neither is there much "borderless worldism".

---

* *Editors' note*: Rupert Murdoch, *The Century of Networking*, Eleventh Annual John Bonython Lecture (JBL), 20 October 1994. The JBL is the Sydney-based Centre for Independent Studies' premier annual lecture.

ଌଌଌ

So much for the immediate post-Cold War period, but five years have passed since the Berlin Wall came down and we are now entering what we shall have to call, inelegantly, the post-post-Cold War era. What is that going to be like? What insights might realism provide as to its nature? Let us start with the two erstwhile superpowers, for much will depend on how they perform, or fail to perform.

The immediate and natural reaction to the end of the Cold War was that the collapse of one superpower left the other supreme. The United States as "the sole remaining superpower" would dominate the world scene and its will would shape the new era. As cool a customer as Richard Nixon declared that "because we are the last remaining superpower, no crisis is irrelevant to our interests." American leadership in the Gulf War initially seemed to confirm this view. True, since then the United States has been much more indecisive and ineffectual, but most commentators have been content to blame that on the incompetence of the Clinton administration, an accidental and temporary factor.

I have argued that this explanation is inadequate and superficial, that for deeper reasons the United States is unlikely to perform effectively the role that this scenario designates to it. It is unlikely to do so because it now lacks the will, the compelling need and drive to play the role of superpower.

This can be put in different ways. One way of putting it is that the phrase "sole remaining superpower" is an oxymoron, a contradiction in terms, at least when applied to the United States. In superpower politics, it takes two to tango. Changing the metaphor, the game is a relational one, not solitaire. If you have two superpowers and you take one away, what you have left is less than a superpower because the incentive, the compulsion to mobilise and deploy resources, and to convert potential into performance is no longer there.

To put this in a slightly different way: as the collapse of the Soviet Union has underlined, the conventional realist way of measuring power is inadequate. It has put too much stress on what is material and quantifiable – manpower, arms, productive capacity – and not enough on motivation. In the case of cancerous states like Napoleonic France, Hitler's Germany or Stalin's Soviet Union, the motivation for dominance is self-generating and insatiable. In normal states it is not; they need the galvanising sense of danger and threat that the presence of a great rival creates. Capacity, potential – these alone do not make a superpower. Otherwise, after all, the United States would have been a superpower back in the 1920s, which, of course, it wasn't.

The United States will, it goes without saying, continue to be an important presence – indeed, the single most important presence – on the world stage. Its natural weight and, for a while, the habits acquired during the Cold War will ensure that. But in the case of the United States, foreign policy needs a great goal to drive it. Hence the obsession with formulating "doctrines" – from Monroe to Reagan – and the endless current demands for enabling "visions". Such a great defining goal is now lacking. In its absence, America will not dominate and stamp its will, and gradually new priorities and inhibitions will affect its pattern of behaviour, setting narrower limits – the need to attend to pressing domestic matters; the reluctance to suffer casualties except when vital interests are concerned; the need for multilateral cover to justify its actions.

All this will be interpreted as weakness or "decline" by those who expected superpower behaviour. But it will really only represent different circumstances, priorities and needs.

Turning to the other erstwhile superpower, Russia, I believe that this is a case in which the realist approach has its dangers. As I noted earlier, realism deals in states, not regimes, and maintains that the foreign policies of states tend to be continuous over long periods, regardless of regime changes. It is not surprising, then, that leading realists – notably Kissinger and Brzezinski – tend to view Russia today with the same suspicion and wariness that they showed towards the Soviet Union. Their expectations of imperialist behaviour are largely shaped by the history of Soviet and, before that, czarist foreign policy, and there is little inclination to give any benefit of the doubt to the struggling democratic government in Moscow.

Questions arise: What were we opposing in the Cold War – a totalitarian regime and ideology, or Russia as Russia? Was not a democratic Russia one of the outcomes we wanted – not only because it would be better for the Russians, but because it would make it an easier country to live with? If so, instead of presuming a continuation of bad behaviour, and basing policy accordingly (notably by the eastward expansion of NATO), should we not be prepared to exercise some patience, and remember Churchill's advice: in victory, magnanimity? Are there not distinctions to be made between imperialist behaviour and a desperate attempt to hold a chaotic country together? And, regrettable as it is, is it not virtually inevitable that a period of great transition will be characterised by some violence and brutality? Think of the British departure from India or Kenya; or the French from Vietnam or Algeria.

These are vitally important questions. Once already in this century, Western countries created a terrible crisis and allowed an unnecessary world war to happen because they assumed that the foreign policy of a totalitarian regime would be no different from that of the struggling democracy it replaced. It would be inexcusable and disastrous if they made the same error in reverse at the end of the century, by proceeding on the assumption that the policy of a struggling democracy was no different from that of the totalitarian regime that preceded it. The great danger with Russia today is not imperialism, but anarchy and chaos – not an assertive, purposeful state, but the collapse of the state.

I've mentioned NATO, so let me turn to that question. Realism is mostly thought of as a safeguard and antidote against utopianism. But there are other things which prevent realists from seeing things as they are, which promote illusions and create distortions. Prominent among them is habit, which causes one to focus on the reality of yesterday, not today.

I believe this is the case with NATO now. NATO was a magnificent Cold War achievement, arguably the most successful alliance in history. But the threat it was meant to contain, and the force it was meant to balance, no longer exist. A Russia which is having its work cut out to quell Chechnya is no threat to world peace. Yet the survival – and indeed the expansion – of NATO is treated as a vital issue; and the continuing political and strategic unity of "the West" is taken for granted as a permanent fact of life, though except during the periods of the hot and cold world wars of this century it has never existed before.

There are, of course, powerful vested interests involved here – many careers and contracts and consultancies and reputations. But the most powerful vested interest is in certain ideas and ways of looking at things with which we are comfortable: yesterday's realism.

A further example of the grip of habit is that people continue speaking of "the West" while simultaneously advancing the incompatible opinion that the structure of the new era will be triangular or tripolar, with North America, the Asia-Pacific and Europe representing the three poles. But, of course, such a tripolar conceptualisation denies the unity of the West and splits it into two separate, competing parts. Now, it is true that Scott Fitzgerald once suggested that the test of a first-rate intelligence is the ability to hold two opposed ideas in the mind at the same time, and still retain the ability to function. But he was speaking as a novelist, not a strategist, and on the whole it is better for strategists to avoid holding contradictory ideas simultaneously.

ৡৡৡ

Speaking of the tripolar model brings the Asia-Pacific region into the picture, and this raises a different and intriguing kind of question. The realist theory of foreign policy was developed on the basis of the experience of Western states, and indeed for several centuries all the principal actors in world politics – all the great powers – belonged to that one civilisation. Power politics was a Western game, so cultural or civilisational factors did not come into consideration because they were a constant, a given. The first significant partial exception to this was Japan in the middle of this century, and its attitude towards diplomacy, war, the treatment of prisoners and so on suggested that all Western generalisations might not hold true for other cultures. Ruth Benedict's famous work, *The Chrysanthemum and the Sword*, was an early attempt to probe this question.

Now, with the political and economic rise of states in other civilisations – particularly in Asia – the question has become urgent. Will the generalisations of realism apply and hold true for non-Western actors who are destined to assume a much greater role in the scheme of things? Will the universal human nature that classical realism posits, or the international anarchy that neo-realism sees as crucial, override the cultural differences between civilisations?

Some raised early doubts in this respect. As long ago as 1968, for example, Coral Bell, herself a realist by temperament, argued that the central realist notion of a balance of power system was foreign to China, with its traditional belief that "there can only be one sun in the sky" and its model of a kind of solar system of imperial dependencies and vassal states around the sun of the Middle Kingdom. But other China specialists, including John Fairbanks of Harvard, disputed such a view, speaking of the "deeply ingrained attitude towards foreign relations as a problem in the balancing of foreign powers against each other to China's advantage." Certainly, Henry Kissinger, no mean judge, has been impressed with the

Chinese grasp of realpolitik. But on the other hand, for long periods of the Cold War, China simultaneously alienated both superpowers, showing no concern for balancing one against the other.

Again, some would argue that the fact that Japan in recent years has become the second most powerful economic power in the world without developing comparable military power, and without engaging seriously in great power politics, shows that it is different in kind. But, of course, Japan has behaved in this way while its security was being looked after by a friendly and dominant United States – in very much the same way that the United States itself, in an earlier age, did not engage very actively in power politics as long as its interests were protected by a friendly British navy. That is, it might not have a cultural explanation but a political and strategic one, and it might not outlive the favourable condition of American protection and American maintenance of an Asia-Pacific balance.

Some argue that as economic growth proceeds and "modernisation" occurs, Asia will become more like us: that modernisation will equal Westernisation – with Westernisation usually taken to mean "liberal and democratic". Again, *perhaps*; though many Asians (and many others) insist that in their case there will be a different synthesis of economic, social and political elements. Whether this is true or not – whether there is only one modernising road or several – seems to me one of the crucial questions of our time. For example, a Western academic at the University of Singapore, David Martin Jones, argues that those who believe that the rising middle classes in Asia will perform the same political functions as they did earlier in the West – that is, pressing for democracy, a civil society and human rights – are doomed to be disappointed, that these Asian middle classes are regime-supporting and stability-oriented. I'm not sure whether he will be promoted, demoted, deported, or caned for saying this.

Before leaving this question of the possible influence of civilisational differences on political behaviour and relations, let me make one further point. These are legitimate and vitally important questions that need to be discussed, especially in a culturally Western country like Australia that exists in a non-Western region. Out of diplomatic delicacy and prudence, it may be necessary for governments to walk gingerly around such questions on occasion. But for people who are paid to think and tell the truth to declare these questions off-limits, and to characterise efforts to discuss them as "racist", seems to me to be professionally and morally disgraceful. I have tried to identify some enemies of realism. Well, a squeamish, deferential, guilt-ridden political correctness is another formidable enemy of the attempt to see things as they really are.

⚭⚭⚭

Let me return briefly to the big picture. At the beginning, I emphasised the initial euphoria at the end of the Cold War and the extent to which realism is an effective antidote to the wishful fantasies of utopians. But its sobriety and coolness is also the best antidote to the doom-laden and rather hysterical prophecies of dystopians, those who see the world as rapidly and unstoppably going to hell. I make the point because, after the initial grand hopes that accompanied the end of the Cold War were disappointed – after Bosnia and Somalia and Rwanda and Georgia and Chechnya – there has recently been a violent swing to doom-saying. Fashionable American intellectuals now talk of "chaos theory". A great deal of attention has been given over the last year, for example, to an article by Robert Kaplan titled "The Coming Anarchy" in the *Atlantic Monthly*.

In my opinion, it is a poor article, the sort of thing that gives pessimism a bad name. Its commitment to a catastrophic view of the future is such that it offers, without any serious argument, contemporary West Africa as a paradigm of the world's future: a world of gross overpopulation, environmental degradation, crime, corruption, and a general breakdown of government and civil society. While it is eloquent on the horrors of West Africa, the success story of East Asia is hardly mentioned. It is a sensationalist, un-argued and pretentious article (and I say this as an editor who has published Kaplan in the past). The problems and dangers that are pointed to are real and serious enough. But like their utopian opposites, what the dystopians do is focus on a few trends, treat them as irreversible, ignore countervailing forces, allow for no surprises, and for no learning and no corrective action.

Realism is a good counter to dystopianism, both because its natural, controlled pessimism acts as an inoculation against extreme kinds of panic-mongering, and because its commitment to trying to see things as they are involves a balanced appraisal, taking account of positive factors as well as negative ones.

I haven't felt it necessary to spell out formally the components of the realist position – and to tell you the truth, I don't think it *is* much of a coherent theory. When academics have tried to make it one, they have soon got themselves into trouble and entangled in contradictions. But if it isn't much of an intellectual position, it is an excellent *dis*position with which to approach foreign policy and international affairs. Let me share a short quotation that encapsulates in vivid form the essence of that disposition.

In the midst of an argument about the appropriate way to respond to someone who was being unpleasant, Dr Johnson once said:

> If a madman were to come into this room with a stick in his hand, no doubt we should pity the state of his mind; but our primary consideration would be to take care of ourselves. We should knock him down first, and pity him afterwards.

There you have much that is central to the realist disposition: its awareness of danger as a natural part of life; its stress on self-reliance and its guiltless acknowledgment of the need to put self-interest first; its willingness to use force prudentially; the overriding priority given to survival; and the consequent recognition that, while humanitarian impulses are fine, they cannot be overriding and must be kept subordinate in the order of things.

In the sense of a basic disposition that assumes these things to be true in human affairs, I don't think that realism is in any danger of becoming outdated or irrelevant any time soon.

India: Relevant at Last?

The National Interest, Spring 1997

This is a year of 50th anniversaries. Soon, and very properly, Americans will be celebrating two decisions that truly deserve the adjective "seminal" – those embodied in the Truman Doctrine (birthday 15 May) and the Marshall Plan (5 June). Taken together, these decisions went far toward defining the epoch of global politics that followed.

Less likely to get much attention in coming months is a third 50th anniversary, that marking the independence of India and Pakistan on 15 August 1947. In its way, though, it is as historically significant as the other two.

The achievement of independence by the Indian subcontinent marked the effective end of the age of European imperialism. Its symbolic significance was enormous: If, in the immediate aftermath of its triumph in the Second World War, the greatest of Western empires was unable to maintain possession of the jewel in its crown, the clear message to the other European colonial powers – nearly all of them recently defeated and occupied in war – was that the game was up. A wholesale, rapid, and somewhat indecorous retreat followed. Within two decades there was scarcely a Western colony left, the number of independent states had trebled, the "Third World" had been invented – and, in retrospect, we were left wondering by what feat of legerdemain had a small number of European states managed to impose their will for so long on such a large segment of the world.

India was the first Third World country and it remains the greatest and most interesting of them. But it has never seized the American imagination – as over the last 100 years its great neighbour, China, so conspicuously has and it has never figured large in Washington's political and strategic calculations.

In one respect this is very odd. The United States and India are the world's two largest democracies. Despite having a bigger population than the whole of Africa, and despite the fact that that population is riven by religious, linguistic, regional, and caste differences (and that half of it is illiterate), India has maintained – with occasional lapses – a functioning parliamentary system, an independent judiciary, a free press, and civilian control of the military. But although this is something that virtually all other Third World states have signally failed to do, and although promoting and sustaining democracy abroad is frequently identified as a major American foreign policy concern, India's conspicuous success in this regard has attracted little American attention or praise. Instead, the American attitude toward India over the last five decades can fairly be described as a variable mixture of indifference and impatience.

It has to be said that in traditional foreign policy and strategic terms this treatment has not been entirely undeserved. A combined diet of Hinduism, the London School of Economics, and Kingsley Martin's *New Statesman* proved to be a bad preparation for conducting foreign policy, and against all the odds the Indian political elite managed to make their country largely irrelevant in world politics.

They made three serious mistakes. First, they failed to secure their back door and have thus remained preoccupied with the threats posed by Pakistan and China, and unable effectively to project their energy outward. Second, for many years they put their money on the Non-Aligned Movement, of which they were one of the founders. This was not only an intrinsically unsatisfactory instrument, but one which, because of the one-country-one-vote rule, was increasingly dominated by smaller, but more numerous and united, African states who were unimpressed by the claims of moral leadership emanating from Delhi. Third, in so far as they moved away from Cold War non-alignment, they chose the wrong side, entering into something resembling a de-facto alliance with Moscow. This they did partly to counter a perceived threat from

China, partly out of resentment at the US-Pakistan connection, but also partly as a matter of ideological – that is, "socialist" – preference.

The same ideological preference made India less interesting than it should have been to Western economic interests. From the beginning – and bear in mind that that the beginning coincided with the heyday of Fabian socialism, as represented by the Attlee government in Great Britain – the Indian political elite opted for central planning, public ownership, tight regulation, and protectionism. As a result its economy lagged, its foreign trade remained modest, and it was both inhospitable and unattractive to foreign investment.

⏊⏊⏊

Given the combination of past neglect and upcoming anniversary, the appearance of a report prepared by a Council on Foreign Relations task force on *A New US Policy Toward India and Pakistan* is timely. The chairman of the group was Richard Haass and its project director Gideon Rose, both of whose names will be familiar to *National Interest* readers.

The new policy in question is thought to be needed because the international situation has altered radically, and, the report argues, because the status of the two countries is in the process of changing. On the one hand, Pakistan is in imminent danger of becoming a failed state; on the other, India is at last demonstrating something that, with different policies, it might have shown much earlier – the potential to become a full-fledged major power.

The report's prescriptions concerning policy toward the two countries are strikingly different. In the case of Pakistan there is simply modest advice to "restore normalcy and close working relations"; in the case of India there is the much more ambitious conclusion that "the time is propitious for the United States to propose a closer strategic relationship", and that "the United States (should) adopt a declaratory policy that acknowledges India's growing power and importance", as well as take a number of significant practical steps to give the relationship real substance.

What justifies the conclusion that "the time is propitious" for such a major change of policy? Two things, one domestic and the other international. First, in recent years India has at last begun to modify its *dirigiste* economic policies – lowering tariffs, reducing restrictions on foreign investment and ownership, engaging in a modest amount of privatisation. There is still a long way to go, and the obstructive powers of the Indian bureaucracy remain formidable. But over the last 17 years the annual growth rate has averaged over 5% and the Indian economy has become progressively more interesting to the West.

Second, US geopolitical interests in Asia have changed in ways that enhance India's importance. The report does not say much about the rising power of China, but it is very much there between the lines, and it, more than anything else, is what enhances the strategic importance of a well-armed and increasingly prosperous India in the eyes of those Americans who see the containment of China as the central mission of US foreign policy in its next phase. Additionally, the rise of a militant and intolerant Hindu nationalism in India in recent years, and the tension it has generated with the Islamic states to the west, cause India to be seen by some Americans as a potential ally against Islamic fundamentalism. As China develops closer relations with Islamic states, it is argued, so it makes sense for the United States to enter into a partnership with India.

Four years ago in these pages, Ross Munro launched an all-out attack on the idea of such a US-Indian strategic partnership. He argued that "such an alignment would imperil US interests, not advance them", and that an ally as weak and vulnerable as India would be "not an asset but a burden". Part of his opposition was based on extreme scepticism about India's economic reforms and their prospects, part on the belief that such an alliance would polarise the region and drive moderate Muslims toward militant Islam. Implicit was the belief that the United States would become hostage to an India that had unrealistic ambitions and an effortless capacity to alienate its neighbours.

There is no acknowledgment of the existence of such arguments, let alone an attempt to confront them, in the main body of the Haass-Rose report, which makes it an intellectually less interesting document than it might have been. A possible reason for this omission emerges when one turns to the unusually large number of "Additional and Dissenting Views" that accompany the main report.

Most of these views are very friendly to India and strongly endorse the proposal of a strategic partnership with it. Their criticism is focused on the other central concern of the report, that of nuclear proliferation. India and Pakistan are now de-facto "nuclear weapons-capable" states. The report argues that the US government should give up trying to reverse that status, both because success is unlikely and because it has the effect of constricting bilateral relations at a time when they need to be developed. Instead, the report maintains, the United States should work to establish "a more stable and sustainable plateau for Indian and Pakistani nuclear relations" – in other words, it advocates attempting restraint rather than rollback.

One would have thought that this would be perceived as a conclusion highly favourable to India. But the interesting thing is that most of the dissenting views – one of them signed by five members of the panel – do not criticise the report for being too generous toward India on the proliferation issue but for being too harsh, as its recommendations, if implemented, would put India at a permanent disadvantage with respect to the full-fledged nuclear-weapons states. (At the same time, most of the dissenters favour a much tougher line toward Pakistan, ostensibly on the not very compelling ground that, unlike India, it has imported some of its nuclear technology.) Given the evident strength of this pro-Indian point of view on the panel, it is reasonable to speculate that it might have been impractical to rehearse a strong anti-Indian case in the report.

That said, it must be acknowledged that on the particular issue of proliferation – as it refers to both India *and* Pakistan – the central argument of its dissenters has force. As they say, "the entire effort of the United States to establish universal non-proliferation regimes that indefinitely perpetuate the inequality between the nuclear-weapons states, including China, and non-nuclear weapons states, including India, is designed to relegate India to second-class status." In the absence of any sign that the United States or any of the other four nuclear forces intend to honour Article VI of the Nuclear Non-Proliferation Treaty (NPT) by moving to reduce and ultimately eliminate their nuclear arsenals, such efforts amount merely to an attempt to perpetuate a five-power nuclear monopoly. They can claim no moral force – no disinterested concern for the "common good" – and while it might be possible to force India to comply by political pressure, there is no reason why the government in Delhi should do so voluntarily. In the negotiations on the Comprehensive Test Ban Treaty, it made it clear that it will not, even if this means standing alone.

In this respect, what I believe the report's treatment of the proliferation issue inadvertently, but usefully, underlines is the difficulty – indeed the impossibility – of reconciling the role of the US government as the protector and promoter of American interests, and the aspirations some have that it should be the disinterested custodian and arbiter of an impartial world order. As the country searches for a foreign policy appropriate to a new era, that is a lesson with an application far beyond the Indian subcontinent. It is one that events are likely to teach us long before the NPT celebrates *its* 50th anniversary.

A Reluctant Realist

The New York Times, 29 March 1998

A review of Abba Eban's *Diplomacy for the Next Century*, Yale University Press, 1998.

For two and a half decades – a very long time in world politics – Abba Eban was a significant player on the international scene. In 1947, as a young man of 32, he was at Chaim Weizmann's side during the crucial United Nations vote endorsing the creation of Israel. In the aftermath of the 1973 Arab-Israeli war, he was still Israel's Foreign Minister. In between, he served long spells as Ambassador to Washington and representative to the United Nations, his country's two most important diplomatic posts.

His finest hour came at the United Nations in 1956, when he had to protect the interests of an Israel abandoned and isolated after the Suez crisis. Conor Cruise O'Brien, who was there, describes him at that time in less than heroic terms, ones that underline just how atypical an Israeli political figure Eban was: "portly in appearance, and rather plummy in public discourse; he looked like Beach the Butler, and sounded like an archbishop." But after this O'Brien continues: "Many people underestimated him; a great mistake." Indeed, he goes on to compare Eban's efforts at damage control on this occasion to those of Talleyrand after the defeat of France in 1814-15 – surely the ultimate compliment for a diplomat.

Eban also played a crucial role in the lead-up to the 1967 Arab-Israeli war, particularly in presenting Israel's case to President Lyndon Johnson in a way that made its ultimate resort to force acceptable. Partly because of their different focuses and priorities, and partly reflecting a difference of style, the hard men directly responsible for Israel's survival did not always fully appreciate Eban's efforts. Generals and diplomats rarely see eye-to-eye, and Yitzhak Rabin and Moshe Dayan tended to dismiss Eban as a mere conveyor of their messages. This was a travesty. In reality, Eban's efforts abroad brilliantly complemented their incredible military feats.

In this short book, *Diplomacy for the Next Century*, Eban gives us the distilled essence of his views. They are those of a realist – that is to say, someone who believes that self-interest is what determines the behaviour of states, that insecurity and rivalry are inherent in the system, and that power is the final arbiter in that rivalry. If I were asked to nominate a brief, readable introduction to what realism in foreign policy means, or should mean, this book would now join a very short list (along with, in the order of their publication, Walter Lippmann's *US Foreign Policy*, Martin Wight's *Power Politics* and George F. Kennan's *Realities of American Foreign Policy*).

Eban's book would be on that list, first and not least, because it is exceptionally well-written. It is entirely free from jargon, obscurity and cliché, and it has a concision and elegance that are rare in writing about international affairs. Even when the point he is making is familiar, he is usually able to give it near-epigrammatic sharpness. Thus on a crucial question, one that has great relevance to today's discussion of "hegemony", he cuts through thickets of obfuscation by simply observing that "the alternative to a balance of power is an imbalance of power, which has usually provoked wars and has never consolidated peace." On one of the serious drawbacks of open diplomacy: "Once your fallback positions are published, you have already fallen back to them"; on deterrence: "The science of things that do not occur"; on the tempo of international politics: "Diplomats touch nothing that they do not adjourn." And to establish where ultimate loyalties reside and the difficulty of transferring them to the "world community", he gently reminds us that "when Americans landed on the moon, they planted their own Stars and Stripes on that bleak landscape, not a portrayal of planet Earth."

Another strength of the book is that Eban is at ease with the history of diplomacy, early and recent, in a way that is rare today. He uses that history not as decoration but to illuminate matters of substance, and he does so with specific examples rather than sweeping generalisations. Thus, reflecting on the "long peace" between 1815 and 1914, he makes the thought-provoking, because counterintuitive, point that it was secured "in an age in which war aroused no moral revulsion." When he wishes to demonstrate the fateful but neglected role that ignorance can play in the affairs of the world, he quotes Woodrow Wilson's admission, "I never knew that there were a million Germans in Bohemia." And he is able to draw attention to a major change in the dynamics of international politics merely by recalling that the leaders of Britain and America in the years leading to World War II, Prime Minister Neville Chamberlain and President Franklin D. Roosevelt, never met. (How many Cold-War-oriented international relations specialists would even have known that?)

Eban is parsimonious with those well-rehearsed set-piece stories of the great that are the bane of most diplomatic writing, but the book is studded with crisp and illuminating characterisations of leaders with whom he worked. The Anthony Eden of the Suez crisis is neatly and exactly summed up as "probably over experienced". Yitzhak Rabin was "more frugal in the distribution of praise than anyone I have ever met." Henry Kissinger's dominance is conveyed by the phrase "the only US Secretary of State under whom two Presidents served." And no progress was made at the Madrid conference of 1992 because "Yitzhak Shamir was having a passionate love affair with the status quo." Perhaps one has to read writing on international affairs for a living to have a full appreciation of the freshness of such prose.

While these qualities are anything but negligible, the most compelling reason for recommending this book is the nature of Eban's realism. Realists come in various shapes, not all of them attractive or illuminating. There are the scholastic and doctrinaire, lost in their elaborate closed systems. There are the cynical and gleeful, delighted to find hypocrisy and gullibility all around them. There are the ostentatiously tough and assertive, forever flexing their muscles. And again, there is the attenuated realism – an accountant's realism, one might say – that insists on reducing all human affairs to what is palpable and measurable, and dismisses such things as ideas and ideals and passions from its calculations.

Abba Eban I would describe as a reluctant realist, and that is the best sort. His understanding of the world has been hard-earned – reached, I surmise, against the grain of both his temperament and background. (He grew up in the Britain of the interwar years, when realism was hardly in the ascendant, and his education culminated in the very liberal atmosphere that prevailed in the Cambridge University of the 1930s.)

What made Eban a realist was Israel's precarious predicament during the whole of the period he served his country. It was a predicament that left no room for illusion or sentiment and little for altruism or optimism.

In its origins, Eban's realism was situational rather than temperamental, and it remains sceptical rather than cynical, pragmatic rather than dogmatic. It is characterised as much by reservation as by assertion. He is cautious about generalisations – "international events, like fingerprints, are marked by particularity, not similarity" – and late in the book he declares, "My most emphatic conclusion about diplomacy is that there are no general solutions for particular cases." Realism is much healthier when it is characterised by the tension that such reluctance conveys, by an ultimate uncertainty and modesty concerning the world. This is especially the case when there is a lot of what Yeats called "passionate intensity" in the air.

All this having been said, I regret having to end with a caveat. *Diplomacy for the Next Century* has 176 pages of text, but the book I have been reviewing to this point ends on page 140. The following pages, which contain two chapters on the Middle East peace negotiations, strike me as markedly inferior in quality of analysis and argument to what has gone before. They are characterised not by the cool detachment of the rest of the book but by a desire for a happy outcome, to be achieved even at the expense of a recalcitrant reality. But then, Abba Eban is not the first man whose admirable qualities shine more brightly abroad than when dealing with matters closer to home.

The Anglosphere Illusion

The National Interest, Spring 2001 [extract]

Based on a presentation at a Hudson Institute seminar in Berkshire, England, an edited version was published in *Prospect* (London) in April 2001. The essay was also reprinted as Appendix Three in Owen Harries, *Benign or Imperial? Reflections on American Hegemony*, ABC Books, February 2004.

During recent months, many people have looked back to the beginning of the 20th century to find parallels with our present circumstances. Thus the position of Britain then – both with respect to its dominance and the first signs of its decline – has been compared to that of the United States today; the significance of the rise of Germany then has been compared to the anticipated emergence of China as a genuine world power in the near future. And Norman Angell's belief – given expression on the eve of World War I – that interdependence was rendering war obsolete has been seen as the equivalent of the current faith in the pacific effects of globalisation and the spread of democracy.

There is another parallel that deserves mention. Today, a few thoughtful and eloquent individuals – among them Robert Conquest and John O'Sullivan – have been making the case for an English-speaking political union. The argument is that the United States, Britain, Canada, Australia, New Zealand and a few other smaller entities have so much in common in terms of political culture, values and institutions that they should draw together and enter into some sort of formal arrangement to act in concert – to create, that is, what some are now referring to as a political "Anglosphere".

Now this line of argument almost exactly replicates one advanced by a group of highly-intelligent, well-educated and well-connected young men at the beginning of the last century. The group – known as Milner's Kindergarten, after its patron, Lord Milner, or sometimes as the Cliveden Set, because of its connection with the Astor family – included among others Philip Kerr (later, as Lord Lothian, Britain's ambassador to Washington during World War II), Lionel Curtis (founder of Chatham House) and Geoffrey Dawson (to be for 26 years editor of *The Times*, when that newspaper still had great political influence).

The historian Norman Rose has recently written about this group in terms that could be applied, almost word for word, to today's advocates of an English-speaking union:

> What they meant by "doing things in the world" was primarily to sustain the Anglo-Saxon fraternity. Dedicated to an intimate partnership between the Dominions and Britain, perhaps federation or even union, and a strengthening of the Anglo-American connection, they aimed in this way to preserve Britain's distinctive role in international affairs.

The similarity extends also to what they disliked and feared: "For Kerr and his friends, France was the bogeyman of Europe. There was an almost paranoid fear that scheming French politicians would embroil Britain in disputes at variance with its genuine interests."

The ideas propounded by the group reflected both the reality of British imperial power and the fear that, unless girded up, that power was doomed to decline. This view of things had enough appeal that at the grand intergovernmental Imperial Conference of 1911 a proposal was made – it was formally put by Joseph Ward, Prime Minister of New Zealand, the smallest and most British of the English-speaking Dominions – for an Imperial Parliament, to be responsible for formulating common foreign and defence policies for the Empire.

The proposal was promptly shot down by Canada and South Africa, both of whom had substantial non-English populations that were not susceptible to the charms of Anglo-Saxon tradition. Indeed, while such an arrangement would have served the interests of Britain, as the strongest party, it was inimical to the quickly strengthening national sentiments of countries that had only just moved from subservient status to independence.

Values and Interests

If the idea of an English-speaking union, based on a common heritage and shared values, was not a goer in 1911, what are its prospects today? A consideration of that question should begin by considering an episode that occurred almost exactly midway between the Imperial Conference of 1911 and the present – the Suez crisis of 1956.

Recall that this crisis erupted a mere decade after the end of World War II. Those Americans and Britons who had worked so closely together to win that war were still running things: Dwight Eisenhower and his generation in Washington; Anthony Eden and his in London. Britain still possessed a vast empire and substantial armed forces based on compulsory national service. Britain and France were America's principal allies. The Cold War was going strong. Within a year the Soviet Union would put Sputnik into space, seriously shaking American confidence.

In that year, 1956, the Egyptian military dictator, Gamal Abdel Nasser, seized the Suez Canal from the company that owned it [in which the British and French had shares] and proceeded to nationalise it. Both the British and French regarded this as an outrageously immoral act. Even worse, they believed it a serious threat to their strategic interests. The British still had substantial colonial holdings in Southeast Asia, close links with Australia and New Zealand, and a vital interest in Middle East oil. They regarded the canal as the "jugular vein" of their imperial system, and Nasser's actions as unacceptable.

After some futile negotiation, the British and French, acting in collusion with Israel, decided to seize back the Canal from Nasser. They did so in secret – partly to maintain military surprise, partly because they believed that the United States would be unsympathetic to what they were doing. They acted – very slowly and very ineptly, it has to be said – but before they achieved their goal the United States publicly denounced their action and led its condemnation at the UN. Even more decisively, by manipulating the currency and oil markets to create a crisis for Britain and France, and by using the US Sixth Fleet to harass the Anglo-French task force as it approached Port Said, Washington forced the abandonment of the military expedition. The upshot was that these two principal allies of the United States, which were also two of the world's leading democracies, were publicly humiliated before the eyes of the world. It was a truly traumatic event, especially for the British, whose pretensions to still being a great global power were never to recover.

Why did the United States act as it did? From a mixture of motives. Partly it was a long-standing distaste for and suspicion of European imperialism, of which this crisis was seen as a clear example. Partly it was a Cold War concern not to alienate the Arab countries and drive them into Moscow's arms. Partly it was a realpolitik concern to displace the British and French as the main influence over the oil-producing countries. Partly it was because of the complicating factor of the Hungarian Uprising, which coincided with the Suez crisis. And, not least, partly it was that the whole thing happened in the middle of a US presidential campaign, which made it more than usually necessary for the Eisenhower administration to appear whiter than white in terms of high principle. (Not long after the event, Selwyn Lloyd, the British Foreign Minister, was left gasping in astonishment when John Foster Dulles, the then US Secretary of State, blandly asked him, "Selwyn, Why did you stop? Why didn't you go through with it and get Nasser down?" A real case of adding insult to injury, one might think.)

ॐ ॐ ॐ

I have recounted this episode at length because it bears on my theme in two illuminating respects. First, it happened at a time when the political and cultural ties between America and Britain were much stronger than they are now. Only a little more than a decade earlier, Britain had hosted over a million US troops on its soil for an extended period; British troops had fought under American generals and Americans under British generals, in what was an extraordinarily intimate arrangement. As well as all that, in 1956 the United States still had what it no longer has: a WASP [White, Anglo-Saxon, Protestant] establishment, with all that meant in terms of tastes and values and affinities. There was no such thing as multiculturalism to cloud the issue; no doubt concerning the superiority of that cultural tradition which derived from America's English origins and which the two countries had in common.

The point is that even in those exceptional circumstances, cultural affinities and shared traditions were not enough to ensure common foreign policy goals, to override hard calculations of national interests. Indeed, that should have become apparent to the British several years earlier, when Harry Truman had abruptly cut off Lend-Lease to Britain almost as soon as the war ended, and when the United States had driven a hard bargain with Maynard Keynes concerning a loan to prevent Britain, bled white by a war it had fought from beginning to end, from going bankrupt.

Now if that were true nearly half a century ago, it must be much truer today, when the common culture that is being appealed to as the basis of association or unity is so much more attenuated – by massive immigration on both sides of the Atlantic of peoples who are unacquainted with that cultural tradition; by a strident and aggressive multiculturalism that insists that the Anglo-Saxon culture and tradition are no better than any other culture and tradition; and, not least, by educational establishments that do not regard the transmission of a cultural heritage as one of their responsibilities.

In these circumstances, it is surely a serious error to believe that a traditional culture is capable of providing the foundation for a worldwide English-speaking union. After all, in the face of the reckless policies of Tony Blair – whom I have characterised elsewhere as the British Gorbachev, in that he believes that statesmanship consists of taking flying leaps into the future without any clear idea of where one will land – that tradition and that political culture are proving incapable of keeping even Britain united. Already the term "British" has a diminished application.

Please understand that I am in no way criticising the United States in pointing these things out. I do so only to try to contest the argument that cultural compatibility can and should form the basis of a common foreign policy. It cannot. Was it Nietzsche or was it De Gaulle who described states as "cold monsters"? In any case, it was Britain's own Lord Palmerston who insisted that

> We have no eternal allies and we have no perpetual enemies.
> Our interests are eternal and perpetual, and those interests
> it is our duty to follow.

That unsentimental formulation is well-known. What is perhaps less well-known is that Palmerston was doing no more than paraphrasing something said several generations earlier by another statesman. George Washington, in his Farewell Address of 1796, had said:

> The nation which indulges toward another an habitual hatred
> or an habitual fondness is in some degree a slave. It is a slave
> to its animosity or to its affection, either of which is sufficient
> to lead it astray from its duty and its interest.

Any case for a foreign policy union or association of English-speaking peoples will have to be made in terms, not of culture, but of the national interests of the parties involved, and those interests will have to be continually re-interpreted and recalculated as circumstances change.

An End to Nonsense

The National Interest, Special 9-11 Issue, Thanksgiving 2001 [extract]

A shorter version of this piece appeared in the *Daily Telegraph* (Sydney) as "A Reminder of Darker Times" on 14 September 2001. A revised version was also published in May 2002 as "The Return to Realism" in *Blaming Ourselves: September 11 and the Agony of the Left*, before being extracted as "The Day the Earth Didn't Change Forever" in *The Australian*, 15 May 2002.

Someone – was it Nietzsche? Henry James? Lionel Trilling? – has observed that those who lack the imagination of disaster are doomed to be surprised by the world. Until September 11 such a lack was very prevalent in the Western world. While it was particularly characteristic of liberals, with their belief in progress and perfectibility, it was by no means confined to them. Indeed, in retrospect, the emergence of a species of optimistic conservatives – a term that until our time had been close to being an oxymoron – may come to be seen as a distinguishing feature of the last decades of the 20th century.

In any case, many people of many political and temperamental stripes were taken by surprise by the awful disaster of September 11. That they were was clearly evidenced by the widespread insistence that the acts of terror in Manhattan and Washington marked the beginning of a new era, that the world would never be the same again, that everything was changed and changed utterly.

With all due respect, this was and is nonsense. It reflects not the reality of the matter but the difficulty that intellectuals habitually have in distinguishing between the state of their minds and the state of the world. It also reflects what the philosopher John Anderson termed the "parochialism of the present", a condition resulting from a combination of ignorance of history and an egotistical insistence on exaggerating the importance of events that more or less directly involve oneself. Horrifying and atrocious as the acts of terror were, it should be remembered that they have happened at a time when people who experienced the Somme and Verdun, the Holocaust and Hiroshima, are still alive.

Far from marking a sharp break with the world in which we have been living for the last decade, this act of terror was an event with which that world had long been pregnant, and there had been many urgent and well-informed warnings of its imminent delivery. Nor were the reasons for such warnings hard to discern.

Once the discipline imposed by the superpower rivalry of the Cold War ended; once the authority and control of many nation-states began to be seriously undermined by transnational and subnational forces; once the movement of people became easy and virtually unmonitored in an increasingly "borderless" world – and all these things happened in the last ten years – the opportunity for terror increased greatly. And as globalisation – which is to say, the Westernisation of the world – proceeded rapidly, producing both fear and powerful resentment as it undermined traditional cultures and authority, the motive for terrorism also strengthened greatly.

The point has often been made that terrorism is the weapon of the weak, of the losers. In this case, terrorism has been employed by members of some (not all) other civilisations who – on religious and cultural grounds, and because the bases of their authority and power are threatened – furiously reject and oppose the triumph of Western ideas, values, institutions and enterprise. Unable either to compete with the West or to hold it at bay, they vent their hatred and despair by terror. Again, the likelihood of this happening was clearly foreseen, notably, though by no means exclusively, by Samuel Huntington.

⚜ ⚜ ⚜

What happened in September was not that the world changed in some fundamental manner, but that, in the most dramatic way, a group of ideas and assumptions about the world that had come to prevail among large sections of Western elites was shown to be at best inadequate and at worst utterly false.

First and foremost, there was the assumption that the world was moving rapidly and surely toward a benign, market-driven interdependence; that a positive-sum game was in progress in which all would benefit and friction would be smoothed away. With the triumph of the West, too, there came the belief that liberal democracy was destined to triumph rapidly and more or less universally. (As his views first appeared in this magazine, I should emphasise that this was not what was argued by Francis Fukuyama in his justly famous "End of History?" essay. He allowed for long holdouts against democratisation in substantial parts of the world. Still, the reception given to his views and their subsequent vulgarisation no doubt reflected and contributed to the attraction of the more simplistic version.)

Speaking of simplistic, there was also the complementary belief that traditional power politics had become old hat. As that human weathervane, William Jefferson Clinton, proclaimed, "the cynical calculation of pure power politics does not compute. It is ill-suited to the new era." It was asserted that "geoeconomics" – a term [coined by Edward Luttwak] that first saw the light of day in [the Summer 1990 issue of] this magazine – had allegedly displaced geopolitics, and that economic wealth and "soft" power were replacing violence and coercion as the ultimate currency of "the global village".

There was, too, the long-standing liberal belief, given a new lease on life by the end of the Cold War, that enmity between peoples was the result of misunderstanding and ignorance rather than of genuine conflicts of interest. Once these were removed by education and increasing contact in a multicultural world, it was assumed, harmony would prevail.

In the United States the ideas outlined above usually go under the label "Wilsonianism", after the president who so vigorously promoted them. They are not, then, exactly newly-minted and, indeed, they were already pretty shop-soiled when Wilson took them up. The "universal interdependence of nations" was proclaimed by

Marx and Engels in their Communist Manifesto of 1848. And long before that the belief that proximity and interaction would promote harmony was sufficiently prevalent for Rousseau to feel obliged to contradict it, observing of the states of Europe in the 18th century that their condition was such that they "touch each other at so many points that no one of them can move without jarring all the rest; their variances are all the more deadly, as their ties are more closely woven." As for the alleged obsolescence of power politics, that is a belief that was widely subscribed to a century ago, on the eve of the Great War.

Especially at a time when American faith in these ideas has received a body blow, it is worth bearing in mind the remarkable durability of such notions. Unfortunately, there is truth in the remark that a truly bad idea never really dies. One can predict with great confidence that these beliefs will survive the present setback and before long will again be advanced as exciting new truths.

But for the immediate future the Wilsonian set of assumptions is not going to be convincing or useful. The belief that conflict is due to ignorance and misunderstanding has been exposed yet again for the nonsense it is. (In today's world, no two groups understand each other more fully than the Israelis and the Palestinians, unless they be the Protestants and Catholics of Northern Ireland.) Far from being adequate for dealing with Osama bin Laden and the Taliban, "soft" power was partly instrumental in creating them. Military power of the old-fashioned kind, as well as intelligence and technical knowledge, which have always been important sources of power, are needed to destroy them.

In which case, what will have happened will not be so much the entry of America into a new era but the end of a brief pause when euphoria and illusion flourished. It will mean a return to an older, more sober, and above all more realistic state of mind about the world.

Appendix

On Prudence and Restraint in Foreign Policy

Sue Windybank talks with Owen Harries, *Policy*, Autumn 2002

SW: Given that this issue of *Policy* contains several articles exploring the use – and misuse – of labels, I would like to begin by discussing your shift from left to right. In a profile of you published in *The Bulletin* in 1984, you were described as a "left-wing Laborite" who became a "star in the American right". When did you begin to change?

OH: You must remember that I grew up in a South Wales mining valley during the Depression, in a place that at one point had an unemployment level of 57%. I don't think I saw a live conservative for the first 20 years of my life. It was only after I came to Australia to take up a teaching position in adult education at the Department of Tutorial Studies at Sydney University that I really started moving away from a leftist position. I had Harry Eddy on one side and Esmond Higgins, who was an ex-leading member of the Australian Communist Party, on the other. In a small department, I was a new factor that was fought over, so to speak.

SW: Who ended up converting you?

OH: I think largely myself, though Harry Eddy was certainly influential. He was an ex-Trotskyist who had moved away to become a very strong anti-communist. He was polemically very powerful and he just out-argued me. At least I had the sense to realise I was being out-argued, and I started to shift.

SW: Despite this shift, you voted for Whitlam in 1972. Why?

OH: It was more push than pull. It was the push of Billy McMahon. I felt it was impossible to vote for him. The Liberals had a very bad spell. They were split internally. Gorton had been a mixed bag, and McMahon was really bad. At that time, I was running a television program on Channel Nine and I was interviewing people every week. One week I interviewed Gough and at the end of the program in the makeup room I told him that at the next election I was going to vote for him. And he said, "Well, Owen, if you're going to vote for me, I'm going to win."

SW: Within a few years of voting for Whitlam you were advising shadow Minister for Foreign Affairs, Andrew Peacock, before becoming head of policy planning in the Department of Foreign Affairs. During that time, you largely wrote the Report of the Committee on Australia's Relations with the Third World, which became widely known as the "Harries Report". Why was it felt that such a report was needed, and what was the reaction to it?

OH: You must remember that from 1973, when OPEC made its first move and forced up the price of oil, when America was very much on the defensive after Vietnam and Watergate, the Third World was at its most militant. It was riding high, it was exerting a lot of pressure on the West, and in those circumstances, it was felt – by Peacock and Fraser – that Australia was particularly vulnerable as a sort of outpost of the West with a lot of Third World neighbours. It was rightly felt that we needed to give serious consideration to what all this meant.

As for the reaction to it, it was very favourable, though not uniformly so. There were some attacks on it from the left, but by and large it got a very good press indeed. It was pointed out that this was the first time that a report like this, a serious intellectual report, had been produced by an Australian government on the question of foreign policy. The British Foreign Office was very interested in it and I conducted a seminar on it for them in London. The Japanese seriously thought of translating it. So it was pretty much a success.

Let me emphasise that while I chaired it, and wrote something like over half of it, there were a lot of other important contributions from other people. Ashton Calvert, who is currently head of the department, wrote some chapters in it. Des Moore was influential on the economic side. It was a very good, very enjoyable year. We worked intensely. It involved interviewing extensively, and sorting out internally on the committee. We only had one member who dissented. Everything else we managed to resolve without smoothing it all out into a bland custard.

SW: You went on to become a senior adviser to Malcolm Fraser, before accepting the post of Australian Ambassador to UNESCO. How long were you at UNESCO?

OH: I was at UNESCO for about a year and a half. I went there at the beginning of 1982, but then Malcolm Fraser lost the election in 1983. As a political appointee I was required to submit my resignation, and the Labor Party wanted to find somewhere for Gough Whitlam to get him out of Australia. So I offered my resignation, it was accepted, and I left. And then it was a question of what I was going to do. I didn't particularly want to go back and teach at the University of New South Wales. I had already become pretty disillusioned at what was happening to universities, so some friends suggested I go to Washington. I joined a think tank there, the Heritage Foundation, where I spent a very happy year and a half getting America and Britain to withdraw from UNESCO.

SW: On what grounds?

OH: That under its Director-General, [Amadou-Mahtar] M'Bow, it was corrupt, that it was grossly inefficient, and that it was grossly anti-Western. America and Britain were paying to get their values undermined and attacked. Even by UN standards, UNESCO was pretty outrageous, and I always argued that even those who believed in the UN should have wanted to criticise and attack UNESCO because it was giving the UN a bad name.

On Prudence and Restraint

SW: How would you describe yourself now?

OH: I would describe myself as a conservative.

SW: What's the difference between a neoconservative and a conservative?

OH: Irving Kristol famously described a neoconservative as a liberal who'd been mugged by reality, and I guess there's an element of that. But I think I became increasingly aware that, as compared with a lot of the neoconservatives that I worked amongst and that I had as colleagues and friends in America, my position tended more towards what you might call classical conservatism. After the Cold War ended, a lot of neoconservatives reverted to their liberalism, particularly in foreign policy, whereas I didn't. In fact, conditions after the Cold War tended to strengthen my realist, conservative approach to foreign policy. I think I spent most of the 1990s arguing not against the left but against the neoconservatives, arguing for prudence and restraint in American foreign policy, as against the rather gung-ho approach they favoured.

SW: When you say that some neoconservatives reverted to liberalism after the Cold War, do you mean that they had an overarching vision of a post-Cold War world in a Fukuyama-style sense – that is, that liberal democracy as the ultimate form of government would triumph?

OH: For as long as the Cold War was on, the presence of the Soviet Union, and the threat it posed, demanded a realist approach from the United States and this set up a sort of intellectual and ideological discipline on American neoconservatives. They operated in the realm of necessity, and the choices were very limited. Absent the Soviet Union, and with America as the sole remaining superpower, they left the realm of necessity and entered the realm of choice, where the constraints were lifted.

What happened in these circumstances is that a lot of neoconservatives remembered that they used to be liberals and went back to a sort of Wilsonian belief in America as a crusader for democracy, America as the founder of a New World Order that would replace realism and replace power politics. Increasingly, you had neoconservatives very strongly arguing that America should use its position of dominance to establish this New Order, to impose its will on the world, to promote democracy very actively.

Now I had two serious objections to this. One was that it is not do-able. Democracy is not an export commodity. It's much more a do-it-yourself project. Americans should have realised this because for several generations they had been using their influence in the Caribbean and Central America, right next door to them and with very small countries, and even there they couldn't do it. So why they thought they could do it elsewhere in the world was a bit mysterious. Also, I don't think the United States is particularly good at understanding other cultures and other societies.

The other thread of the argument is that if you are the sole remaining superpower, you should be very careful and restrained in the use of your power. As anyone who has studied international history and politics knows, the fate of dominant powers that are very active and assertive is that they're balanced sooner or later by coalitions of powers against them – and that this was likely to happen to a United States that insisted on imposing its will on the world. This is where, again, American exceptionalism came into it. They couldn't believe that it would happen to them. They thought that America would be an exception to this rule. It might have happened to Spain under Phillip II, it might have happened to France under Louis XIV and Napoleon, it might have happened to Wilhelm II's and Hitler's Germany, but it wouldn't happen to America.

SW: What about Britain? It didn't really happen to Britain.

OH: Britain got away with it, you might say, by exercising a very considerable element of restraint and prudence, a policy of "splendid isolation". Britain was active on the outskirts of the world, but pretty inactive in the heartland of Europe. Britain stood aloof from the alliance systems of Europe – and perhaps it stood aloof too long – but it was certainly not an assertive European presence where the game was played.

SW: There were those who argued, when the Cold War ended, that the United States should pull back, that it was time to "bring the boys back home". And since September 11, some commentators have subscribed to what the CIA calls "blowback" – the unintended consequences of past American foreign policy and intervention overseas – and have subsequently argued that the "best defence is to give no offence". What do you think of this view?

OH: That's not my position. What I call for is not isolationism, not withdrawal, but restraint and discrimination. You should pick and choose and depend not on doctrine, but on circumstance. I don't argue for a minimalist foreign policy for the United States, I argue for a discriminating foreign policy. It's only in the context of the intellectual forces at work in the Washington environment in which I worked for 16-17 years that you might be able to appreciate the stress I put on prudence because I saw so much of the contra position. That, combined with the sort of fecklessness and fakery of the Clinton years – pretending to be doing something they weren't doing, being busy without being effective – influenced my views to a great extent.

SW: You recently referred to the Clinton years as the "Saxophone years", a kind of "wasted decade" [*The Age*, 18 December 2001]. What do you think could have been done differently?

OH: The United States under Clinton had a profoundly unserious foreign policy, and it was implemented by what I think was the most second-rate team that America's had in foreign policy since World War II. What you had was a policy of gesture masquerading as a serious policy, pinpricks being presented as massive hammerblows. And it all got quite silly. Even in the attitude towards a serious subject like, say, China, swinging from treating China as the main rival to treating it as a strategic partner, there was a profound lack of seriousness in it.

SW: Clinton famously claimed not to be a foreign policy president, sensing that Americans were tired after the Cold War and that it was time to focus on pressing domestic issues.

OH: All the more reason why there was a need for discrimination and a careful selection of issues, not generalised busyness.

On Harmony and Clashes

SW: You are now a Senior Fellow at a classical liberal think tank, yet foreign policy doesn't seem to be a natural area for some classical liberals, unlike domestic issues. What is it about international relations that some classical liberals can't seem to come to grips with?

OH: Well, historically, of course, classical liberals of the 19th century – people like Richard Cobden and John Bright – rejected the belief that international politics had to be about power politics, and believed in what we now call globalisation – that the more the capitalist system became globalised, the more interdependent countries would become, the more harmonious relationships between countries would be, and that both the barriers between countries and the ignorance about each other that some liberals tend to believe is the cause of war, would be dissipated and become less and less influential.

There is a sort of utopianism built into classical liberalism, as far as international politics is concerned, in the belief that more interdependence means more harmony. This is a doctrine that E. H. Carr in his great realist tract called "a harmony of interests" theory. I just think that's wrong. I think Rousseau got it righter in the 18th century when he argued that the more states had to do with each other, the more interdependent they became, the more scope for aggravation and irritation between them. People who talk of a "global village" as if all will be sweetness and light have no experience of real villages.

SW: The terrorist attacks on September 11 would surely prove the "harmony of interests" theory wrong.

OH: The violence and the Muslim reaction to the Western world is precisely a function of closer contact, and the greater impact of the West on the Arab world.

SW: Do you think the September 11 attacks have proved Huntington's "clash of civilisations" thesis – that the next era of conflict will be fought over cultural values, and, in particular, that it is inevitable that the West and Islam will clash?

OH: That is a clash of civilisations, but I don't know that I would generalise the thesis to be the be-all-and-end-all of conflict from here on in. My view of Huntington has always been that the "clash of civilisations" was a bold and interesting thesis, that one should accept it as such and welcome the light it threw, and not criticise it in detail, but try to look at the central truth that it contained. I'm sure that if you try to push everything into that framework then you will find that some things would not fit, that there would be exceptions and contradictions. What he was arguing was that after nearly a century of ideological confrontation, we were now going to have cultural confrontation. I think there was an element of truth in that.

SW: In a recent column in the *Sydney Morning Herald*, Gerard Henderson wrote that some people are drawing parallels between the war on terrorism and the Cold War, with Islamic fundamentalism replacing communism. Do you find such parallels useful?

OH: I'm struck much more by the differences than the similarities. Looking back at one of the great central questions of the last century, it is striking how responsibly and cautiously the two main actors behaved throughout the Cold War. They handled their enormous power very carefully. I guess the boldest move was the Soviet policy that led to the Cuban Missile Crisis, but even that, once it came to a crisis point, was handled very delicately and sensibly and quickly. The Soviet Union, at least until the very end, was a vicious and evil system, but in its international behaviour it was essentially a cautious actor that calculated the correlation of forces carefully. It was both at the same time. Flying two aircraft into those towers in New York is an animal of a different breed.

SW: Perhaps one similarity is that to prevail against terrorism, the United States must try to keep a coalition together that cuts across civilisational lines, just as it did in the Cold War.

OH: This comes back to what we were talking about earlier about prudence. Because the Soviet Union was as powerful as it was, the United States readily recognised that it needed allies and that it had to act in multilateral ways. I think there is a danger now that the United States is so supreme in terms of all-round power that the temptation of unilateralism is greater than it was. There are some people in Washington – some of them are my friends and some occupy senior positions in the [Bush] administration – who believe that the United States can, and should if necessary, dispense with allies and proceed on its own.

SW: Which do you think will prevail – multilateralism or unilateralism? Take the current debate about action against Iraq as a case in point.

OH: What would worry me about Iraq is (a) what America might have to do in order to get rid of Saddam Hussein and that might involve killing a lot of innocent people; and (b) what you would do with Iraq afterwards. To be responsible for a country of that size, and to put something together that would work with the Kurds and the Shiites, would involve America in an avoidable exercise in what we now call nation-building, and I doubt it could be brought off successfully.

At the same time, I also think there is a real and serious problem. Saddam Hussein is a vicious dictator. I think that if he thought he could get away with it, he is not above using biological and chemical weapons, even against America, and then there's the question of whether he has nuclear weapons. And in so far as he dominates and he's mortal, think if he should suddenly discover he had a terminal illness, think of what he might do before he died. It's a horrifying thought.

SW: The European reaction to possible American action against Iraq has ranged from apprehension to opposition from some quarters. Does this foreshadow an uncertain future for the Atlantic alliance? You have written, for instance, that if the EU project is successful, Europe could become a major rival, and that it could cause serious problems for the US.

OH: I think one of two things is going to happen to the European Union. They're either going to bring it off, and make it work, in which case they will be a very serious rival; or the whole thing will disintegrate. The EU project has been an elite-driven thing that has been foisted upon Europe essentially by the political elites. If it collapses, those elites will be discredited and you'll have rival elites of the extreme left and extreme right there to exploit the situation, in which case you'll have a tremendously unstable continent. Either scenario is bad. So I guess the best one can hope for is that the thing just limps along in the middle somehow, not failing, not succeeding.

SW: The French government clearly hopes that the EU will act as a "second pole", a balancer against the US and what they call the "dollar hegemony". Is it necessarily a bad thing for the EU to act one day as a balancer against the preponderance of American power?

OH: I guess I have to say no. It's not a bad thing. I think some sort of balance is desirable. And Europe is a better balancer, a more reliable balancer, than China, which despite all its talk about its eternal civilisation and about it being the oldest state in the world and so on, has extraordinarily little experience in living with other states in a quasi-competitive/co-operative environment. China has always thought of itself as the centre of power.

Back to the Future?

SW: During the 1990s there was a lot of talk about the pacific forces of globalisation, multinational companies and NGOs, all eroding the relevance of national borders and thus the nation-state. At the same time, states no longer have a monopoly on force, given the rise of warlords, transnational criminal networks, and the like. Certainly, in many parts of the world it appears this way, with states breaking down or failing. What do you make of this?

OH: Let me respond to the much-heralded demise of the nation-state first. A lot of people have talked about this as a return to a sort of medievalism.

Instead of power being monopolised by states, it's now become diffuse and you have a variety of agents applying power and applying force. I think there's some truth in this, and it's not just power in the military sense. One of the great features of our age is the decline in secrecy and the decline in the monopoly governments have had over information. It's very hard to keep secrets nowadays, and access to information for people who know how to go about it is much greater than it's ever been. This is to a large extent why NGOs have increasing influence in the world, because they have woken up to this very quickly and have made maximum use of the information that they can now get hold of.

So in a sense nation-states are being attacked from above and below: above by pseudo, quasi, international or universal organisations – we have international courts, we have international this and that – but also from below, with all these forces coming up to challenge the power of the nation-state – everything from environmentalists to drug gangs.

Second, although a lot of people have wanted to see the decline and disappearance of nation-states, we may still live to discover that there are worse conditions than a world of nation-states – a world where you have a malign anarchy, where all sorts of irresponsible and uncontrollable agents have significant power without responsibility. The Westphalian system of nation-states at least established a set of ground rules and at least there were some constraints exercised on governments by their populations. Many of these new agents are utterly irresponsible. So it's starting to look like a very strange world. Perhaps the most that we can hope for is that nation-states can at best control the situation.

SW: Should policymakers and leaders try and explain this complexity instead of presenting complex issues as simple moral slogans? I'm thinking of Bush's "axis of evil", even Reagan's "evil empire".

OH: It depends very much on the situation. It can be a drawback. It's not helpful in some situations of great complexity and where there are many shades of grey involved. On the other hand, people often overcomplicate international affairs, and I think there is a European tendency, particularly, to believe that making moral distinctions is in some way terribly unsophisticated and a sign of simplicity and naivety. And so you lapse into a sort of relativism and it can very often immobilise you, because who is to say that one thing is better than the other? Who is to decide? You end up with a sort of phony tolerance, which leads to paralysis.

As for Reagan's evil empire, I think that was a good statement because after a very bad decade when the US had lost in Vietnam, when they'd had Watergate and lived through four years of Jimmy Carter, American conviction needed some simple, bold statements. Reagan's evil empire, on the one hand, and his use of the "city on the hill" image on the other were very good in reminding Americans of what they were and what they were against.

The axis of evil was, I think, one of those smart phrases that Bush's State of the Union address, which was going fine on its own, could well have done without. As far as I know, there is no axis. I don't know of any strong connection between Iraq and North Korea, for example. Words should have meaning. I know the person who wrote it and he has since resigned from the speechwriting team.

Of course, "axis" evoked the 1930s and fascism, but I don't think it made conceptual sense. And I don't think that one should assume that all evils are joined, that they are united. They're not. What America has had to start on after September 11 is very complicated and difficult. It needs a lot of very hard and clear thinking to sort out what exactly you're against and how you're going to go about it. I think that's still a work in progress.

Australia and the United States

SW: Moving on to the relationship between Australia and the United States: You wrote recently that cultural affinities and shared traditions are not enough to ensure common foreign policy goals between countries, to override national interests. I think many Australians – certainly some media commentators – woke up to this with East Timor when they realised that the US intended to keep its distance (although the US provided logistical support and helped in other ways behind the scenes). That was a clear case of America's national interests diverging from Australia's. I wonder what would happen the other way around in a conflict between China and Taiwan. What if the US military went in to support Taiwan and asked the Australian government for help? Should we get involved, or would our interests diverge to too great an extent?

OH: Well, there are two things there. First of all, American behaviour: how much one should expect a sort of generous appreciation of one's past help to influence America. States don't work like that. And they shouldn't work like that. We shouldn't expect them to. It was an American, George Washington no less, who explained why you can't expect generosity from countries when he said: "The nation which indulges toward another an habitual hatred or an habitual fondness is in some degree a slave ... It is a slave to its animosity or its affection, either of which is sufficient to lead it astray from its duty and its interest." America is no exception. That should set limits to the belief in goodwill as any sort of generalised factor in international politics.

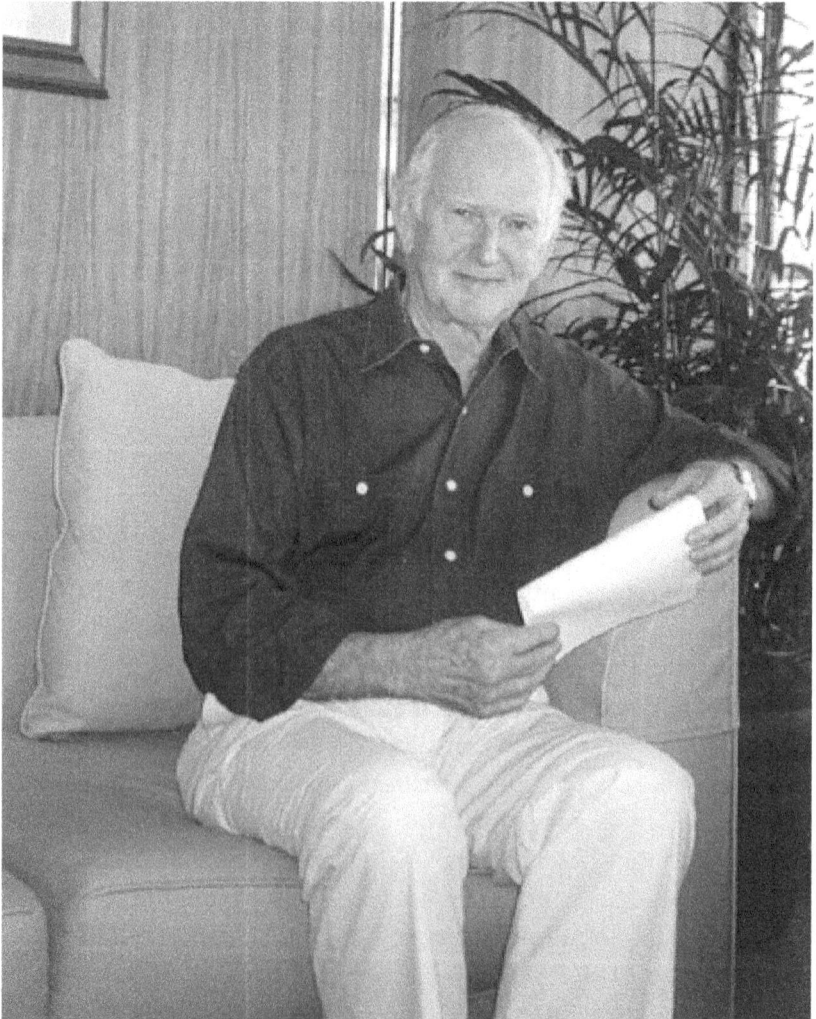

As far as China and Taiwan are concerned, on the general question, and before coming to the Australia part of your question, this has been an intensely-argued issue that divides people who'll agree on most other things. My own view is that America's relations with China should not be dictated by the Taiwan issue. That would be a case of the tail wagging the dog. America should not allow Taiwan to have control over its relations with China, which has many dimensions – broad strategic dimensions, economic dimensions, and so on.

Taiwan now has de facto independence in virtually every respect. The only limit on it is that it's not a member of the UN and a couple of other international organisations. To me that's no big deal. Now I think the United States should be prepared to defend that de facto independence in the event of any Chinese excursion against it. But I don't think it should be prepared to intervene in order to extend that *de facto* independence to a *de jure* independence. If the Taiwanese insist on pushing things to complete independence and create a situation of conflict, then I think that's their business and I don't think any Americans should die for that cause. To all intents and purposes, they've got independence now.

SW: President Bush recently re-affirmed American support for Taiwan in the event of a conflict with China.

OH: I think an unqualified commitment of that kind is a mistake, and could act as an incitement to the Taiwanese to push it to the limit. I'm a believer that there's a great deal of sense in leaving the question ambiguous, in a calculated ambiguity in America's Taiwan policy. We have lived with it for the last 20 years, or virtually, and it's been to everyone's advantage. The Taiwanese have moved from being a dictatorship to a democracy, China has immeasurably improved from what it was like in the late 1970s, and the United States has got on fine. So I'm very sceptical about America getting involved, unless the Chinese behave outrageously and without extreme provocation and turn on Taiwan, which is very unlikely. The Taiwanese now have something between 50 and 60 billion dollars invested in China, movement between the mainland and the island is increasing all the time, and economic relations are thickening.

SW: But just say things did go really badly. What should Australia do?

OH: My answer to that is, "Keep well clear of it all."

SW: Would that mean a rupture in the alliance?

OH: It shouldn't, it wouldn't. We should calmly look them in the eye and say, "This is your East Timor. Good luck, chaps. We're solidly clapping from the side-lines." And it would make good sense. Australia is much too small militarily to get involved in such a game. It would be completely out of its class, for one thing. Secondly, when the dust has settled, Australia has to live with China, and it should bear that in mind and not get involved.

SW: What about Australian support at a tokenistic level?

OH: What's the point of a token? I would say that perhaps Australia is too keen on tokenism with the United States, and too eager to be part of everything. Australia too should act with discrimination.

Bibliography

1950s

"Our Nearest Neighbour", *Current Affairs Bulletin*, 30 April 1956, pp. 3-15.

"Oil, Sand and Power", *Current Affairs Bulletin*, 6 August 1956, pp. 115-127.

"The Fallacy of Two Percentism?", Editorial, *The Australian Highway* [Journal of the Workers' Educational Association], July 1958, p. 33.

"Anderson and Andersonianism" [Editor's Note], *The Australian Highway*, Special Issue, September 1958, p. 49.

Editorial, *The Australian Highway*, December 1958, p. 77.

Editorial, *The Australian Highway*, March 1959, p. 1, and "Highwayman's Diary", pp. 7-8.

Editorial, *The Australian Highway*, April 1959, p. 25, and "Highwayman's Diary", pp. 30-31.

Editorial, *The Australian Highway*, May 1959, p. 49, and "Highwayman's Diary", p. 53.

"China: The Communes' Success", *The Observer*, 16 May 1959, p. 297.

Editorial, *The Australian Highway*, June 1959, p. 73, and "Highwayman's Diary", p. 80.

"Education Week", Editorial, *The Australian Highway*, July 1959, p. 97, and "Highwayman's Diary", p. 102.

"University Politics", Editorial, *The Australian Highway*, August 1959, p. 125, and "Highwayman's Diary", p. 131.

"Educational Progress?", Editorial, *The Australian Highway*, September-October 1959, p. 149, and "Highwayman's Diary", p. 154.

"Why Russia is Ahead" [Review of James Gavin, *War and Peace in the Space Age*, Hutchinson, 1959], *The Observer*, 31 October 1959, p. 696.

Editorial, *The Australian Highway*, December 1959, p. 177, and "Highwayman's Diary", p. 182.

1960s

Editorial, *The Australian Highway*, February 1960, p. 1, and "Highwayman's Diary", pp. 5-6.

"Faith in the Summit", ibid., pp. 2-5.

"Safety in the Law", Editorial, *The Australian Highway*, April 1960, p. 21, and "Highwayman's Diary", pp. 26-27.

"The Summit: Divided They Rise", *The Observer*, 30 April 1960, pp. 15-18.

"The Summit: Khrushchev's Victory", *The Observer*, 28 May 1960, p. 18.

"Education and Television", Editorial, *The Australian Highway*, June 1960, p. 49, and "Highwayman's Diary", p. 56.

"Television and the W.E.A.", Editorial, *The Australian Highway*, September 1960, p. 77.

"Faith in the Summit: Some British Attitudes", *Foreign Affairs*, October 1961, pp. 58-70.

"Six Ways of Confusing Issues", *Foreign Affairs*, April 1962, pp. 443-452. Reprinted in *Survival* [London], July 1962, pp. 163-168.

"Faint Breath of Liberalism" [Review of Evan Luard, *Britain and China*, Chatto & Windus], *The Bulletin*, 2 June 1962, pp. 61-62.

"Social Change and Adult Education", *Australian Journal of Adult Education*, July 1962, pp. 20-26.

"Do the Soviet Leaders Misunderstand the West?", *The Australian Outlook*, August 1962, pp. 199-206.

"Swapping True Clichés for Wrong" [Review of Erich Fromm, *May Man Prevail?*, George Allen & Unwin], *The Bulletin*, December 1962, pp. 33-34.

"The Cold War and Its Origin" [Review of D.F. Fleming, *The Cold War and Its Origin*, Allen and Unwin, 1962], *The Australian Highway*, April 1963, pp. 25-27.

"Conscience or Whore? 50 Years of New Statesmanship" [Review of Edward Hyams, *The New Statesman: The History of the First Fifty Years 1913-1963* and *New Statesmanship: An Anthology*, Longmans], *The Bulletin*, 1 June 1963, p. 40.

"Snakes & Ladders" [Review of Vance Packard, *The Pyramid Climbers*, Longmans], *The Bulletin*, 27 July 1963, p. 43.

"The Chink of Grasshoppers?", *The American Scholar*, Summer 1963, pp. 397-406. Partly reprinted in the *Sydney Morning Herald*, 7 December 1963.

"A State of England" [Review of Anthony Hartley, *A State of England*, Hutchinson, London, 1963], *Quadrant*, September 1963, pp. 85-87.

"The Case Against Germany: Hatred and Doubt in Adenauer's Make" [Comments on Gudrun Tempel, *Speaking Frankly About the Germans*, Seeker & Warburg, and Lionel Kocher, *The Struggle for Germany*, Edinburgh], *The Bulletin*, 14 December 1963, pp. 47-48.

"Jewish Perspectives" [Comments on the Jewish Labor Bund's journal *Perspectives*], *The Bulletin*, 30 May 1964, p. 57.

"Reign of Terror" [Review of Brigitte Granzow, *A Mirror of Nazism: British Opinion and the Emergence of Hitler 1933-1939*, Gollancz], *The Bulletin*, 20 June 1964, pp. 52-53.

"An Old Debate", *Quadrant*, October-November 1964, pp. 23-31.

"Seminar in Port Moresby", *Quadrant*, March-April 1965, pp. 78-80.

"A New Guinea Journal" [Review of Peter Hastings, editor, *New Guinea*, vol. 1, nos 1 and 2, Council on New Guinea Affairs], *The Bulletin*, 7 August 1965, p. 57.

"Britain from the Fifteenth Floor" [Review of Anthony Sampson, *Anatomy of Britain Today*, Hodder & Stoughton], *The Bulletin*, 25 September 1965, pp. 58-59.

"Commitment in Vietnam, Part 1", *Current Affairs Bulletin*, 27 September 1965, pp. 146-160.

"Commitment in Vietnam, Part 2", *Current Affairs Bulletin*, 11 October 1965, pp. 162-176.

"The Australian Debate on Vietnam", in Sibnarayan Ray, editor, *Vietnam: Seen from East and West*, Thomas Nelson (Australia) Limited, Melbourne and Sydney, 1966, pp. 153-162. Reprinted in *Quadrant*, May-June 1966, pp. 39-46.

"The Visible Saboteurs" [Review of David Wise and Thomas B. Ross, *The Invisible Government*, Jonathan Cape, and Henry L. Stimson, *American Secretary of State*], *The Bulletin*, 5 March 1966, pp. 44-45.

"The Menace to Australia's Security" [Extracts from "Is Asian Communism a Threat to Australia?", Address to the 33rd Summer School, Australian Institute of Political Science (AIPS)], *The Australian*, 30 January 1967. Reprinted in *Tharunka* [UNSW], 14 March 1967, p. 7. "Owen Harries Replies", [Response to critique], Letter to the Editor, *Tharunka*, 30 March 1967, p. 6.

"Is Asian Communism a Threat to Australia?" in John Wilkes, editor, *Communism in Asia: A Threat to Australia?*, Proceedings of the 33rd Summer School, AIPS, Angus & Robertson, Sydney, 1967, pp. 118-

131, with "A Response to the Discussion: Is Asian Communism a Threat to Australia?", pp. 154-157.

"Miss Murdoch's Realism", *Quadrant*, May-June 1967, pp. 10-14.

"Militarism and Owen Harries" [Response to Sol Encel, "Militarism and Society", *Tharunka*, 5 September 1967], Letter to the Editor, *Tharunka*, 19 September 1967, and "Discrepancies", Letter to the Editor, *Tharunka*, 3 October 1967.

"Welsh Nationalism – Winds of Change in Llanfairfechan", *Quadrant*, July-August 1968, pp. 49-54.

"Should the US Withdraw from Asia?", *Foreign Affairs*, October 1968, pp. 15-25. Reprinted in *Quadrant*, November-December 1968, pp. 40-46, and *Survival* [London], December 1968, pp. 397-403.

"Menzies and the Suez Crisis", *Politics* [Journal of the Australasian Political Studies Association], November 1968, pp. 193-204.

"Leaving the Aussies in the Lurch", *Interplay*, March 1969, pp. 9-12.

"America and the Intellectuals: A Seminar at Princeton", *Quadrant*, March-April 1969, pp. 43-48.

"American Policy and Australia's Security", Institute of International Studies, South Carolina, 1969.

"Trouble-Makers", Letter to the Editor, *The Bulletin*, 29 May 1969.

"Mr Wilson's War" [Review of Anthony Howard and Richard West, *The Making of a Prime Minister*, Jonathan Cape], *The Bulletin*, 29 May 1969, p. 56.

"What Liberal Democracies Are Up Against" [Review of Robert O'Neill, *General Giap: Politician and Strategist*, Cassell, Australia], *The Bulletin*, 7 June 1969, p. 69.

"A Scotsman, an Irishman and a Welshman" [Review of H. J. Hanham, *Scottish Nationalism*, Faber and Faber, London, 1969], *The Bulletin*, 18 October 1969, pp. 65-66.

"The Teaching of Adults in Adult Education", in *The Political Education of Australians*, Canberra, 1969, pp. 37-44.

1970s

"Ten Days in Vietnam", *Sydney Morning Herald*, 9 March 1970.

"The Eagle and the Lotus" [Review of J. F. Cairns, *The Eagle and the Lotus: Western Intervention in Vietnam 1847-1968*], *The Australian Quarterly*, March 1970, pp. 120-125.

"Reply to Carey", Letter to the Editor [on Vietnam], *Tharunka*, 18 March 1970.

"Road to Paris" [Review of Henry Brandon, *Anatomy of Terror: The Secret History of the Vietnam War*, Deutsch, 1970], *Sydney Morning Herald*, 18 April 1970.

"After the Moratorium", *Quadrant*, May-June 1970, pp. 40-43. Reprinted in *Woroni* [ANU], 8 September 1970, pp. 2, 9.

Review of Henry Albinski, *Politics and Foreign Policy in Australia: The Impact of Vietnam and Conscription*, Duke University Press, 1970, in *The Australian Outlook*, December 1970, pp. 347-349.

"The Great Powers and Southeast Asia", *Quadrant*, January-February 1971, pp. 27-34.

"Looking for the Threat", *The Bulletin*, 13 November 1971, pp. 18-19. Reprinted in slightly expanded form as "On Threats", in Henry Mayer and Helen Nelson, editors, *Australian Politics: A Third Reader*, Cheshire, Melbourne, 1973, pp. 771-773.

"World in Focus: How to Understand a Four-Power System", *The Bulletin*, 1 January 1972, pp. 30-31.

"We Shall Miss You", Letter to the Editor co-signed with Richard Krygier and David Stove, *The Bulletin*, 5 February 1972.

"Down with Parsing!", Letter to the Editor, *Sydney Morning Herald*, 11 February 1972.

"American Perspectives on Asia", in Richard L. Walker, editor, *Prospects in the Pacific* [International Relations Series Number 2, Institute of International Studies, University of South Carolina], Heldref Publications, Washington DC, 1972, pp. 54-86.

"The Embattled University" [Based on a paper presented to the Workers' Educational Association in late 1971], *Current Affairs Bulletin*, 1 March 1972, pp. 290-301.

"Shift on Vietnam Protest", Letter to the Editor, *Sydney Morning Herald*, 30 May 1972.

"Tutors: The Academic Shop Stewards?", *Vestes* [The Bulletin of the Federal Council of University Staff Associations of Australia], 1972, pp. 128-135.

"Reactions to Mr Nixon's China Policy", *Quadrant*, June 1972, pp. 50-54.

"New Guinea's Foreign Policy", Letter to the Editor, *Sydney Morning Herald*, 27 June 1972.

"Waiting for the Dust to Settle" [Review of Bruce Grant, *The Crisis of Loyalty: A Study of Australian Foreign Policy*, Angus & Robertson], *The Bulletin*, 9 December 1972, p. 49.

"The Sino-American Détente: Genesis and Prospects" [Comment on Allen S. Whiting's paper at a conference on China and the World Community, 10-12 June 1972], in Ian Wilson, editor, *China and the World Community*, Angus & Robertson and the Australian Institute of International Affairs, Cremorne [Sydney], 1973, pp. 89-92.

"The Whitlam View of the World", *Sydney Morning Herald*, 29 January 1973.

"Fragmentation and Organisation: A Discussion on the Political Future of Papua New Guinea" [With Eugene Ogan, Peter Lawrence, Fancy Lawrence, Ian Grosart, and Edward P. Wolfers], *Quadrant*, March-April 1973, pp. 43-51.

"Asia and Australia: The Whitlam Approach", *Art International* [Paris], May 1973, p. 86.

"Mr Whitlam and Australian Foreign Policy", *Quadrant*, July-August 1973, pp. 55-64.

"Democracy and Education", Letter to *Alumni* [UNSW], December 1973, pp. 10-11.

"W.H.C. Eddy" [Obituary], *Quadrant*, January-February 1974, p. 72. Reprinted in *In Memorium: W.H.C. Eddy, 1913-1973* [booklet], W.H.C. Eddy Memorial Appeal/Workers Educational Association, Sydney, 1974, pp. 26-27.

"Harry Eddy", *WEA News*, March 1974, p. 6. Reprinted, ibid., p. 26.

"Nixon's International Legacy ... 1. Detente May Lead to Disaster", *Sydney Morning Herald*, 17 September 1974.

"Nixon's International Legacy ... 2. Is Our Foreign Policy Blinkered?", *Sydney Morning Herald*, 18 September 1974.

"Decency, Peace and Historical Inevitability: The Vietnam Debate Revisited", *Quadrant*, June 1975, pp. 8-11.

"Santamaria and Foreign Policy", *Quadrant*, July 1975, pp. 19-30.

"Australia's New Guinea Question", in W.J. Hudson, editor, *Australia's New Guinea Question*, Thomas Nelson Ltd and the Australian

Institute of International Affairs, West Melbourne and Sydney, 1975, pp. 143-160.

"The Self-Criticism of E.G. Whitlam", *Quadrant*, August 1975, pp. 42-44.

"Australia's Foreign Policy Under Whitlam", *Orbis – A Journal of World Affairs*, Fall 1975, pp. 1090-1101.

"Australia, Israel and the UN", *Quadrant*, September 1975, pp. 8-10.

"Introduction" as editor, *Liberty and Politics: Studies in Social Theory*, Pergamon Press for the Workers' Education Association of New South Wales, Rushcutters Bay [Sydney], 1976, pp. 1-6.

"Australia's Foreign Policy and the Elections of 1972 and 1975", in Howard R. Penniman, editor, *Australia at the Polls: The National Elections of 1975*, American Enterprise Institute for Public Policy Research, Washington DC, 1977, pp. 257-275.

"The Conference in Perspective", *Sydney Morning Herald*, 13 February 1978.

Australia and the Third World: Report of the Committee on Australia's Relations with the Third World, Committee on Australia's Relations with the Third World [chaired by Owen Harries], Australian Government Publishing Service, Canberra, 1979.

1980s

"The Ideology of the Third World", Appendix U, *Australia and the Third World*, ibid. Reprinted in *Quadrant*, January-February 1980, pp. 21-29.

"A Comment on the King-Indyk Critique" [Response to Peter King and Martin Indyk, "Australia's Relations with the Third World – A Critique of the Harries Report"], *Current Affairs Bulletin*, May 1980, pp. 26-29.

"The Third World Report and Its Critics", *The Australian Outlook*, August 1980, pp. 154-158.

"The US and UNESCO at a Crossroads", *Backgrounder* No. 298, The Heritage Foundation, Washington DC, 19 October 1983.

"Gough's New Job: Surviving the UNESCO Jungle", *The Bulletin*, 8 November 1983.

"The Menzies Foreign Policy: A Study in Realism", *Quadrant*, December 1983, pp. 23-33.

"European 'Sophistication' vs. American 'Naiveté'", *Commentary*, December 1983, pp. 46-50.

"US, Quit UNESCO", *The New York Times*, 21 December 1983. Reprinted as "Why the US Should Pull Out", *The Age* [Melbourne], 30 December 1983.

"UNESCO: Whitlam's Odd Role in World Body", *The Bulletin*, 6 March 1984, pp. 84, 87-88.

"Best-Case Thinking", *Commentary*, May 1984, pp. 23-28. Reprinted as "The Case Against Best-Case Arguments", *The Bulletin*, 5 May 1984, pp. 97-98, 100, 102.

"Europe and America: 1984", in Steven C. Munson, editor, *The State of the Nation* [Proceedings of the national conference of the Committee for the Free World, 11-13 May 1984], University Press of America Inc., Maryland, 1985, pp. 32-41. Reprinted as "Europe and America: 1984", *Quadrant*, July-August 1984, pp. 17-20.

"Conservative Critics of NATO", *The American Spectator*, June 1984, pp. 12-14.

"A Primer for Polemicists", *Commentary*, September 1984, pp. 57-60. Reprinted as "12 Rules for Winning", *Quadrant*, December 1984, pp. 19-22, and in "Tactical Notes No. 10", the Libertarian Alliance, London, 1991. Revised as "How to Win Arguments and Influence Debate", *Australian Financial Review*, 1 February 2002.

"Harries Replies", Letter to the Editor [Response to a profile by John Edwards], *The Bulletin*, 23 October 1984.

"Crisis in the Pacific", *Commentary*, June 1985, pp. 47-54.

"Neoconservatism and Realpolitik", *The National Interest*, Fall 1985, pp. 124-127.

"Enough Unreality in the South Pacific", *The New York Times*, 2 October 1985.

"How Has the United States Met Its Major Challenges Since 1945?" [Contribution to a symposium with Lionel Abel, W. Barrett, Peter L. Berger, W. Berns, Midge Decter, J. Epstein, S. Garment, Nathan Glazer, Sidney Hook, and Jeane J. Kirkpatrick], *Commentary*, November 1985, pp. 44-46.

"The Uncertainty Principle", *The National Interest*, Winter 1985-86, pp. 125-128.

"A Conservative's Guide to the Third World: The Term Means Just What It Says", *The American Spectator*, January 1986, pp. 14-15.

"Neither Marcos Nor Aquino", *The New York Times*, 23 February 1986.

"Bookshelf: Butter, Not Guns", *The Wall Street Journal*, 13 March 1986.

"Line of Shame that NATO Will Regret", *The Times* [London], 17 April 1986. Reprinted as "The Line of Shame Route Flown to Hit Libya Shows How US Allies View NATO", *Los Angeles Times*, 17 April 1986.

"Doctrine Overdose: How to Kill a Foreign Policy", *The New Republic*, 5 May 1986, pp. 17-18.

"The Idea of a Third Force", *The National Interest*, Spring 1986, pp. 3-7.

"ASEAN Nights. There are Limits to the Reagan Doctrine", *The American Spectator*, June 1986, p. 15.

"Will Thatcher Melt on S. Africa? She May Soon Have No Choice but to Back Sanctions and Weep", *Los Angeles Times*, 22 July 1986. Reprinted as "Thatcher May Weep Once Again", *Toronto Star*, 2 August 1986.

"A Flawed Endgame", *The National Interest*, Summer 1986, pp. 110-112. Reprinted in *Quadrant*, October 1986, pp. 77-79.

"Playing It for History", *The New York Times*, 7 October 1986.

"A Conversation with Zbigniew Brzezinski", *The National Interest*, Fall 1986, pp. 28-35. Reprinted in *Quadrant*, January-February 1987, pp. 35-39.

Contribution to Midge Decter, editor, *Thinking about East/West* [Proceedings of the national conference of the Committee for the Free World, Washington DC, 22-24 November 1985], The Orwell Press, New York, 1986, pp. 15-18; 27-28.

"Tribute to Richard Krygier", *Quadrant*, November 1986, pp. 26-27.

"At the Bloody Crossroads" [Speech to *Quadrant* 30th Anniversary Dinner], *Quadrant*, December 1986, pp. 81-82.

"Summits and Troughs", *The National Interest*, Winter 1986-87, pp. 107-111.

"The Other Ocean", in Midge Decter, editor, *The United States and the World* [Proceedings of the fifth national conference of the Committee for the Free World, 1-3 May 1987], The Orwell Press, New York, 1987, pp. 49-56.

"Anthony Eden and the Decline of Britain", *Commentary*, June 1987, pp. 34-43.

"Principle and Circumstance", *The National Interest*, Summer 1987, pp. 108-112.

"Why Should Congress Be Exempt from Truth-Telling?", *The New York Times*, 15 July 1987.

"Dealing with the Soviets" [Review of William G. Hyland, *Mortal Rivals: Superpower Relations from Nixon to Reagan*, Random House, New York, 1987], *Commentary*, November 1987, pp. 66-69.

"Gorbachev and Botha: Two of a Kind?", *The Wall Street Journal*, 7 December 1987.

"The Rise of American Decline", *Commentary*, May 1988, pp. 32-36. Reprinted in *Quadrant*, July-August 1988, pp. 3-7.

"New Game for Divining Russia's Future", *The Wall Street Journal*, 9 May 1988.

"The Coming Dominance of the Pacific", *The National Interest*, Spring 1988, pp. 124-128.

"Exporting Democracy – and Getting It Wrong", *The National Interest*, Fall 1988, pp. 3-12. Reprinted in *Quadrant*, March 1989, pp. 48-54, and in R. James Woolsey, editor, *The National Interest on International Law and Order*, Transaction Publishers, New Brunswick and London, 2003, pp. 254-266.

with Dennis L. Bark, "Introduction" as editors, *The Red Orchestra: The Case of the Southwest Pacific*, Hoover Institution Press, Stanford University, 1989, pp. xix-xxiii.

"Lee Kuan Yew Interviewed by Owen Harries", *IPA Review* [Journal of the Institute of Public Affairs, Melbourne], June 1989, pp. 18-24.

"Between Paradigms", *The National Interest*, Fall 1989, pp. 101-107. Reprinted as "Foreign Policy Beyond the Cold War?", *IPA Review*, October-December 1989, pp. 35-39.

Strategy and the Southwest Pacific: An Australian Perspective, Pacific Security Research Institute, Sydney, 1989. Reprinted as "The Unstable Southwest Pacific", *Quadrant*, November 1989, pp. 14-25.

with David Anderson, "A 'Hawk' By Any Other Name", Letter to the Editor on behalf of the Pacific Security Research Institute, *Australian Financial Review*, 27 October 1989.

"As Ideology Dies, Analogies Rise", *The New York Times*, 29 October 1989.

with William F. Buckley Jr., "Is the Cold War Really Over?", *National Review*, 10 November 1989, pp. 40-43.

"The End of the World as We Know It", *The Australian*, 10 November 1989.

"Parts of the Berlin Wall Will Crash in the Pacific", *Australian Financial Review*, 23 November 1989.

"Is There a Future for the Reagan Doctrine?", in Midge Decter, editor, *After Reagan – What?* [Proceedings of the sixth national conference of the Committee for the Free World, 18-20 November 1989], The Orwell Press, New York, 1989, pp. 49- 51.

1990s

"Students Should Know More about the Real World than Past History and Geography", *NASSP Bulletin* [Publication of the National Association of Secondary School Principals], January 1990, pp. 16-20. Reprinted as "What American Students Should Know About the World", *Momentum* [Journal of the National Catholic Educational Association], Washington, February 1990, pp. 21-25, and in John Fonte and Andre Ryerson, editors, *Education for America's Role in World Affairs*, Office of Educational Research and Improvement, Washington DC, 1994, pp. 97-102.

"Revolution Redux: The Anatomy of an Analogy", *The New Republic*, 2 April 1990, pp. 19-21.

"Credit Ratings", *The National Interest*, Summer 1990, pp. 109-112.

"Perspective on the 'New World Order': The Little Guys Are Calling the Tune: If Japan and Germany Can't Stand up to Iraq, Then the Dominance of Economic Over Military Power is Nonsense", *Los Angeles Times*, 28 December 1990.

"Of Unstable Disposition", *The National Interest*, Winter 1990-91, pp. 100-104.

"Introduction" as editor, *America's Purpose: New Visions of US Foreign Policy*, ICS Press, 1991.

"On the Scene: A Woman for Four Seasons", *National Review*, 15 April 1991, pp. 22-23.

"Defining the New World Order: Impossibility" [Contribution to a forum edited by Ian Buruma], *Harper's Magazine*, May 1991, pp. 60-61.

"Drift and Mastery, Bush-Style", *The National Interest*, Spring 1991, pp. 3-7.

"The New World Order of George Bush", in *US Foreign Policy Options and Australian Interests*, Occasional Paper No. 7, Pacific Security Research Institute, Sydney, 1991, pp. 17-23.

"The New World Order? Take Your Pick" [Extracts from The John Latham Memorial Lecture, University of Sydney, 12 September 1991] *Sydney Morning Herald*, 19 September 1991.

"The Cold War and the Intellectuals", *Commentary*, October 1991, pp. 13-20.

"The Fog of Peace" [The John Latham Memorial Lecture, see "The New World Order?"], *Quadrant*, November 1991, pp. 10-16.

"Lower Case: The Third World, R.I.P.", *The National Interest*, Winter 1991-92, pp. 109-112.

"Learning from Communism's Fall", *Wilson Quarterly*, Winter 1992, pp. 7-9.

"Yugoslavia and the Politics of Memory: Revival of Sleight, Honor, Feud and Revenge", *The Washington Times*, 28 June 1992.

"The Day of the Fox", *The National Interest*, Fall 1992, pp. 109-112.

"Fourteen Points for Realists", *The National Interest*, Winter 1992-93, pp. 109-112.

"The Clash of Civilisations", *The Weekend Australian*, 3-4 April 1993. See also "Cultural Conflicts – But Not Conspiracies", Letter to the Editor [Response to Greg Sheridan, "'Culture Wars' a Product of the Conspiracy Junkies", *The Australian*, 7 April 1993], *The Australian*, 14 April 1993; and "Blind Prophets Unable to Even Judge the Truth of Our Past", Letter to the Editor [Response to Richard Woolcott, "We Must be the Odd Man In", *The Australian*, 17 April 1993], *The Australian*, 23 April 1993.

"China is a Real Threat" [Letter in response to Ross Munro, "Awakening Dragon: The Real Danger in Asia is China", *Policy Review*, Fall 1992], *Policy Review*, Winter 1993, Heritage Foundation, Washington DC, p. 90.

"The Strange Death of Soviet Communism: An Autopsy", A Special Issue, *The National Interest*, Spring 1993, p. 3.

"Shattered Illusions", *The Washington Post*, 16 June 1993. Reprinted in *The Australian*, 25 June 1993.

"Poets on Power (and its loss)", *The National Interest*, Fall 1993, pp. 115-120.

"The Collapse of 'the West'", *Foreign Affairs*, September-October 1993, pp. 41-93. Extracted as "'The West' Is Only a Flag of Convenience", *The New York Times*, 28 August 1993, and as "Survival of 'West' Doubtful Now Cold War is Over", *Straits Times* [Singapore], 2 September 1993.

"Struggletime in Washington", *The Australian*, 24 December 1993.

"Making Sense of Foreign Policy: Work Gives US History a Clear-eyed Examination" [Review observations on Warren I. Cohen, series editor, *The Cambridge History of American Foreign Relations*, Cambridge University Press; Bradford Perkins, Vol. 1, *The Creation of a Republican Enterprise*; Walter LaFeber, Vol. 2, *The American Search for Opportunity, 1865-1913*; Akira Iriye, Vol. 3: *The Globalizing of America*, 1913-1945; Warren I. Cohen, Vol. 4, *America in the Age of Soviet Power*, 1945-1991], *The Washington Times*, 26 December 1993.

with Michael Lind, "Realism and its Rivals", *The National Interest*, Winter 1993-94, pp. 110-112.

"An Anti-Interventionist No More: America's Credibility is Now at Stake", *The Washington Post*, 21 April 1994.

"Power and Civilisation", *The National Interest*, Spring 1994, pp. 107-112.

"Huntington and Asia: Prediction or Warning?", Paper presented to the Eighth Asia Pacific Roundtable, Institute of Strategic and International Studies, Malaysia, 5-8 June 1994, *mimeo*, 16 pp.

"The Next Cold War? Asia v. the West", *National Review*, 1 August 1994, pp. 28; 30; 32-33; 36-37. Reprinted as "Asia v. the West?", *Quadrant*, October 1994, pp. 33-38.

"My So-Called Foreign Policy: The Case for Clinton's Diplomacy", *The New Republic*, 10 October 1994, pp. 24-31. Reprinted as "Triumphs Amidst Disaster: Clinton's Foreign Policy Success", *Current* [New York], 1 January 1995, pp. 12-18.

"A State of Mind", *The National Interest*, Winter 1994-95, pp. 111-112.

"The Australian Connection", in Christopher C. DeMuth and William Kristol, editors, *The Neoconservative Imagination: Essays in Honor of Irving Kristol*, The AEI Press, American Enterprise Institute, Washington DC, 1995, pp. 35-45. Reprinted in *Quadrant*, November 2009, pp. 19-26.

"Realism in a New Era" [Inaugural Richard Krygier Memorial Lecture, La Trobe University], *Quadrant*, April 1995, pp. 39-46. Revised as "Does Realism Have a Future?", in Kenneth Minogue, editor, *Conservative Realism: New Essays on Conservatism*, HarperCollins and the Centre for Policy Studies, London, 1996.

"What Kind of Hawk?", *The New York Times*, 15 June 1995.

"Expanding NATO: An Exchange between Odom and his Critics" [Contribution to a Symposium with Stephen Sestanovich, Ted Galen Carpenter and William E. Odom], *The National Interest*, Summer 1995, pp. 102-104.

"Establishment Gadfly from Arkansas" [Review of Randall Bennett Woods, *Fulbright: A Biography*, Cambridge University Press], *The Washington Post*, 13 August 1995.

"On Letting Go", *The National Interest*, Fall 1995, pp. 109-112. Reprinted as Appendix One in Owen Harries, *Benign or Imperial? Reflections on American Hegemony* [2003 Boyer Lectures], ABC Books, Sydney, February 2004, pp. 95-102.

"Senator Dole is a Hypocrite", *The Spectator* [UK], 25 November 1995, pp. 20-21.

"Pat's World", *The National Interest*, Spring 1996, pp. 108-11.

"An Offer Castro Couldn't Refuse – Or Survive", *The National Interest*, Summer 1996, pp. 126-128.

"Bookshelf: Policy Skirmishes Along the 38th Parallel", *The Wall Street Journal*, 15 July 1996.

"Does Realism Have a Future?", 1996. See "Realism in a New Era", April 1995.

"Bob Dole's Calculated Pragmatism", *The New York Times*, 22 September 1996.

"The Cracking of the Coalition" [Review of Robert Nisbet, *Conservatism: Dream and Reality*, University of Minnesota Press, Ann Arbor, 1995], *The Washington Times*, 15 December 1996.

"Madeleine Albright's Munich Mindset", *The New York Times*, 19 December 1996.

"China Rising" [Review of Richard Bernstein and Ross H. Munro, *The Coming Conflict with China*, Alfred A. Knopf, New York, 1997], *The New York Times*, 16 March 1997.

"India: Relevant at Last?", *The National Interest*, Spring 1997, pp. 115-118.

"The Anti-China Syndrome: How Not to Handle China", *National Review*, 5 May 1997, pp. 35-38. Reprinted as "The Anti-China Syndrome", *Prospect* [London], 20 July 1997, and in *Quadrant*, July-August 1997, pp. 11-15.

"Lost in the Mists of History" [Review of Alice Thomas Ellis, *A Welsh Childhood*, Moyer Bell, 1995], *The Washington Post*, 8 June 1997.

"A Larger NATO? It Will Enlarge Spending and Endanger Europe" [The No Case by Owen Harries and the Yes Case by Joshua Muravchik], *The American Enterprise*, July 1997, p. 18.

"Virtue by Other Means", *The New York Times*, 26 October 1997. Reprinted as "America Must Stay the Course of Engagement", *The International Herald Tribune*, 27 October 1997.

"The Dangers of Expansive Realism", *The National Interest*, Winter 1997-98, pp. 3-7. See also Letter from George F. Kennan, *The National Interest*, Spring 1998, p. 118. Both reprinted in the *Congressional Record*, Washington DC, 3 March 1998.

"A Reluctant Realist" [Review of Abba Eban, *Diplomacy for the Next Century*, Yale University Press, New Haven, 1998], *The New York Times*, 29 March 1998.

"US is Drifting and Incoherent" [Extract from address to the Australian Institute of International Affairs, Sydney], *Australian Financial Review*, 8 April 1998.

"America and the Euro Gamble", *The National Interest*, Fall 1998, pp. 125-128.

"Creating a Monetary Monster? If Europe's Common Currency is a Failure the Consequences will be Dire", *National Post* [Toronto], 4 November 1998. Reprinted as "America and the Euro: Double or Quits?", *Australian Financial Review*, 5 November 1998.

"A Gorbi Streak Neutered Newt", *Australian Financial Review*, 23 November 1998. Reprinted as "The Gorbachev of US Politics: Newt

Gringrich Has the Same Serene but Misplaced Self Confidence", *National Post* [Toronto], 28 November 1998.

"Faking It: Do We Really Care About Kosovo?", *National Review*, 3 May 1999, pp. 30, 32, 34. Extracted as "The Balkans Require More Reflection", *Australian Financial Review*, 28 April 1999. See also "So, What Do We Do Now?" [Reply to Eliot A. Cohen], *Slate* [online], 27 April 1999. Featured in "Letterbox", *Australian Financial Review*, 30 April 1999.

"First Kosovo. Then Russia. Now China.", *The New York Times*, 16 May 1999.

"Harry Lee's Story", *The National Interest*, Summer 1999, pp. 153-159. Extracted in "Notebook", *Australian Financial Review*, 7 June 1999 and 22 November 2000.

"Three Rules for a Superpower to Live By", *The New York Times*, 23 August 1999. Reprinted as "Dangers for the US With its Near Absolute Power", *Australian Financial Review*, 26 August 1999.

"A Year of Debating China", *The National Interest*, Winter 1999-2000, pp. 141-147. Extracted as "Calm Down, Spying is the Way the World Works" in "Notebook", *Australian Financial Review*, 12 May 2000. Reprinted as Appendix Two in Owen Harries, *Benign or Imperial? Reflections on American Hegemony* [2003 Boyer Lectures], ABC Books, Sydney, February 2004, pp. 103-117.

2000s

Contribution to "American Power – For What?: A Symposium" [With Elliott Abrams, William F. Buckley Jr, Eliot A. Cohen, Francis Fukuyama, Frank J. Gaffney Jr, Jacob Heilbrunn, Robert Kagan, Zalmay Khalilzad, Jeane J. Kirkpatrick, Charles Krauthammer, William Kristol, Michael Ledeen, Edward N. Luttwak, Walter A. McDougall, Joshua Muravchik, Joseph S. Nye Jr, David Rieff, Peter W. Rodman, Robert W. Tucker, Paul Wolfowitz], *Commentary*, January 2000, p. 21.

"A Letter from Wales", *The National Interest*, Fall 2000, pp. 127-132.

"A Long Time Between Murders", *The American Scholar*, Winter 2001, pp. 71-79. Reprinted in *Quadrant*, October 2001, pp. 56-60.

"The Anglosphere Illusion", *The National Interest*, Spring 2001, pp. 130-136. Extracted as "Anglosphere Illusions", *Prospect* [London],

April 2001, and reprinted as Appendix Three in Owen Harries, *Benign or Imperial? Reflections on American Hegemony* [2003 Boyer Lectures], ABC Books, Sydney, February 2004, pp. 118-132.

"Over and Out", *The National Interest*, Summer 2001, pp. 5-7.

"Time to Reconsider Our US Ties", *Australian Financial Review*, 10 September 2001.

"A Reminder of Darker Times", *Daily Telegraph* [Sydney], 14 September 2001.

"Guts to Say No Before It's Too Late", *The Australian*, 28 September 2001.

"An End to Nonsense", *The National Interest*, Special 9-11 Issue, Thanksgiving 2001, pp. 117-120. Revised as "The Return to Realism", in Imre Salusinsky and Gregory Melleuish, editors, *Blaming Ourselves: September 11 and the Agony of the Left*, Duffy & Snellgrove, Sydney, May 2002, pp. 23-31, and then extracted as "The Day the Earth Didn't Change Forever", *The Australian*, 15 May 2002.

"The Wasted Decade", *The Age*, 18 December 2001.

"How to Win Arguments and Influence Debate", *Australian Financial Review*, 1 February 2002. See also "A Primer for Polemicists", September 1984.

"Who Says We Are in the Doghouse?", *The Australian*, 4 February 2002.

"Be a Realist, Not a Lap Dog", *The Australian*, 4 March 2002.

Understanding America [Lecture for the Centre for Independent Studies (CIS), 3 April 2002], CIS Occasional Paper No. 80, Sydney, April 2002. Extracted as "Turning on Axis Distorts Aim: US Must Exercise Prudence and Restraint in the War on Terrorism", *The Australian*, 4 April 2002, and as "American Pie Losing Its Flavour", *The Age*, 4 April 2002.

"Hearts, Minds and Immigration", *Quadrant*, October 2002, pp. 9-14. Reprinted in Leonie Kramer, editor, *The Multi-Cultural Experiment*, McLeay Press, Sydney, 2003, pp. 55-70.

"We Must Dance with the Devil", *The Australian*, 29 October 2002. Revised as "Facing Reality in Indonesia", *The National Interest*, 27 November 2002.

"Introduction" as editor, *China in The National Interest*, Transaction Publishers, New Brunswick, 2003, pp. vii-xii.

"What It Means to be Conservative", *Policy*, Winter 2003, pp. 28-37. Extracted as "What Conservatism Means", *The American Conservative*, 17 November 2003, pp. 13-16.

"And Then There Was One…" [Extract from Lecture 1, 2003 Boyer Lectures, Australian Broadcasting Corporation], *The Age*, 14 November 2003.

"America's Utopian Mission" [Extract from Lecture 2, 2003 Boyer Lectures], *The Age*, 21 November 2003; see also "America's New Game Plan for Domination Rests on Success in Iraq", *Sydney Morning Herald*, 21 November 2003.

"Can the US Export Democracy?" [Extract from Lecture 3, 2003 Boyer Lectures], *The Age*, 28 November 23; see also "Past Failures Are Where the Real Lessons Lie for Democracy's New Enforcers", *Sydney Morning Herald*, 28 November 2003.

"Dreams of World Peace and a Global Culture Are Just That – Dreams" [Extract from Lecture 4, 2003 Boyer Lectures], *Sydney Morning Herald*, 5 December 2003.

"America's Challenge from Within" [Extract from Lecture 5, 2003 Boyer Lectures], *The Age*, 12 December 2003; see also "A New Threat to the US – from Within", *Sydney Morning Herald*, 12 December 2003.

"Buddies with the US at All Costs, and Wide Open to Attack" [Extract from Lecture 6, 2003 Boyer Lectures], *Sydney Morning Herald*, 19 December 2003.

"Rhetoric Matters" [Reply to Edward Rhodes, "American Grand Strategy: The Imperial Logic of Bush's Liberal Agenda"], *Policy*, Summer 2003-04, pp. 42-43.

Benign or Imperial? Reflections on American Hegemony [2003 Boyer Lectures], ABC Books, Sydney, February 2004. Extracts reprinted as "The Perils of Hegemony: Washington Learns That Democracy is Not Made for Export", *The American Conservative*, 21 June 2004, pp. 14-20. Extracted version reprinted in Gary Rosen, editor, *The Right War? The Conservative Debate on Iraq*, Cambridge University Press, 2005, pp. 73-86.

"Punching Above Our Weight?", in *Benign or Imperial?*, op. cit., chapter six, pp. 77-92. Extracted as "The Men Who Shaped Our Place in the World", *The Australian*, 16 January 2004. Reprinted with chapter two, "Taking on Utopia", pp. 16-30, as "Australia and the Bush Doctrine: Punching Above Our Weight?", in Mel Gurtov and Peter Van Ness, editors, *Confronting the Bush Doctrine: Critical Views from the Asia Pacific*, Routledge Curzon, London and New York, 2005, pp. 227-244.

"Don't Get Too Close to the US", *The Australian*, 17 February 2004.

"Why Power is America's Weakness", *Financial Times*, 27 July 2004. Reprinted as "Lesson in the Limits of Power", *The Australian*, 2 August 2004.

"Australia's Alliance with America: Indispensable Ally to the Indispensable Nation?", Transcript of contribution to Foreign Policy Forum held by the Centre for Independent Studies, Sydney, 8 September 2004, *mimeo*.

"Iraq is the Failure the US Had to Have", *Sydney Morning Herald*, 7 January 2005.

Morality and Foreign Policy [Extended version of the first George Shipp Memorial Lecture for the Workers' Educational Association, Sydney, 29 October 2004], CIS Occasional Paper No. 94, Centre for Independent Studies, Sydney, February 2005. Extracted as "It Pays to be Prudent When It Comes to Morality in World Politics", *Sydney Morning Herald*, 21 February 2005; "Iraq Adventure is Rich in Dangerous Precedents", *The Age*, 21 February 2005; and as "Morality in Foreign Policy", *Australian Financial Review*, 4 March 2005. Edited versions published as "Morality and Foreign Policy", *Policy* [Sydney], Autumn 2005, pp. 24-29; "Power and Morals", *Prospect* [London], April 2005; and "Power, Morality and Foreign Policy", *Orbis* [Philadelphia], Fall 2005, pp. 599-612.

"Losing Our Way" [Review of John Lukacs, *Democracy and Populism, Fear and Hatred*, Yale University Press], *The Washington Post*, 17 April 2005. Partly reprinted as "America's Big Problem", *Australian Financial Review*, 22 April 2005.

"Costs of a Needless War", *The Australian*, 18 July 2005. Reprinted as "Two Women and a War", *The American Conservative*, 29 August 2005, pp. 26-27.

"Suffer the Intellectuals", *The American Interest*, September 2005, pp. 80-84. Extracted as "The Parochialism of the Present", *Australian Financial Review*, 16 September 2005, and reprinted as "Suffer the Intellectuals: Why Predictions by Intellectuals So Often Turn Out to be Wrong", *Policy*, Autumn 2008, pp. 44-47. Revised as "Don't Panic. It's Only Prophecy", *The Spectator Australia*, 24 April 2010.

"The Failure of the Bush Doctrine", *The Age*, 28 October 2005.

Contribution to "Defending and Advancing Freedom" [With Paul Berman, Max Boot, Niall Ferguson, Francis Fukuyama, Frank J. Gaffney, Reuel Marc Gerecht, Victor Davis Hanson, Mark Helprin, Daniel Henniger, Stanley Hoffman, Paul Johnson, Robert Kagan, Rich Lowry, Edward N. Luttwak, Martin Peretz, Richard Perle, Daniel Pipes, Richard Pipes, David Pryce-Jones, Arch Puddington, Natan Sharansky, Amir Taheri, Ruth Wedgwood, George Weigel, James Q. Wilson, and R. James Woolsey], 60th Anniversary edition, *Commentary*, November 2005, pp. 34-35.

"Donald Horne (1921-2005)" [Extracts from speech at the State Library of NSW, 3 November 2005], *The Australian Author*, April 2006, pp. 8-9.

with Tom Switzer, "Loyal to a Fault", *The American Interest*, 1 June 2006.

"Different Battles, Different Response", *The Australian*, 5 July 2006.

with Tom Switzer, "Little Magazine Leaves Big Mark", *The Australian*, 3 October 2006.

After Iraq [Adapted from a speech to the Lowy Institute, Sydney, 29 November 2006], Lowy Institute Perspective, 30 November 2006. Extracted as "The End of Simplicity", *The Australian*, 1 December 2006, and "Don't Think It's Over", *The Australian*, 19 December 2006.

Contribution to "What Does All This Mean for Australia?" [Panel discussion with Ross Garnaut, Elsina Wainright and Allan Gyngell], *Global Forces 2006: Proceedings of the ASPI Conference*, Australian Strategic Policy Institute, Canberra, December 2006, pp. 72-81.

"Global Discontinuities" [Discussion with Itamar Rabinovich, Niall Ferguson, and Scott Barrett], in Francis Fukuyama, editor, *Blindside: How to Anticipate Forcing Events and Wild Cards in Global Politics*, Brookings Institution Press, Washington DC, 2007, pp. 143-145.

Reply to Peter Hartcher, "Bipolar Nation" [*Quarterly Essay* 25, January 2007], *Quarterly Essay* 26, May 2007, pp. 99-101.

"Mass Destruction, Mass Distribution" [Review of William Langewiesche, *The Atomic Bazaar*, Farrar, Straus and Giroux], *The Wall Street Journal*, 22 May 2007.

with Tom Switzer, "US Alliance Will Change", *The Australian*, 4 October 2007.

"The Global Outlook", in *Australian Voters' Guide to International Policy*, Lowy Institute Paper, Sydney, October 2007, pp. 3-4. Extracted as "Bush Not the Only Problem", *The Australian*, 19 October 2007.

"Foreign Policy After Bush" [Response to Barry Posen, "The Case for Restraint"], *The American Interest*, November-December 2007, pp. 22-23.

"Anglo-Saxon Attitudes: The Making of the Modern World" [Review of Walter Russell Mead, *God and Gold: Britain, America, and the Making of the Modern World*], *Foreign Affairs*, January-February 2008, pp. 170-174.

"Suffer the Intellectuals", *Policy*, Autumn 2008. See "Suffer the Intellectuals", September 2005.

"How to Judge a President-To-Be", *Australian Financial Review*, 1 September 2008.

"The False Choice Between Realism and Morality", *The Interpreter* [online], The Lowy Institute, Sydney, 19 February 2009.

2010s

"Don't Panic. It's Only Prophecy", *The Spectator Australia*, 24 April 2010. See also "Suffer the Intellectuals", September 2005.

with Tom Switzer, "US Strikes the Right Balance on China", *The Australian*, 21 January 2011.

"A Tribute to Coral Bell", *The Spectator Australia*, 6 October 2012.

with Tom Switzer, "Iraq's Lesson to America", *The Drum* [online], ABC News, 19 March 2013.

with Tom Switzer, "Leading From Behind: Third Time a Charm?", *The American Interest*, May-June 2013, pp. 7-15. Extracted as "US Foreign Policy Staying at Home", *Australian Financial Review*, 10 May 2013.

Acknowledgements

We are privileged to have known, worked with, and been guided by Owen Harries. This book is a tribute not only to his contribution to intellectual life in Australia and America, but also to a friend and mentor.

Assembling a collection of Owen's best essays and articles has been a time-intensive but immensely important project. We are grateful to Michael Easson for supporting the project, and for compiling a bibliography of Owen's writings amounting to some 300 entries. Michael also sourced and digitalised a lot of the original articles. Many that made the final cut were republished as shorter pieces or op-eds, and several of these are included here given size constraints on the book. Some essays and articles appear as extracts for the same reason. We would like to thank CIS Research Assistants Anjali Nadaradjane and Yuki Cheng for retrieving the remaining articles on our shortlist and helping to convert and proof them.

We would also like to thank Ward O'Neill for the use of his 1978 sketch of Owen on the front cover, and Michelle High in Washington, who worked for Owen from 1997 to 2001, and provided some photographs from the 1990s. Michelle also drew our attention to the reprinting of Owen's article on NATO expansion, and George Kennan's response, in the *Congressional Record*. Closer to home, we are grateful to the Lowy Institute's Executive Director, Michael Fullilove, for letting us use images of two letters of congratulation that Owen received from Henry Kissinger and George Kennan for his articles in the late 1990s on China (pages 124-134) and NATO (pages 135-146) respectively. Owen joined the Institute as a Visiting Fellow in 2003 and later donated the letters, which are displayed at their Sydney office.

On the production side, we are grateful to Michael Gilchrist for the care he took during layout, and to publisher Anthony Cappello for his guidance since the book was first proposed.

Source Acknowledgements

We are especially grateful to the editors or representatives of the following journals, magazines, newspapers and think tanks who kindly granted us permission to reprint Owen's writings, either in full or extracted form. Without their support, this book would not have been possible.

In America: Jacob Heilbrunn, Editor of *The National Interest*, whom Owen hired in 1989; Steven Palma for *National Review*; Ronald Burr on behalf of *The American Conservative*; and Grace Wisbey at the American Enterprise Institute.

In Australia: Michelle Gunn, Editor of *The Australian*; Michael Stutchbury, Editor-in-Chief of the *Australian Financial Review*; James Chessell, Managing Director of Publishing at Nine, for the *Sydney Morning Herald*; Keith Windschuttle, Editor of *Quadrant*; Rowan Dean, Editor of *The Spectator Australia*; and the Lowy Institute's Executive Director, Michael Fullilove, and Chief Operating Officer Sarah Hipsley.

Thanks also to the estate of Owen Harries for the use of three *New York Times* pieces, an op-ed from the *Financial Times*, and the chapter "Punching Above Our Weight" from *Benign or Imperial? Reflections on American Hegemony* [2003 Boyer Lectures], ABC Books, 2004.

Finally, we wish to thank the following publishers for permission to reprint extracts from the copyright material listed below.

pages 116-123: "My So-Called Foreign Policy: The Case for Clinton's Diplomacy". From *The New Republic*. © 1994 New Republic. All rights reserved. Used under license.

pages 211-219: "The Collapse of 'the West'". © 1993 Council on Foreign Relations, publisher of *Foreign Affairs*. All rights reserved. Distributed by Tribune Content Agency.

www.ingramcontent.com/pod-product-compliance
Lightning Source LLC
Chambersburg PA
CBHW060837100426

42814CB00016B/407/J